The Mythology of the Ifugaos

By

Roy Franklin Barton

PHILADELPHIA

AMERICAN FOLKLORE SOCIETY

1955

Printed in Germany *at* J. J. Augustin, Glückstadt

MEMOIRS OF THE
AMERICAN FOLKLORE SOCIETY

VOLUME 46

1955

Foreword

"The Mythology of the Ifugaos" is the last to be published of the three major manuscript volumes which the late Roy Franklin Barton preserved through his Japanese captivity in the Philippines and brought back to America to revise and edit in the few years that remained to him before his untimely death in 1947. "The Religion of the Ifugaos" was published in 1946 as Memoir 65 of the American Anthropological Association, and "The Kalingas" in 1939 by the University of Chicago Press.

Barton possessed an extraordinary gift for entering into rapport with primitive peoples and their institutions and for portraying these with their psychological implications. This faculty shows throughout the present volume. He lived eight years with the Ifugao, all told, spoke the language, and collected all myths in text.

From the point of view of literature, the semi-poetical recitatives of myths 1 and 2 are of outstanding interest. They are presented with the Ifugao and English in parallel columns in line-for-line equivalence, enabling the reader to taste for himself the literary quality of the Ifugao text in Barton's marvelously exact and vivid translation, which does equal justice to native content and native form. That the near-metrical form was wholly aboriginal seems doubtful now, in view of what Fred Eggan has recently published from the Sagada Igorot, and Richard Howell on Ainu verse form, also in the *Journal of American Folklore*. But whether these attempts at narrative poetry originated spontaneously or under stimulus of foreign influences, they are equally interesting for their bearing on the philosophy of literature.

The third and fourth myths in the present volume also retain the Ifugao text as well as its English translation, and thus provide a sample of Ifugao "prose."

Barton had kept the Ifugao original also in myths 7, 29, and 30. This the present writer has reluctantly sacrificed in order to keep down cost of publication; but the three texts are being deposited with the University of Chicago in its Anthropology Department.

In Part I, Barton analyzes the qualities of Ifugao mythology from several angles. He considers the myth as an instrument of ritual magic. He goes at some length into the form, style, and literary attributes of the mythology. And he discusses the classification, affiliations, and possible origin of the principal motifs in the Ifugao corpus of myths. These he divides into "general" or widely spread motifs and "recent" or locally developed ones. The latter group he subdivides into "traditional," "invented," and "contest type." The names of the classes are unusual, but it is quickly evident what they represent, and Barton substantiated his interpretations by interesting analyses of several narratives.

Throughout, we are brought in contact, through a vigorous and original mind, with the products of the active mythopoeic faculties of an also vigorous and original native people. Barton thoroughly respected Ifugao creativity, without sentimentally overvaluing it, and thereby earns the respect of scholars for his role as transmitter and interpreter.

A. L. Kroeber

The officers of The American Folklore Society
wish to express their gratitude to A. L. Kroeber for
undertaking the difficult task of editing the author's
posthumous manuscript.

The publication of this work is made possible through generous subventions by the Bollingen Foundation, Inc., and the Philippine Studies Program (supported by the Carnegie Corporation) of the University of Chicago.

Preface

The myths contained in this work were nearly all collected while on a field trip that was supported by grants from the Social Science Research Council and the National Research Council. They were saved from loss during the Japanese invasion only through the fact that a copy of them had been sent to this country. My other myth recordings, including some that I had intended to embody in this work, were lost to the enemy.

A large part of the work of preparing this volume for publication was done during a term as Lichtstern Fellow, at the University of Chicago.

All myths were recorded in the native language and then translated. For reasons that will appear in the body of this work, they could not be recorded from their recitation in the rituals, but every effort was made to get informants to repeat them as ritually used. There are a few references to a manuscript of Kankanai myths that was partly lost. I have let them remain, as I hope to recover the lost portions or again record the myths and publish them.

Acknowledgements are gratefully rendered to the sources of support named above, to Professor A. L. Kroeber, Professor Fay-Cooper Cole and Professor Fred Eggan, whose criticisms have been exceedingly valuable, to the informants whose names appear in the headings to the various myths, especially to Ngidulu, Kumiha and Balogan, my principal informants, to Mr. Francisco Bugbug, who recorded two myths at my request, and to Mr. Marco Manghe, who put in my hands his excellent recording of the "Virgin Birth," the best ever made of an Ifugao myth.

University of Chicago,   Roy Franklin Barton

February 18, 1947.

Contents

Part I
Qualities of the Mythology

1. INTRODUCTION

The Ifugaos, about 80,000 in number, inhabit a steep mountain region near the center of the northern third of Luzon, the northernmost large island of the Philippine Archipelago. They have lived in this isolated region for many hundred years certainly, perhaps for well over a thousand. Their principal social unit is the bilateral kinship group; there is no institutionalized community organization, although there is, of course, a tie of locality and neighborhood, largely unrecognized in the people's consciousness. The greater part of the tribe grows rice by irrigated terrace cultivation, but several thousand Ifugaos raise "dry" upland rice, in clearings. In addition to rice cultivation, all Ifugaos make mountain clearings in which they grow the camote (the tropical sweet potato), corn, mung beans, cassava and less important crops. Subjection of the tribe to colonial rule, begun in a sporadic, indecisive way by the Spaniards shortly after the turn of the last century, met effective resistance, both passive and active, and was only effected by the Americans, during the period 1903–1907. Until this date there was little acculturation of any kind, nor is it very important even now.

There are definite indications that Ifugaoland was settled by migrations from various directions that displaced the aboriginal Negritos. Of these migrations, the following are to be distinguished:

1) A migration of Kankanai, or proto-Kankanai, from across the Cordillera to the west. An indication of this stream is the very close kinship between the modern Kankanai and Ifugao languages. This stream also brought stone terracing. The walls of Western Ifugao resemble those of the Kankanai and Bontok in their approach to the vertical. I measured walls in Central Ifugao and found the pitch to be about twice as great as in Western Ifugao. Beyer has pointed out the greater age of the western fields and the fact that their walls are built of hard river stones, mainly diorite, that have a high resistance to weathering. To the east the walls contain progressively more and more split stone, mainly sandstone or granite. The reason for the

difference is interesting. When an Ifugao builds a new field, he walls the terrace with whatever stone is most conveniently at hand, which is almost always from a landslide, exposed folds, or from boulders on the ground which he sometimes cracks by the use of fire and water. When this stone crumbles in the wall, however, he replaces it with the much more resistant stones carried up from the bed of a river or stream. The fact that walls in Western Ifugao are almost entirely of this type is therefore evidence of their greater antiquity. Further-more, although the mountains there are steeper, the fields are larger than elsewhere, since smaller ones, through generations of labor, have been combined so as to utilize the area formerly occupied by the walls and at the same time eliminate a source and means of access of pests.

2) The Ifugaos of the Lamot Valley, to the south, speak a different language from other Ifugaos and build terraces without the use of stone. Being without retaining walls, the terraces are necessarily lower and narrower than in districts where stone is used. This folk practices tree burial of infants and has its own distinctive ritual and no doubt mythology.

3) Thirty years ago the Ifugaos of Ligauwe had a secret language for which they were famous and in which a few of them could converse. It barely survives today as a prestige language in certain rituals.

4) The dry rice cultivators of the eastern foothills, the "Silipanes" have a different religion and speak a different dialect from other Ifugaos.

5) The Mayaoyao folk have a markedly different pantheon and ritual, a different dialect with some lexical differences, different color preferences and ornamentation. This is the only district in Ifugao, where cairn burial is occasionally to be found and here a shack is especially built as a girl's dormitory

6) Several hundred people have migrated into the Tinok region, from Benguet, during American times.

While there is sufficient somatological and cultural unity between these various migrations to justify including them under a single tribal name, still amalgamation is far from having run to completion, and this is especially true with respect to mythology. When applied in this work to ritual and myths, the term "Ifugao" is to be under-stood as applying only to the people of the middle course of the Bula River, the part immediately west of Ligauwe Gap, or, specifically, to the inhabitants of the Kababuyan River Valley and Kudug on the north side of the river and to Kiangan and Nagakadan Valleys on the south side.

The Ifugaos have no form of writing, but they have an enormous body of literature, notwithstanding. It consists of the mythology; the

Alim, a series of ballads in jocular-romantic vein that may properly be chanted only by the wealthy; folktales; the Hudhud epics, a series of loosely joined incidents remotely suggestive of the Ramayana or Mahabharata, but not drawn from these, sung by a leader but with the ends of the verses repeated by the commonalty as a refrain; satirical songs, some of them rather subtle; and children's rhymes and songs.

This distinction between myth and folktale is always clear in the mind of the Ifugao. Myths – I think all of them – are used ritually; they enter into the framework and constitution of the culture and its world viewpoint; they are taken seriously, they are never, as myths, related for diversion. I have found only two myths that have folktale versions. In these instances the folktale versions are not taken seriously – the true version is believed to be the mythical one.

I hesitate to say that there exists in the mind of the Ifugao the distinction that Boas asserts always to exist in the mind of the American Indian, namely that the myth "relates incidents which happened at a time when the world had not yet assumed its present form and when mankind was not yet in possession of all the arts and customs that belong to our period. The other group [folktales] contains tales of our modern period."[1] It will herafter be seen that the Ifugao, on account of the manner in which he uses myths in ritual, is continually switching from present to past, and sometimes he muddles the two. Some anthropologists believe that primitive man always distinguishes clearly between ritual and practical measures in his medicine, agriculture, technology and the like, between the ghost world and the real one. I doubt that the Ifugao always does. I once heard a bonesetter, an alert and intelligent young man, decry the usefulness of manipulation and splints: he said, "The prayer is the thing – if it be right, the recovery will be right." It is true that in vital essential matters, all peoples do take some practical measures, else they would cease to exist. That they always distinguish between practical and ritual ones or between a mythical period and the world's present form I do not believe. I have recorded two Kankanai myths in which the informant's great grandfather was an actor; I am sure that he *was* the great grandfather, or at least so taken. I do not believe that the Kankanai consider that the customs of society nor the laws of the world were different at that time.

I have just characterized Ifugao myths, but that characterization does not fit Kankanai myths. Some of these are not used ritually and *are* narrated for diversion, yet are taken seriously and enter into the frame-work of the culture. It is very hard to make an inclusive definition of a myth, but since for the purposes of this work it is

1*

necessary, I define myths by the criteria of credence and function. A myth is a narrative that is believed, at least by the unsophisticated, and which enters into and bolsters the framework of the culture and its concept of the world.

The recording of Ifugao myths was begun by Juan Villaverde, Dominican missionary in Kiangan during the periods 1868–1872 and 1891–1897. He died en route to Spain in 1897, leaving a manuscript entitled, "Supersticiones de los Igorrotes Ifugao." This manuscript was edited by Julian Malumbres, who had been for some years his companion in Kiangan and was afterward for many years archivist of the Dominican Order in Manila, and was published in *El Correo Sino-Anamita*, Manila, pp. 293-455.

Villaverde did not record the myths in the native language; they appear incidentally in his sometimes unorganized but otherwise excellent account of the "supersticiones". It must be remembered that he had no chance to edit or reorganize his manuscript; perhaps he had not even finished it. It is evident that when he was writing about a rite or belief, he would bring in the myth that bolstered or confirmed it and that while recording this myth he would follow off leads into other material. Consequently it is sometimes difficult to distinguish which is myth and which is explanation. His work contains 14 myths, several of them variants of myths published here.

Villaverde noted [with some amazement] that a number of Ifugao myths contain motifs found in biblical narratives.

Professor H. Otley Beyer has published four Ifugao myths.[2]

The Reverend Mr. Lambrecht has published 56 myths from Mayaoyao in his series, "The Mayawyaw Ritual."

The author of this work has hitherto published 13 myths from Kiangan or Central Ifugao.[3]

2. THE MAGICAL AND FUNCTIONAL ROLES OF IFUGAO MYTHS

Myths enter into nearly every Ifugao ritual, even into those of decidedly minor importance. The myth itself is called *uwa* or *abuwab* [in Kankanai *susuwa*]; its recitation is called *bukad*. Before the recitation there is a *gonob* or simple invocation of the names of all the characters mentioned in the myth or in any way connected with it.

Many myths have individual names that are sometimes of real significance, but I did not know this when I began recording and have in other cases overlooked obtaining the names. The English titles under which the myths appear in this work are translations of the Ifugao names that appear at their left, unless the titles are starred, in which case I myself have bestowed them.

From one to fifteen or more priests officiate in the rituals. If the ritual be a purely family affair, as most rituals are, then [until recently] only related priests are present, and these are drawn from both husband's and wife's kindred.

1. *Invocation of the ancestral spirits*: each priest invokes the ancestors of his own lineage.

. 2. *Possession by the ancestors*, who drink wine and promise benefits through the priests. [But such possession occurs only at rituals at which one or more pigs or a good many chickens are killed].

3. *One of the priests takes the leadership* and allots the classes of deities to be worshipped among the assembled priests. There are at least 1500 deities known by name and they are divided into about 40 classes. Only in the greatest rituals are approximately all of them invoked, but several hundred may be invoked on occasions of moderate importance. On minor occasions, a small number of classes are invoked.

4. *After the allotment*, each priest invokes his messenger deities, and sends them to summon the classes of deities that have been given him to invoke.

5. *Invocation of the Deities*: Each priest, simultaneously with the other priests, invokes the classes that have been assigned to him. He does this by naming the deities in groups of 3 to 5, for the most part, adding his injunction to them, after which he again invokes a little group and repeats his injunction, re-adapting it to the slightly different nature, perhaps of the group, and so on.

6. *Possession of the priests by the deities allotted them*: The priest drinks a sip of rice wine for each little group — or, rather, in the theory of the religion, the deities themselves drink the wine, using the priest's body — whereupon the deities promise compliance with whatever the priest enjoined in number "4" above. [But possession is conditional, as in "2" above].

7. *Idiosyncratic or extraordinary rites* such as the *baltong* chants the invocation of a cock,[1] oblations, "fanning" with a chicken, spear-swinging, chanted odes and the like. These are carried out by the priests having the greatest prestige.

8. *Sacrifice of the victims*: while these are in their death throes the priests name the deities, or principal ones of them, to whom the victims are being sacrificed, as rapidly as possible.

. 9. *Myths connected with the "Raw Eaters"* are recited before chunks of raw meat from the victims. Before beginning these or any other myth recitations, there is an invocation of the myth characters, incidents or objects.

10. *Rites of "Quenching" and "Dispatching the Steam"* occur immediately after the meat has been cooked.[2]

11. *Recitation of myths except "Raw-Eater" myths*: the myths are recited before large shallow baskets of cooked rice, on which is piled the cooked meat.

The priests always sit on a mat of parallel runo reeds, laced together, even though the rites occur in forest or field. Usually the mat will be laid under the shelter of house or granary. The priests squat on their haunches back of the baskets of rice and meat; in their midst are jars of rice wine and large wooden bowls into which the wine is occasionally poured out. In the wine bowls float coconut-shell drinking cups whose rims are symmetrically notched to accomodate the drinking mouth. In war or sorcery rites the priests hold bolos, sharp edge forward, and flourish them whenever they utter a *fiat*, or "clinching phrase." In some rites wooden granary idols stand on the mat, or there may be a sorcery box containing war charms or a ritual trough containing granary charms. On box or trough are piled large clusters of freshly plucked betel nuts or betel flowers, together with pepper vine leaves.

Before the myth recitation begins, there is an allotment of the myths among the priests. At a mock-headfeast I saw in Bitu in 1937 over forty myths were recited by 16 priests. Each priest recites his myth simultaneously with the rest and when he has finished one myth, he begins another. The result is a babble in which the words are indistinguishable. Boys or youths sometimes snuggle alongside a priest, turn their ear to him alone so as to listen only to his myth and in this way begin their education for the priesthood. The Ifugao man who is not a priest is an exception.

The myth recitation consists of short phrases barked out by the priest in two or three musical intonations — those of the young priest probably in a falsetto, those of an elderly priest in a deep rumble. If you should approach one of the little villages in which a myth recitation is going on, you would first hear a faint hum like that of swarming bees. As you came nearer, the hum would grow into a murmur and the murmur would grow into a roar like that of an approaching mob on the stage. Arriving in the village you would note that, despite the fact that the stories were all being lost in a general jumble, there would nevertheless be an audience of women and children sitting underneath neighboring houses, gathered to listen. The Ifugao's habitat is a most beautiful part of the earth to the eye (though I am pretty sure the Ifugao sees no beauty in landscapes or scenery), and here is a beauty for the ear of even the foreign visitor in the blended voices of the myth recitation of many priests. Aside from the fact that the monotony of daily life is broken by them, the Ifugao enjoys myth recitations because he appreciates the babble of them as a rising and falling sound. The voices, he says, "rise and fall like the sound of the bamboo harp."

But the enjoyment of the audience falls far below that of the priests themselves. Ngidulu, one of my informants explaining in his autobiography the motives that led him when quite a young man to become a priest, said: "Partly I think it was because I wanted to hear my own voice and to be heard by others." Further he relates that he was, at first, dissatisfied with his voice: "... it was too boyish, too high-pitched. I used to go down to the tributary (a stream) and train it there, all by myself. There, too, I practiced different styles of recitation or enunciation, because it is a great relief to a priest, during a prolonged series of invocations and myth-recitations, to be able to change his style of chanting. The older priests advised me to train so."[3] I have often noted that as a myth-recitation draws to an end, so that voices begin to drop out, some priests are timid and bring their recitations to a hurried close while others, bolder, contrive to prolong their myths, delighting in the chance of making a solo display of their voices and of their energy of recitation.

The Ifugao myth is fundamentally sympathetic magic. It tells about hero-ancestors or gods or other supernatural beings who in the past were confronted with problems similar to those which worry the Ifugao in the present, and of how they resolved the problems. The language of the myth is in the present tense, but it is of the nature of a historical present. There can be no doubt about that for a priest sometimes drops into the past tense inadvertently, showing that he conceives the action as occurring in the past. I do not believe, though, that the historical present is used as a matter of rhetoric: it seems more likely that the motivating idea is something like that behind the celebration of the Mass — that the recitation is, in a way, a repetition anew of a past event.

However that may be, the myth sets up parallels in magic, and these are "clinched" and made effective by phrases which I term "*fiat*" (*poltak*). In Central Ifugao, the *fiat* is introduced by the word "*Batdakana*", which may be analyzed with a fair degree of plausibility into the ancient Indonesian prefix *b*, the root *at*, meaning "like" or "do", the pronoun *daka*, "thou" and the contraction (*h*)'*na*, from *hina*, meaning "that which is nearer to the person spoken to than to the speaker". Thus the word means, "Be (or act) thou in that way," and it is most often addressed to omens, events or magic forces, or, as we shall see, sometimes to the myth itself or to powers that stand back of the myth. Often the words come from the mouth of an actor in the myth and his clinching phrase seems to be considered to have an effect in the present.

In Kiangan, besides *batdakana*, another phrase is often used: "It is not there but here in our village of ..., so that ...", the priest naming whatever benefits it is desired to secure. The number of *fiats* thus interjected into a myth varies according to the region and according to the priest — some priests interject *fiats* at every possible, even far-fetched parallel, while others, more temperate, use only one at the end of the myth. In Central Ifugao, the interjected *fiats* are used more often to clinch good omens that occur as incidents in the myth than to clinch parallels.

Many myths are followed by a *tulud*, the purpose of which is to bring to the place of the rites the principal actor of the myth, or else the mana or talisman power about which the myth relates, or the powers or beings that stand behind the myth. The primary meaning of *tulud* is "pushing," but it also means "compelling."[4] In Kiangan, it is mostly the actors who are brought, and they declare through the priest that they will confer the benefits of which the myth relates, and that it shall be now as it was in the past. In "pushing" the myth character from the scene of the myth to the site of the recitation, the priest "pushes" him from place to place, has him going uphill, down-hill, across a valley, over a ridge, wading streams, going round a mountain without changing altitude, walking on rice-terrace dikes and so on, according to the character of the country. In populated regions every acre or hectare in the habitat has its name, in unpopulated regions the named areas are larger. I was told that the priest dare not omit naming a place on the route lest the myth character get away from him or fail to come, but this is probably a rationalization, for, as a matter of fact, it is only when the character reaches the priest's home region that every place is named; before that, only the "high spots" are hit.[5]

In Central Ifugao the *tulud* usually takes a repetitive form — the form of subordinate appended myths, that are essentially repetitions of each other. I did not there find myth characters brought to the site of the recitations, but only the mana of charms, objects having inherent power, such as granary images (*bulol*), and personifications of magic or mana called *dinakwat* ("Endowments" or "Obtainments"). In this form of *tulud*, somebody living between the site of the myth recitation and the place where the myth action supposedly occurred, borrows the talisman or *dinakwat* or obtains it as a gift and takes it home. There it repeats its wonder-working and, being much heard about, is borrowed by another Ifugao who lives still nearer the site of the myth recitation. And so, by three or four stages, each essentially a repetition of the former ones, it is finally brought home. The last obtainer is, of course, he for whom the rites are being done [Myth 2, The Self-Beheaded].

It is apparent that both these forms of *tulud* serve the function in magic of bridging from the past to the present and from the "there" to the "here." The myths are in the historical present, the *tulud* are in the present tense. There is, moreover, a third kind of *tulud*, which is independent — not preceded by a myth: Nos. 17, 25, 28, and 29 are good examples.

At the end of myth, myth-*tulud*, or *tulud* recitation, there is a final, clinching phrase. In Kiangan this follows the formula: "Be' it not then, but now; not there but here, so that .... [the desired benefits are named]. In Central Ifugao the ending is most often, *Tabina* ..., "It was the source (or cause)" of such and such benefits, followed by *Kalidi*, a compelling or clinching word, after which the priest enu-merates the benefits that ought to follow the recitation and ends with the final phrase, "because thou art being mythed" or, "for there — ye have been mythed this myth of ours."

To whom are these endings addressed? Sometimes to the powers standing back of the myth, sometimes to the characters of the myth, sometimes to the myth itself, and sometimes to the incidents or even objects mentioned in the myth.

Thus, in the myth, "Sun and Moon Quarrel" [15], in which Moon sets a trap in which Sun is impaled, not only Moon and Sun are invoked in the preliminary *gonob*, but also *Niknaan Umalgo hi Kabunian*, "The Trapping of Sun-God of the Skyworld;" *Nunhikhi-kadan-na*, "His Kicking;" *Nunhighigokan-na*, "His Hiccoughing;" *Numpitpitagan-na*, "His Floundering;" *Nunlinglingotan-na*, "His Sweating;" *Nunututogan-na*, "His Vomiting." After invoking these incidents of the myth, the priest goes on to invoke the parts of the deadfall, the main posts, the weight, the action, the trigger, and so on.[6] These myth-incidents and myth-objects are thus considered as deities. Indeed, under the expansive trend of his religion, the Ifugao deifies pretty nearly everything in his cosmos and myth characters, incidents and objects constitute about one-fifth of his overgrown pantheon.[7] He calls them *mabaki* — "prayables." But they are not on precisely the same level as the other deities, being more subject to the compulsion of magic, especially the recitation of the myth in which they appear.[8]

The ritual significance of the myth may be summed up as follows; first, there is sympathetic magic in the myth as a whole and in some of its situations that may afford parallels with the present; second, the characters and sometimes the incidents and objects of the myth are regarded as supernatural entities that can be controlled by the myth recitation; third, there is mana or magic power in the myth itself. The myth recitative is conceived as setting all these into action. It is, however, rather a violent procedure to draw a distinction between these kinds of magic: in the mind of the Ifugao the three aspects are intermeshed and indefinite, with magic merging into worship and worship passing into magic, with confusion between the personal and impersonal, between entity and force, symptom, action or feeling.

Among the Kankanai and Nabaloi tribes, the myth is not often conceived as maintaining parallels for sympathetic magic — the abridged myth is itself conceived as a means to power or compulsive magic.

The Ifugao uses myths as magic to a greater extent than has been reported for perhaps any other people. In some measure this situation may be more apparent than real, owing to the fact that the ritual use of myths may frequently have been overlooked due to the recording of myths outside their functional setting by investigators who were solely interested in the myth content. But even making due allowance for this sort of recording, the Ifugao use is still excessive and exceptional. Why should it be so ?

I think it is so because of the expansive trend of the Ifugao religion operating over a long period of time. This trend has arisen partly from the fact that ritualizing is an outlet for masculine exhibitionism and partly from the fact that the Ifugao leans a little more heavily on the supernatural than do most peoples: he is rather uniquely helpless in the respect that, besides all the usual ills of primitive folk, he has an unusually low political development, so nearly lacking as he does, local and community organization. In this helplessness, with the normal human tendency to wishful thinking and laziness, he has turned to the supernatural with the result that his god-creation and ritual have proliferated extraordinarily.

Utilization of myths as ritual recitatives is also correlated, in all probablility, with the lack of spectacles and masked dances as outlets for exhibitionism. There exists, I believe, only one mimic dance — the cockfight dance. It accompanies the recitation of myths relating contests between Full-Grown Cock and Fledgling, between Cobra and Python, Hardstone and Softstone, and so on — but only on great occasions. At other times the myths are recited without a dance performance. It may be that dances more frequently accompanied myth recitations in the past, but that, not being sustained by spectacular masks, they have fallen into disuse, leaving only the cockfight dance to survive because of the striking costume that the dancers wear in it. It may be, too, that in some instances a myth recitation has replaced a dance.

We are on less conjectural ground when we suspect that one way in which myths came to be used as magic was through the substitution of spoken magic for enacted. For example, in one myth the husband of a woman in difficult childbirth goes up the mountainside, chops down a tree of a sort corresponding to our "slippery elm," peels the bark from the trunk and tosses it downhill. It slides easily and smoothly, thus furnishing a parallel for the "travelling" of the "Other-townsman," the baby being born. It is hardly necessary to suppose that formerly such a log or section of a log was actually prepared and slid down an inclined plane or that some sort of magic was enacted with it. But it is safe to say that some such manner of relieving difficult birth was conceived and embodied in a myth according to the pattern of the culture. It is in the line of least resistance to tell about magic acts rather than go to the exertion of performing them. The basis for verbal magic is primordial and firm. Marr[9] and Levy-Bruhl have convincingly argued that a magical quality was attributed to beginning-speech. Malinowski, on the basis of more tangible data, argues that the experiences of the child, in both its prearticulate expressions of its discomforts and needs and in its learning to talk, inculcate an attitude toward speech that is essentially magical in nature[10] and reborn in every generation.

3. THE MYTH AS A RECITATIVE

The manner of reciting the myth — in barked-out, terse phrases or clauses — determines, and is determined by, the myth's literary form. Although I have punctuated the translations in order to make them more readable and have carried over the same punctuation so far as possible into the Ifugao text, I am not at all sure that my punctuation conforms to the Ifugao's means of expression. I cannot make up my mind whether the text consists of a vast number of short, complete sentences, nearly every one of which corresponds to a "bark" in the recitation, or whether it consists of exceedingly long sentences, only two or three to the episode, and that these long sentences consist of short coördinate clauses which we would ordinarily set off by commas or semicolons.

These sentences, or clauses, as the case may be, have 2, 3, or 4 accents — most frequently 3. The meter is fairly regular. The predominating tendency is toward the dactylic foot, but a considerable number of syllables may be crowded into the place of the short unaccented syllables. The priest can bend almost any combination to the intonation to which he recites, but there can be no doubt that, not consciously, probably, but rather, physiologically, he likes the

meter to be regular. To help obtain this regularity, meaningless
words, such as *kánadi, dáye, tatáowa*, and the like are inserted, singly
or in combination. The first has an accommodating accent which may
be shifted from the first syllable to the second in order to conform to
the meter. Phrases composed of meaningless words appear to be used
sometimes from sheer love of repetition, sometimes for the purpose
of bringing the priest back to the regular swing of the intonation
after it has been interrupted by irregular meter, and not infrequently
for the non-esthetic but exceedingly practical purpose of giving him
time to recall his lines when his memory has suffered from the too
many sips of liquor he has taken when being possessed by a hundred
or so gods during the rites that have preceded.

The verses of the myth are "barked" to a fundamental intonation
in which each line ends in a downward inflection and to a secondary
variant having a rising inflection, which relieves the monotony. The
latter usually begins with a line in which there is a naturally rising
inflection, as for example at the end of a question, and this rising inflection continues throughout several succeeding lines until the priest
begins again on the fundamental.

As has been said, the priest, when tired out, can relieve his voice
by changing to an entirely different style of reciting. This different
style of recitation is rarely used and did not sink deeply enough into
my memory to maintain itself during the months that have passed,
so that I cannot say anything about it. I can vouch for the one
ordinarily used, however.

From phonograms which I made in the Folklore Section of the
Institute of Ethnography, Leningrad, of the beginning lines of the
myth of the Virgin Birth, Miss Zinaida Victorovna Evald made the
following transcription and analysis:

"There are two fundamental intonational formulae:

and a third, which is found only once:

"The two fundamental formulae do not always have the same
rhythm, for this depends on the number of syllables and accents in
the declamation. At the same time, II has the stabler rhythm (owing

to the periodically recurring line, "Dola-dad Kiangan") and appears
to close a period of more variable recitation.

"The tonic and quantitative principles enter in on an equal basis:

sometimes ♪ ♩ and sometimes ♩ ♩."

FORM, STYLE AND CONTENT ILLUSTRATED BY A MYTH

Myth No. 1, the Virgin Birth, was recorded by Hon. Marco Manghe,
presidente of Burnai, who was a pupil of mine when I was a teacher
in Ifugaoland during the period 1908–1915. His is a better recording
than I have ever been able to attain. By giving the priest, Malingan,
a "grandfather" of his, [when a kinship term is enclosed in quotation
marks, it is to be understood in its extended Ifugao sense] the impression that he, Manghe, wished to prepare for the priesthood, he
was able to secure a remarkably accurate version that includes all the
meaningless words which contribute to the perfecting of the meter.
In my own recordings the priests have inclined to leave these out.
It is certain, however, that Malingan used many more of these words
than priests ordinarily do. But even aside from the better recording,
Malingan's version of the myth manifests a literary quality con-
siderably higher than that of the ordinary run of myths. Malingan
must either have had literary talent rising almost to genius or else
someone in the line of priests through which the myth descended to
him must have had such talent.

Manghe's reason for recording the myth is significant. He said: "I
recorded it in order to have it to read over and over to myself — it
is so beautiful!"

The reasons must be given for my presentation of the myth in a
more or less poetic form. I am as suspicious as anybody of poetizations
of native texts, for I always fear that they do no little violence to
the original. And leaving scientific accuracy out of the question,
there is the consideration that such poetizations can hardly rise above
a second rate poetry.

It was impossible for me to do anything else. Manghe had recorded
the Ifugao text in lines corresponding to the priest's recitation. Even
though I began translating into prose form, I found that with the
drone of myth recitation inevitably brought into my ears as I read
the original, I was falling into a corresponding rhythm in the English.
Then it occurred to me that for the purpose of illustrating the style,
form and literary qualities of the myth, a degree of poetization which
should attempt a correspondence to the degree of poetization in the
original would be permissible and desirable. But I set myself strict
limits in order to prevent distortion: (1) the meaningless words must

appear in the English translation — in only one or two instances has one of them been omitted; (2) every line must be translated as a unit — there must be no carrying over of ideas expressed in one line to another in the translation; this was a rigorous requirement; (3) Ifugao figures and metaphors must be left Ifugao — not interpreted in European equivalents. The last was the most difficult of all, but no more difficult, perhaps, than in ordinary translation, in prose form.

I have not felt bound, however, to adhere to grammatical constructions, but have substituted phrases or even clauses for single words, or vice versa, in order to help the meter. The result is a translation that is well within the bounds of the literal. In one respect the "poetization" is more literal than my translations in prose form, for in these latter, in the interest of brevity, I have omitted repetitions of the subject and other parts of speech and have often used a single word where the Ifugao has a whole sentence.

I have preserved Mr. Manghe's spellings and grouping of speech elements (although I often disagree with them) except in cases where they would leave the meter in doubt, as in the case of a two-syllable word which he spelled *die*, which I have changed to *diye*. Mr. Manghe attaches elided prepositions and particles, such as *ad* and *an*, to the preceding word, whereas I write them independently without the vowel and without an apostrophe in the place of it, simply as *d* and *n*. Bernard Shaw and the Russians have set an example of getting along without this use of the apostrophe. In my own recordings I try to keep the speech elements separate. Thus I append the pronominal suffixes by means of a hyphen, writing *"Dola-da d Kiangan"* (their village of Kiangan) where Mr. Manghe writes *"Doladad Kiyangan."* Likewise I would write *"Mamilipili-da y hin-tulang"*, (the sisters choose and choose) *y* standing for contraction of the article *hi* or *di*, whereas Mr. Manghe has written *"Mamilipiliday hintulang."* It goes without saying that my *y*, *n*, or *d*, should be pronounced with the word which precedes it.

The Ifugao title of the myth is "Gahidu," the name of a class of deities who "feel the way for," or direct, the givers of omens, whose good offices the Ifugao hopes to secure by myth recitation. The accent of both text and translation is marked throughout the first two episodes and the accent of native words throughout the whole translation. Consonants have, roughly, their English sounds, and vowels their continental sounds. The accent is, regularly, on the penult; where irregular, it is marked. The native text, naturally, has the better rhythm. The intonational formulae already given can be applied to the translation and the reader is advised to master these and to try to apply them.

4. LITERARY ATTRIBUTES OF THE MYTHS

The most important literary quality of the Ifugao myth is a not unsophisticated employment of repetition. Repetition is the fundamental structure in poetry, music and the dance. Alliteration, rhyme, rhythm, the chorus or refrain, dance movements — all these are merely forms of repetition.

Alliteration and rhyme are probably never intentionally constructed by the Ifugao in myths; his only purposeful attempt at these, I think, is by using puns.[1] But when by accident they do occur, the Ifugao loves them and continually reverts to them. Thus, in the myth of the Virgin Birth, the alliterative lines,

> An mangadadi-da, They're always refusing,
> An mamilipili-da, Too strict in choosing.

recur whenever it is possible to bring them in, as also, in "The Self-Beheaded," the rhymed lines,

> An manayutayu, Dancing and dancing,
> An mondayudayu, Rejoicing and rejoicing.

In all myths there are phrases such as, *Kon-na panalpalíwan*, "Goes, not noting time's passage," *Kánadi kanú tataówa* (meaningless), *Dola-da d Kiangan*, "Their village at Kiangan" and the like, which are favorites because of their alliteration.

Prized, too, are phrases containing names of places; and, so far as I have been able to ascertain, all of these that are attributed in the myths to the earthworld really exist.

As has been intimated, irregularities of rhythm require an added effort in the recitation and are irritating physiologically, accordingly the priest irons them out. Thus, an unconscious tendency toward economy of effort and rhythmic gratification, acting through many generations, may be assumed to have brought about the present comparative regularity in meter.

There is another sort of repetition which gives the impression of being quite sophisticated, a repetition of movement, of progress in unfolding the story. It may be illustrated by the passage in the "Virgin Birth" which relates the rapid progress of Bugan's pregnancy. The sisters are coming out of their bath in the river and Bugan has just remarked, "My loincloth's too little — must be thy loincloth, Magapid." Magapid's answer corresponds to a movement as if she were balancing first on one foot, then on another — or perhaps it would be better to say that it is as if she were advancing one foot, bringing the other up even, and then taking another half-step:

Kánadi the answer
Of her sister Magapid,
Kánadin says she,

"We haven't mixed loincloths —
Look — this is my loincloth,
For its hem's a little crooked."

Kánadibon says Magapid,
Kánadin says she,

"Look at thy loincloth —
Its hem is even!"

Kánadibon continues Magapid,
"Why, thy body is swollen, Bugan!"

This is not the inevitable balance of dialogue — it is a balance in the speech of a single person. It occurred earlier when Maíngit was breaking the news to Bugan about her condition:

Kánadin answered Maíngit,
Kánadin "That's right!" he answered.
Abúnadimo kanú ya kanádi
Kánadin continues Maíngit,
"If thou shouldst give birth, Bugan,
Don't go wrong on the name."
Kánadin continues Maíngit
"Name him Balitok," he says.

It occurs when Amtalao notices Bugan's condition and again in Amtalao's talks with his grandson and in other incidents. But it occurs not only in monologue or conversation:

Kánadi kanú díye
Their go to their granary,
Their granary at Dókyag;
Kánadi arrive there
At their granary place in Dókyag.
Kánadimo Búgan of Kiángan
Opens up their granary
Their granary at Dókyag,
Kánadi kanú tatáowa
Rests her hand on the upper rice layer,
Of their granary at Dókyag.

A somewhat different movement is often observed, which might be termed "inching along":

The sisters go into their dwelling,
Kánadimo kanú tatáowa
Take down their utensils
And go ahead and eat,
They finish eating,
Then put things away.
Kánadimoh kanú tatáowa
They chew their betel quids,
In their village of Kiangan,
Turn them red and thick-spittled.

There are bold "steps" forward at times, too, especially in Balitok's testing of the mana he has received from his father, in the curses he calls down on his enemies, and in the battle.

Now all these movements in the myth are just the movements that are basic in the Ifugao dance: the half-step; the "inching along" (in the case of the male dancers a short hop; in the case of the females a pulling themselves along with the toes, both feet flat on the ground); a balancing of the weight on first one foot then the other while swinging and dipping the extended arms; and, sometimes, bold full steps forward. The basic movements of the one are the basic movements of the other. The Ifugao myth *dances* along — just like Self-Beheaded.

The mood is sprightly — usually in a minor key. In the "Virgin Birth," for example, there are no appeals to any deep emotions until we come to the feud with the covillagers and combat. There is even no censure, or only the mildest, for the girl's refusing and refusing — a most abnormal thing to the Ifugao. There is certainly no sympathy for her plight after eating the betel. There is no commendation of Maíngit for standing by the girl in her trouble, nor any expression of admiration for his really matchless bedside manner when he acts as accoucheur.

The only emotional situations to be found in any myths are those connected with the increase of the pigs, the chickens and the rice, the collection of debts (or the reverse — escape from the clutches of creditors), the overcoming of enemies, the shunting aside of sorceries, evil spirits and sickness. When it comes to these matters, the key changes to major, the priest presses the throttle to the footboard and throws on all the power. He overwhelms his enemy with an avalanche of destructive metaphors, pronounces on him a magnificent curse and, having invoked utter extermination followed out to the rootlets of that one's family, "including the boy-babes," he adds the final insult of his sardonic pity: "We will keep hearing about it; when the Sun is halfway, we will pity them." It is in this part of the myth, in its

application to the basic desires of the Ifugao's heart, the subjects of
his thoughts and the purposes of his life, that the metaphors are
concentrated. They are strong, unusual to our concepts, drawn from
the Ifugao's own environment and often hard to translate.

The Ifugao is quite obviously playing with another literary device
— suspense — but is not very skillful with it. Thus, in Myth 16,
Balitok in quest of a "pacifier" is passed on from deity to deity, until
finally he comes to the right one. We see a somewhat more skillful
suspense in Myth 11, when the hero has to make two attempts to seal
the gods of the winds into their cave, and again in the bargaining of
the latter for their freedom. These devices are favorites and continually recur.

From a literary standpoint, the tendentious ending of Ifugao myths
is objectionable; it is an inevitable accompaniment of the use of
myths as magic. Still more objectionable is the three or four times
repeated Central Ifugao type of *tulud* (as in Myth 2) — a repetition of
practically the identical material of the myth itself. Still, the repetitions are never verbatim — there is always the abridgement of
some matter and enough freshness in the repeated version, for the
Ifugao at least, to lessen the monotony a little.

The dialogue is usually vapid and insipid, and traces of ingenuity
are rare. But the most serious literary defect is the inclusion of an
enormous number of tiresome details. If the myth relates the setting
forth of a character on a journey, it has him pound his rice, winnow
it twice, put water in a pot, sift in the rice, fire the pot, force the fire,
boil the rice, take off the pot, set it by the fire to roast ["dry"],
paddle the rice out into a basket or wooden bowl, eat, put the utensils
away, untuck his hipbag, take out betels, lime them, place the quid
between his teeth, crunch it, turn the spittle red and thick and then
spit it out. After that the character packs up what he wants to carry
on his journey, tucks on his hipbag, "follows" this act by belting on
his scabbard, takes his spear in hand, descends from his house, crosses
the outskirts of his village, and the reader will thank God that his
hero is at last on his way and will hope for something interesting. But
his hope will die a-borning, for the journey itself will be described in
like detail — uphill, downhill around the hill, up and down, along the
rice dikes, across streams, the naming of many places — and the
character will sit down once or twice to chew betels in equal detail
and perhaps even cook and eat again. And when he returns by the
same route, it is all to do over again. The same overloading with
detail enters into descriptions of rituals and techniques. I have spared
the reader so far as I conscientiously could.

The descriptions in the myths of rituals, while usually (and fortunately!) abridged, are occasionally fairly complete and of ethnographic importance. There is an excellent summary of the ritual that precedes a hunt (at present used only before the first hunt of the year) in 28 and in 16 and 17, descriptions of the preliminary ritual of the prestige feast which, combined, attain a fair completeness. Some of the technological descriptions are also good. Number 17 begins with a description of the processes of making rice wine. In 9 we are given a description of the process of making knives and spearheads out of the Chinese cast-iron kettle, the form of iron which apparently reached the Ifugao first — at least the form he first utilized for these puposes. I suspect he really cast the iron, for it is doubtful that he could have reduced the carbon content by any means within his power. However, he projects his present process of working imported steel back to those days. Amtalao, having decided to make weapons for his sons, kicks a cast-iron kettle out the backdoor of his house; it falls and is broken into pieces. He feigns a hypocritical distress as if an accident had occurred in order to avoid a row with his wife. He gathers up the pieces and hammers them into shape. The Ifugaos believe that by hammering and heating alternately, in the old days, their forefathers were able to reduce the brittleness of the iron to malleability. Spears made from this iron exist to this day and are precious heirlooms: they are sold for very high prices and may be sold only with the consent of the owner's kindred. Title passes after the performance of rites similar to those which accompany the sale of inherited lands or of other heirlooms. The spears are very brittle; they take a high polish.

Despite the fact that the Ifugaos' habitat is one of surpassing beauty — according to my own standards, the most beautiful part of the earth's surface — the myths lack any reference to beauty of landscape or of natural objects. I noted this early during my long stay among this people and was always trying to ascertain whether or not the Ifugaos appreciate natural beauty in any degree. I feel fairly certain that they do not. It is true that when an Ifugao stops to rest on his steep mountain trails he seems to choose a jutting point, open so far as possible on all sides, and giving a good view. There he will sit, recovering his wind, fanning himself with the free end of his g-string, chewing betels and spitting all around and gazing out, now over flooded terraces that clamber tier after tier up the rugged mountain sides to the number sometimes of over a hundred, again over dainty tree ferns standing alone or in clusters, now over little thatch-roofed villages perched on hillocks or spurs, or over a verdure of mountain forest. But I am convinced that he gazes vacantly, that the scene arouses no emotion in him. He probably chooses the point as his resting place because the breeze is good, because it is relatively safe from ambush, and because he simply feels less shut-in than he would elsewhere. I have never heard him speak of a landscape's beauties — and if he did he would have to use, for that kind of beauty, a word borrowed from a lowland language which in turn got it from Spanish — *napintat, (from pintado)*, a word not very widely known.

It is also true that in those villages that have the *atul* stonepaved lounging place or the *bantag* large wooden bench or platform, where the folk gather, sit, and chat, these are usually placed in that angle of the village where the view is best. But the location is chosen, I think, because the folk want to be able to see who is coming, who is going, who is doing what.

So far as my observation goes, the Ifugao's esthetic appreciation does not extend much beyond designs,[2] fine workmanship, strong *magic-charged* figures of speech, rhythm and, in less degree, melody. To a slight extent, as if it were incipient, there is an appreciation of the beauty of the human figure and of a limpid complexion; the woman's long hair and shining ornaments — the latter more frequently than the former — are mentioned sometimes in the myths and oftener in the epics. As regards natural things there appears to be an appreciation of only those things which have good implications in magic for the kinship group, and these the Ifugao sees, not as beautiful in our sense of the word, but as symbolically and magic-chargedly beautiful.

Thus, in myths and invocations, the flourishing clump of giant bamboo, protected by its tangled and impenetrable growth of thorny lower branches, stands as a symbol for that unassailability and impregnable unity that he desires for his kinship group. In like manner, the *baliti* tree, a kind of banyan (*Ficus religiosus*), strangling the tree on which it grows parasitically and sending down creeper after creeper to take root and fortify its further spread, is a symbol for dominance over enemies, for the exuberant increase of the kinship group and its ability to exploit other groups. "Rice fields mounting the hills" is a symbol for the increase in wealth and numbers of his group, as also is "smoke from a myriad clearings." Though these are to him primarily symbolical, they doubtless arouse an emotional response which may fairly be assumed to be akin to an appreciation of beauty. It should be unnecessary to add that non-appreciation of the beauty of landscapes is not an inherent or racial trait: Ifugaos have it who have been educated to it, and the lowland Filipinos, of the same race, have given the world some noteworthy artists and writers.

The myths contain passages that strike us as anti-climactic or as profoundly naive: for example,

> Lobwag descends at Bahelna,
> Taking his spear and shield,
> And runs away at Bahelna.

Or

> There are the pretty ones,
> Bugan and Magapid,
> Lousing each other,
> They whose beauty 's profound.

Or the following from the final clinching phrase of the "Tinikman" myth (16), whose purpose is to insure a peaceable drinkfest and a not too tardy departure of the guests:

"... and the drinkfest guests become very drunk. But be closed tight their hands, and be they unconscious of their knives and be they unconscious of their way, so that they be carried home face upward on backs, or with one or more bearers at either end of them, by their children and women folk. And we brothers to each other or fathers and sons to each other who have accomplished the prestige feast will be left alone like the heartwood of a [rotting] tree."

Well, the Ifugao has no pride against admitting fear and running away when there is danger — provided he does not abandon a kinsman. And there is no more naiveté in the last two situations than there is to us in a woman's combing her hair or in our calling a taxi to "speed the parting guest." And who of us has not sometime thought of himself as heartwood as compared with the guest ?

5. CLASSIFICATION, NUMBER AND LENGTH OF THE MYTHS; MYTH CREATION AND TRENDS

At least outside of Europe, it is the myth motif, not the myth, that is the unit of historical connections in mythology.

Ifugao motifs may be regarded as belonging to two groups: 1) those brought into the present habitat and, 2) those that have grown up since the imigration. The first kind of motifs we call "general," because they are also found throughout Indonesia, Polynesia, both Americas, Europe, Asia and Northern Africa. The second kind we call "recent."

When we speak of general *myths*, it is only in the sense that such myths contain general motifs. If we speak of the general myths of this or that area, there can be no implication of any great similarity of narrative, because the narratives reflect different traditions, environments, cultures, and the minds of different myth builders. Even *identical motifs* may be only formally similar — the contents may differ greatly.

The second type of myths, called "recent," are idiosyncratic and particular for each people, since they contain no general motifs or, in Ifugao, sometimes, only one motif, greatly re-interpreted. The recent myths of two or more peoples can be compared only with respect to function, style and general characters.

Ifugao myths of this type fall into three classes: "recent traditional" based apparently on tradition; formulary or "invented" which are as if made-up, manufactured outright, for a ritual purpose or cultural reinforcement; and "contest."

Many of the "invented" myths are little more than formulae — and may be either the beginning of invention or the final product of the degeneration that sometimes results from the use of myths for the exclusive purpose of ritual.

The "contest" myths appear to be founded on the observation that things and creatures, in nature, are at war with each other. Myth 26, telling of the contest between Hardstone and Softstone, is a good example. It is possible that these myths are a degenerate form of the "trickster stories" almost universally found elsewhere, a simplified form having grown from their use as magic.

Any kind of classification in the field of mythology is bound to do a considerable amount of violence to an exceedingly intricate and involved reality. Still, it is desirable to have an approximate conception of the amount of the total myth body that falls under each

Classification of 55 Myths on the Basis of Types and Ritual Use.

Used in Rituals Pertaining to:	General	Doubtful or Mixed	Recent Tradit.	Recent Invented	Contest	Total
Sickness	5		1	6		12
War, sorcery	4	2	2	3	7	18
Prestige feasts			1	3		4
General Welfare and agricultural	1		1	2		4
Debt collection			1	1		2
Transfer of field				1		1
Hunting				1		1
Love charm	1					1
Marriage and peace making		1				1
Wounds, snakebite	1					1
Death				4		4
First haircutting	1					1
Property protect.				1		1
Birth				4		4
	13	3	6	26	7	55

of the classes named above and of the various ritual uses to which myths are put. But it must be remembered that many myths are used for two, three, or more ritual purposes, so that the use here attributed is only that one for which the myth is adapted by the tendentious ending that *happened* to be recorded.

We shall now attempt an approximate quantitative estimate of the total amount of myth material that exists in any single locality in the part of the Bulâ valley where these myths were recorded. As has been said, I have recorded 92 myths in this region. I noted, toward the end of my stay, that when I asked an informant to relate a myth, he would begin, more often than not, on one I had already recorded. To a certain extent this might perhaps be explained on the ground that I had already recorded the more important myths, but in part it must have been a result of my having already recorded a large part of the material.

At a mock headfeast in Anao — a gala affair! — I heard over 40 myths recited. It is fair to assume that this pretty well exhausted the war myths of that locality. Sickness myths are yet more numerous, despite the fact that (for reasons that will be stated later) they do not appear so in our table. Let us suppose there are 60 of these. Agricultural myths may be taken as 4 or 5 times as numerous as those shown in our table, say about 20. All the rest may be considered as being about three times as numerous as shown in the table — say about 60. This gives a total myth body of about 180 myths, many of which are stereotyped repetitions of a single formula.

Let us glance again at the table. We have shown a total of 13 general myths, of which are reproduced in this volume (nos. 1, 3, 5, 6, 10, 13, 14, 15, 19, 22; "doubtful" are nos. 9, 11; "based on recent tradition" are nos. 4, 7, 12 of this volume). I doubt that there are many more general myths that I have not recorded — perhaps only two or three more. We may, then, conclude that these myths comprise less than 10 per cent of the total myth body. This small percentage, however, both to the Ifugao and to the general reader, exceeds all the rest of the mythology in plot interest. [Still, the most interesting *single* myth, especially to the Ifugao, is one of which I have found no counterpart elsewhere — myth No. 7 — based probably on recent tradition].

Myths vary greatly in length. Length is determined mainly by whether or not the rites in which the myth is used are largely attended or not. Largely attended occasions are: certain ones of the war and sorcery rites, of the agricultural rites, all public prestige rites, marriage and peacemaking rites, first haircutting. Such rites as sickness, debt-collection, property protection, birth, death hunting rites and many others are of more or less private character and, though not usually secret, are ill-attended. The priests naturally see no reason for putting on a show when there are no spectators, so the myth versions used at these are short. Besides, there is an added reason for brevity in the fact that only one or two or at most three priests are present at such rites. These few priests have often a large number of myths to recite: if they are to finish within a reasonable time, the myths may not be too lengthy. The number of myths used in sickness rituals is especially large because the Ifugao does not trust his diagnosis of causative agents any more than a poor doctor does. And, like the latter, he relies on shotgun prescriptions — relies on a great number of rites and ceremonies, some one of which, he hopes, will be the right one to relieve the sickness.

The result is that some of the myths used in agricultural or prestige feasts or public war and sorcery rites are fully 7 or 8 times as long as the myths of nearly all of the invented or formulary type that are used to cure sickness or in minor agricultural rites, which are household affairs, or in the preliminary rites for prestige feasts, which also are private. General myths, when used in private or petty occasions, retain their length — the Ifugao either does not know how to abridge them or does not want to. Some of the invented myths used on public occasions are quite long — one of those used in agricultural rites is the longest myth I have recorded. There is little or no interest in its plot; it consists of a repetition of pictures of prosperity such as are of the stuff of the Ifugao's daydreams.

The paradoxical lack of invention in invented myths may be due in part to the jumbled, simultaneous recitation of myths, incomprehensible to the audience, so that there is no spur to invention from this source. However, the audience is not the only spur to invention. The priests throw in little improvements to please *themselves* — in some of the myths. For example, in the "unwanted child" or Iron Eater (14), the adoptive parents express a hypocritical pity for the child they have tried to kill: "What a pity for the child — so deft and competent in our village in the Upstream Region." This happens when there is sufficient plot nidus to stimulate the priest's fancy. If this be lacking, then there is use only for such a meter or rhythm as shall be physiologically agreeable and economize energy expenditure. If there be need for more length, it can be supplied by adding repetitions to the tulud.

The overwhelming majority of myths are of the invented type and this is true to a far greater extent than our table shows. For since these are usually dull myths, I frequently passed them up, when recording, as soon as their character revealed itself. Still, although

the majority are formulary and follow stereotyped patterns, there
are a few of these invented myths that are of exceeding interest,
since they appear to show how myths are sometimes built.

The origin of this interesting type of myth is explicable on the
ground that some time in the past, some striking, grotesque or
terrifying object or behavior has impressed the animism and magic
soaked mind of an Ifugao worried well-nigh unto death by fear of
his enemies or creditors and that hope and wishful thinking have
suggested that back of what he has observed there are powerful
supernatural forces that might aid him. On this basis, apparently, he
has laid the foundation for a new myth or else has incorporated his
hope in an existing one, greatly changing the latter in order to make
it accommodate his hope.

The behavior of the drake of that variety of ducks raised by the
Ifugaos, when he meets a hen-duck, is almost uncanny. It consists of
grotesque head-thrustings and evil-sounding hissings that give the
beholder a creepy feeling.[1] This behavior has been incorporated in a
myth (14) of composite motif-source in which eight neck-thrusting,.
hissing, drake-like beings destroy enemies and creditors.

A swollen-to-monstrous-proportions beheaded corpse, its neck-
stump bubbling and bubbling in the tropical heat, suggested, one
may easily believe, a supernatural similar being that would liquidate
enemies. Thereupon, possibly, a pre-existing myth built on the widespread incomplete body motif (the one-sided man, the bodiless head)
was modified to conform with this wish-fantasy. Or, it may be, a new
myth was built outright — at all events, the myth of the Self-
Beheaded (No. 2) resulted.

Likewise the fantasy possessing a priest as he looked over a row of
swine lying hog-tied and trammelled on the ground near some ritual
performance, awaiting sacrifice in which they would be done to cruel
death by having a stick rammed repeatedly into their vitals — the
fantasy that he would like to see his enemies in just such a situation,
waiting to be sacrificed along with the swine — must have given rise
to the tulud "Pinading" (myth 17).[2]

Myth creation takes place in the following grammatical milieu:
1) all Ifugao myth narratives are in the present tense, but this tense
is a historical present; 2) as we have already shown, a tulud is a
repetition of a myth in the present tense.

Now I believe that while some *tulud may* have grown up as a
means of clinching (section 2) the magic involved in myths, other
tulud begin in magic and develop into myths. That is to say the
tulud is final product in some cases and beginning in others.

Let us illustrate by means of the *tulud* "Pinading" (17). The plot.

is as follows: Two spirits of the class called *pinading* make a contract
while drunk for the intermarriage of their children. One of them is
poverty-stricken, the other is rich. Time passes and the children are
to be married by a prestige feast. The poor one is unable to contribute the animals for sacrifice at this feast which he is obligated to
furnish as prospective co-father-in-law. He goes, along with a kinsman, to all his relatives (who are also poor) in the attempt to borrow
pigs, but one passes him on to another, and so he goes on without
success. But all the while he is coming nearer and nearer the place
where the Ifugaos are making rites of sorcery, till finally in the *tulud*
recitation, he is made to arrive at the house of a relative in the very
neighborhood. This relative directs him to the house of the Ifugaos
where the ritual is under way. The Ifugaos send him to take their
human enemies and use them as porcine *ersatz*. He does so and delivers
the Ifugaos' enemies to his co-father-in-law-to-be, and they are
trammelled and laid in a row with the swine to be sacrificed. The
place spirits praise his contribution; great prosperity follows.

Now, bearing in mind the poverty of human inventiveness and
remembering that inventions of any complexity are always accretions,
let us consider how such a *tulud* may very likely have grown. We may
fairly suppose that the first priest who acted on his fantasy simply
voiced his wish about the use of his enemies as offerings in the form
of a prayer to one of the local *pinading* deities (place-spirits), directing
that deity to go and bring the enemy and place him among the hogs.
The prayer took root and became an established rite. We may
suppose that it could the more easily do this because it corresponded
to the wish-fantasy of many another man.

But prayer is considered a weak measure and the Ifugao does not
put much confidence in it as a means of securing results. For no more
than human beings do the deities act disinterestedly in one's behalf.
Prayer is usually accompanied by some kind of offering — a sacrifice
or at least a sip of rice wine, and then it has not so much the nature
of a supplication as of a statement of what is wanted in return for
something given. It is far more effective — and cheaper — to give
the deities a selfish motive for doing what is wanted and to put them
in such a position that they will want to do it. And so a rationalization
with this end in view begins. The *pinading* needs pigs because he is
poor and has none. He needs pigs for his contribution to his child's
father-in-law for a prestige-wedding feast. But how could a poverty-
stricken deity's child be engaged in marriage to the child of a wealthy
deity? Oh — of course they were drunk when the engagement pact
was made — and rationalization continues in this manner. Probably
many generations were needed to perfect the fully rationalized plot,

for no Ifugao sets out deliberately to develop an agency of magic or ritual. But in the course of time a plot is developed which does put the deity in the most delicate situation as regards his pride that the Ifugao can conceive of — the position of a poor man obligated to contribute to a prestige feast in which his child marries into a wealthy family. And so, finally, the once simple prayer develops into a *tulud*, in accordance with the pattern of the ritual. As a rule, the prayer might more likely, in Ifugaoland, develop into a deity,[3] but the fantasy back of this one not only has a universal appeal but incites the imagination.

We have, as yet, only a *tulud*. Because it has a universal appeal, it spreads to some distance from its origin. It is used in public war ritual, at headfeasts and in headlosers' rites — it "rates" more length. So it is lengthened and adapted to ostentatious ritual according to the pattern of the culture; the *pinading* is brought by stages to the rites.

How might the *tulud* become a myth, in the future ? By a simple change from the present tense to the historical present. The invention or addition of an interesting new incident might constitute a catalyzer that would set the reaction going.

This particular *tulud* seems to be on the make. Its appeal, its importance in public ritual, together with the general pattern of the culture, are likely to change the first episode to a myth. This change appears to have occurred in the case of the "Self-Beheaded" (2).

Like everything else, the Ifugao myth contains the seeds of its further change. Its process of change is subject to the general law that development of ideological elements does not proceed independently but is constantly conditioned by the more basic factors of culture, especially cultural trend and the socio-economic relations, and is dependent on these for its opportunity to pursue its own course.

One seed of change in the Ifugao myth is in its use as a recitative. This use creates rhythm, elaborates plot to a rather slight degree, figurative language probably, and other literary qualities, and leads it along the road of development into the epic, the ballad, the lyric, the narrative — to creative literature. Another seed of change is in the use of the myth as magic. This tends to make the whole myth magic and nothing else, eliminating its detail and plot and converting it, as a final product, into a mere formula, spell, spoken charm or, sometimes, superstitious belief. From our viewpoint we would call the first road one of development and the latter one of decay. But, paradoxically, in some cases, the final product of what we would call "decay" may be a nursery rhyme — more immortal, certainly, and perhaps more important, than ninety-nine per cent of literary creations.

In Ifugao culture, the development of the latter, "degenerative" contradiction in the myth is held in check by those conditions of Ifugao society which find in the present myth-complex a needed outlet for exhibitionism, which make for a numerous priesthood and which make kinship groups suspicious of foreign priests. Let these conditions change and the myth will change.

The Nabaloi and Kankanai, with whose myths we correlated our Ifugao myths, illustrate this fact. With these people the territorial principle of social organization is well developed: the village is the principal social unit and in some localities has a governing council. Exceedingly wealthy individuals control the people, directly as overlords or indirectly through the council. Since the kinship principle is no longer dominant in the social organization, the people have lost their fear of foreign priests with the result that the number of priests is 30 to 50 times smaller than among the Ifugaos, being on the average two men and one woman to about 500 inhabitants.[4] As we have seen, the myths of these tribes are greatly abridged: they have lost plot and detail — the whole myth is magic (and not much else but magic) — power magic, charm magic. Not myths but dialogued songs and improvisations constitute the channel for exhibitionism and literary creativeness.

The predominance of sympathetic magic in the Ifugao's myths appears to be a reflection of the very principle on which his society is organized — the principle of the identification of one kinsman with another and with the whole kinship group. Do something, then, to one and you do it to another and, most likely, to the whole group. The Ifugao sees phenomena grouped together as men are, in his society. Indeed, such would appear to be the general foundation of sympathetic magic. Rain, dust in the air, wind, thunder, the wriggling of a snake, lightning, the trilling of frogs, clouds, falling tears — all of these the man in early tribal society conceives as a "clan" or "kinship group" of phenomena. Set one in action, whether you pour water from a high place, whirl a bull-roarer, throw dust into the air, hold a wriggling snake in your mouth, whip frogs, throw up feathers or cause a rain of tears as did the Aztecs, through sacrificing children, and you set the whole "clan" into action and get the rain.

The total magic is, of course, more intricate, embracing survival of primitive word magic and transmissions of other kinds of magic from quite differing cultures. Furthermore, no purely tribal societies exist. Ifugao society is one of the purest of them, because of the low development of other principles of organization. It seems to me that it is safe to say that sympathetic magic is the dominant form in societies organized on the blood-tie principle.

Feudal and slave societies are characterized by unique, paramount individuals who, controlling the tiny, narrow world of their subjects, seem to the latter to embody the highest imaginable powers — individuals inherently high and singular, whose very blood is different from that of ordinary folk. In dealing with them or with the supernatural beings who are created or recreated in their image, all depends on a correct approach, on knowing secrets of access, on saying the right words in the right way. Magic reflects this new society by superimposing a layer of a new sort on the accretions of the past, a layer which, reflecting the new relations of men to their masters and overlords, is characterized by powerful master words, signs, charms, secret names and formulae and the like. The magic of the past does, indeed, continue on, because the old social relations on which it was based continue on — these have been dominated and limited, but by no means destroyed by the new order. But the preferred magic is that which is created in the image of the times, and much of the old magic is also reinterpreted in that spirit.

In the fact that the Ifugao myth is already, in some degree, itself, considered to be a magical entity rather than as merely affording parallels for sympathetic magic, in the degeneration of some myths to the form of "invented" ones, in the tendency of some priests and of some regions to use few "clinching" phrases for magic parallels, in the wholesale invention of myths to serve as magic alone, we see the development of the myth toward that form of magic which is the characteristic contribution of slaveholding and feudal societies, reflecting the rise in Ifugao society of large properties and of powerful individuals.

Likewise, in Mr. Marco Manghe's excellent recording of a myth of outstanding literary quality (Myth 1), and in the delight he took in it, in poetizations by Deputy-Governor Luis Pawid of several myths (one of which I had intended to include in an appendix to this work but cannot on account of its having been lost during the Japanese invasion), and in the interest manifested by a number of other young Ifugaos in the mythology of their fathers *as literature* — an interest which needs only a little encouragement to make it flower — and finally, in the poetic qualities we have seen and shall continue to see in the myths themselves, there is confirmation of the views expressed above regarding a more positive and creative trend in Ifugao mythology.

6. AFFILIATIONS OF IFUGAO MYTHS

It is to be doubted that dissemination of general motifs is due to any great extent to borowing, because:

1) The borrowing of a myth *as a myth* would involve the borrowing of a new world viewpoint or at least a change in the old one. It would involve a displacement and a re-integration, almost impossible to achieve. In comparison, the borrowing of a new language would be easy. Men are usually satisfied with their world viewpoints and are not looking for opportunities to change them.

2) *Folktales* do not encounter these difficulties: it is quite possible that myth narratives may be borrowed in the role of folktales. And yet I doubt that even the borrowing of folktales happens as much as is generally believed. I have known the Ifugaos for over thirty years. I have read them folktales, have given literate Ifugaos folktales to read; the textbooks used in the schools have contained the folktales of kindred Malayan peoples. But a collection of over thirty folktales recorded in 1937 and 1941 did not gather in a single folktale borrowed from any of these sources. Still, folktales are borrowed sometimes; no doubt myth narratives are borrowed sometimes and function as folktales. It is barely possible that the latter, with revision and gradual integration, sometimes cross the line and become myths again among their acceptors. Here again, the Ifugao material hardly supports the last conjecture. It would be hard to imagine a more favorable influence for this process than the expansive trend of Ifugao ritual. About everything that has presented itself at the mill of the Ifugao religion has been accepted as grist except — a few borrowed folktales that could be worked into beautiful myth-magic by recourse to the tendentious endings that the Ifugao is so adept at contriving: for example, Jack and the Beanstalk, the Magic Flight, the Ogre-Killer. It is barely possible that a myth version of these tales may exist unrecorded, but very unlikely.

3) The distributions of myths of sufficient similarity to suggest borrowing is often such that their having been borrowed is an impossibility. For example, making due allowance for cultural and environmental differences, a Bella Coola myth[1] and the Icarus myth of the Romans; or, our Ifugao Myth 1 and a Wyandot myth,[2] are sufficiently alike to suggest borrowing. Conversely, adjacent tribes often have myths built largely on the same motifs that differ so much as to make their having been borrowed an improbability. Thus, the Kankanai cognate of our Myth 1, although containing a number of the same motifs, is too variant to have been borrowed, and less like the Ifugao myth than the Wyandot myth just mentioned.

The material I can present in a work like this is far too meager to sustain a hypothesis, yet I must present the hypothesis in order to make clear certain terms that I must use in discussing the affiliations of Ifugao myths. It is as follows:

Myths carrying these general motifs were built in a region that gave streams of migrants to many quarters and which was crossed and recrossed by streams of migrants. Throughout human history ethnic groups have continually assembled and dispersed, formed and re-formed, have given off streams to other groups, have dispersed or been dispersed. Every migratory stream carried its own culture, including its myths. All this has gone on many times and the streams have travelled far. Whenever a group received a sizable accession or whenever a group was formed from the pouring of migrant streams into a relatively vacant territory, there was, in addition to the normal and incessant variation in myth versions, a particularly sharp clash of versions, a confusion and fragmentation of the myths, followed by a re-assemblage of motifs in different order, perhaps, or at least with re-interpretation, and the growth of quite variant versions, some of which won greater popularity in the ensuing competition than others did.

During the period of re-assemblage and myth-rebuilding, the following processes occurred:

1) Intrusion of extraneous motifs from other myths.

2) Strained integration, or "faulting," due to the difficulty of making the old motifs fit together in a new story, a difficulty that has often been awkwardly rationalized.

3) Reshuffling of the motifs, so that they appeared in different order. But the ancient motifs were associated in men's minds and this association persisted though the myths themselves had broken down, so that there was a tendency for the motifs to cling together. This fact imposed a degree of limitation in the re-assemblage, and sometimes the motifs fell with similar order and similar interpretation, just as similar hands of cards may fall in the course of many shufflings.

4) Re-interpretation of motifs. But a motif did not permit of infinite interpretation because the very statement of it imposed limitations.

Definitely to determine the validity of this hypothesis would be a work of cosmic proportions, and possibly so little of the myth and folklore material of the world has been well recorded that it could not be done at this time.

We shall note a very few of the regional and global affiliations of three of the myths published in this work. The motifs of these myths are designated, the first by letters A–Q, the second by letters R–Z and the third by letters a–j.

MYTH 1. THE VIRGIN BIRTH

A.[3] Girl refuses all suitors.

B. She and sister louse each other.

C. Son of Thunder gives her a betel quid from which she conceives.

D. Deity announces her conception and the name of the child-to-be.

E. Rapid advance of pregnancy.

F. Girl ridiculed by villagers.

G. Birth away from home.

H. Deity acts as midwife.

I. Girl bears a hodgepodge of objects and creatures having significance as omens.

J. Birth signified by a celestial phenomenon [the rainbow].

K. Child bathed in jewels.

L. Rapid growth of child.

M. Child asks and receives top from grandsire.

N. Contests in which the child wins over the village children lead to taunts about child's paternity and a fend.

O. Grandfather makes a weapon for the child.

P. "Father"-deity endows with power by giving parts of his body to child.

Q. Child darts out lightning, blasts enemies. Tendentious ending.

MYTH 6. ORIGIN OF IRRIGATED RICE

R. Ifugao hunters kill pig in Skyworld, divide meat with deities.

S. Ifugaos cook meat; deities eat their portion raw, having no fire.

T. Ifugaos trade fire for Skyworld rice.

U. Ifugaos teach use of fire, deities teach cultivation of rice.

V. Ifugao tells wife to sit under blanket without moving [strained integration].

W. Ifugao makes fields rapidly with automatic implements.

X. Wife moves, spoiling supernatural field-building.

Y. Ifugao upbraids wife.

Z. She replies that they have enough fields for the present generation [strained integration].

Z.[2] God provides irrigation water by striking spear into bank. Tendentious ending.

MYTH 14: THE IRON-EATER

a. Deity is disgusted with son because latter eats guest's spears and knives.

b. Deity washes son down to earth by means of a heavy rain (cf. Myth 3).

c. Boy, adopted by Ifugaos, again manifests his abnormal appetite.

d. Ifugao takes boy wood-getting, fells tree on him.

e. Boy recovers, carries tree home, chops it into firewood.

f. Ifugao takes boy fishing, drops boulder on him.

g. Boy recovers, throws off boulder.

h. Boy floats downstream.

i. Boy creates 8 mythical monsters from bamboo nodes.

j. Boy brings monsters and rescues "parents" from enemies and creditors.

Mayaoyao Affiliations: — In his series, the "Mayaoyao Ritual," the Rev. Mr. Lambrecht has published 56 myths. The Mayaoyao are a group numbering about 12,000, who, as has been said, inhabit the extreme northeastern corner of Ifugaoland. Constituting one of the later migrations, they differ rather markedly from the Central Ifugaos in mythology and religion. Their myths fall, like Ifugao myths, into "general" and "recent," the latter predominating to an even greater extent than among the Ifugao, since only six of those recorded can be classified as general. Three general motives, however, immortalization by fire, endowment with parts from deities' bodies, and the fighting twins motif, appear rather frequently, and often quite awkwardly, in the recent myths. The hero of all the Mayaoyao myths so far published is "Wigan the Ifugao", and his dealings are primarily with "Wigan of the Skyworld," a deity.

The motifs of the three Mayaoyao myths that are cognate to the Ifugao myths analyzed above follow, each one designated by the same letter as in one or another of the Ifugao myths. Where motifs are practically the same, only the letter is used to designate them, otherwise they are particularized. Intrusives are indicated by "♯."

THE VIRGIN BIRTH MYTH — USED RITUALLY, ON OCCUPYING A NEW HOUSE

A.

♯ Amtalao builds a house for his daughter. [Strained integration, apparently an attempt to adapt the myth to its ritual purpose. The girl has no need for a house, since she will not marry, hence this motif does not jibe with the rest of the story]. Cf. the chants of Wigan, the housebuilder, in Barton, 1946, pp. 69, 149, which, however, are used in arthritis and sorcery rites.

C. Deity blackens girl's teeth (an attention of courtship) and touches her navel, wherefore she conceives.

I. Girl bears a hodgepodge of creatures and objects, all of ominous significance, and finally a baby.

J. (?) Hardly present, but the Rainbow is among the things born.
♯ Cf motif "g." But it is the hodgepodge, not the hero that makes
the trip downstream.

M. "Elder brothers" — that is the hodgepodge born preceding the
baby — threaten to "thwart" the child. Marked faulting and strain
of integration here, but possibly comparable to the Ifugao Myth,
when Amtalao says

> "Do not ye us," he says,
> Slaughter on this day,
> For ye'll kill us tomorrow."

P. "Father"-deity endows child with power by giving parts from
his own and other gods' bodies. [Strained integration: the motif
comes most awkwardly into the plot, also ineffectively, because the
child remains helpless and timid].

♯ Boy marries — hence needs a house [tendentious].

♯ Boy is thwarted by elder brothers: he fears he will die. Grandfather says he will intercede with the omen hodgepodge, builds house
for boy, puts poison on roof. But the "thwarters" still harass the boy.
House location is changed several times, but "thwarting" continues.
[The repetitions remind one of the repetitive *tulud*, of Central Ifugao,
but are more confused and planless]. Finally the house is set on a
rock in the underworld, the grandfather makes the proper sacrifice
to the "thwarters" and the myth closes with the clinching phrase,
"On account of this, Bugan and Wigan are living at Dukligan and
their rice, their chickens and their children multiply."

SUPERNATURAL FIELD-BUILDING [AGRICULTURAL RITE]
MAYAWYAW RITUAL, p. 69

R. (?) Ifugao steals rice from neighboring place spirits. Is detected
by Wigan the Deity. Tendentious.

V. Deity builds two fields rapidly, telling Wigan, the Ifugao, to
remain asleep.

W. The Ifugao is awakened and spoils the supernatural field-
building.

X. Deity upbraids the Ifugao, but the latter says two fields are
enough.

♯ Awkwardly tendentious. Deity promises successful harvest and
his promise is fulfilled.

THE UNWANTED CHILD [USED IN SORCERY AGAINST ENEMIES]
MAYAWYAW RITUAL, p. 110

A.

C. Conceives as in Mayaoyao Virgin Birth Myth.

I. Birth of the child without any hodgepodge as in myth just named.

M. Asks and receives top from grandsire.

N. Child breaks top of enemies. [The myth now switches, with very strained integration, to the Unwanted Child motifs]:

♯ When morning the day, says Amtalao (the grandsire), "What did you do, Wigan?" Says Wigan, "I threw down all the tops of the people." This act the Grandfather considers likely to embroil them with the enemies, wherefore he desires to get rid of the boy. This desire is utterly inconsistent with the tendentious ending.

f. Says, Amtalao, "Let us go to fish." He lets a rock fall on the boy.

g. Father-deity commands boy to rise and carry rock home.

d. Grandsire fells a tree on boy.

e. Father-deity commands boy to rise and carry tree home.

♯ Tendentious and strained: Amatalao carrying his top, Wigan the Ifugao carrying his rock, and Wigan the father-deity carrying the tree, go against and destroy the enemies.

These myths have the best plots, poor as they are, of all that Lambrecht publishes. Only through reading the myths themselves can the meagerness, confusedness and inconsistency of Mayaoyao plots, the flatness and colorlessness of their diction and the strains and faultings of the transitions from motif to motif be fully realized. There is none of the vigor, metrical phrasing and figurativeness of Ifugao myths.

Ifugao influence is apparent; it is noteworthy that the motifs are, for the most part, in the same order, though with many gaps, as in the Ifugao myths. Still more noteworthy is the confusion that our hypothesis assigns to the reconstruction of a migrant stream's mythology. The Mayaoyao have evidently become quite conscious of the Ifugao ritual and magical mechanism, but are quite awkward in their tendentious adaptations.

There has been little if any direct intermarriage with the Central Ifugao regions where the myths of this work were recorded, but there has been an indirect intermarriage by way of the intermediate regions of Dukligan, Haliap and Montabiong. I know that many folk of distant Kiangan claim ancestors from Mayaoyao — indirectly, through Ligauwe and Burnay, however.

If the Mayaoyao borrowed the myths they use ritually, why did they not do a better job of borrowing? Of this I feel pretty sure: the Mayaoyao have not borrowed directly from the Ifugaos. The latter people does not, or until recently did not, allow outsiders at their rites. The borrowing, if any, must have been done in intermediate regions with which both Mayaoyao and Ifugao have intermarried.

We could learn a great deal, probably, about the processes of myth building — and I believe it might be solid, non-speculative knowledge — if somebody would:

1. Determine, if possible, how recent the Mayaoyao immigration is and whence it came.

2. Record cognate general myths as found in (a) Ligauwe, Burnay or Mampolia; (b) the intermediate regions of Montabiong (or Humalapap) and Dukligan; (c) in Bunhian, and Natonin in Bontok Subprovince, beyond Mayaoyao. The myths should be sought in both ritual and non-ritual forms.

3. It would be in especially desirable to learn whether the Mayaoyao have non-ritual versions of the general myths they use in ritual and if so, to record these.

Affiliations with Northern Kankanai Myths. — The Kankanai use myths as ritual, but not to so great an extent as the Ifugao. Nor do myths so dominate their literature, which is also unwritten. Folktales, ballads, and poetical stories of a romantic nature are more polished and more highly regarded by the adults. Among the Ifugao, the telling of folktales hardly reaches to adults.

The Kankanai seem to revel in stories of the mistreatment of children by their parents and wicked uncles, of the children's hardships and of their ultimate rise to wealth and dominance and their triumph over those that have misused them. The stories have a mawkish, sentimental character that thrusts itself on one at every turn. The style is less natural and free than among the Ifugao, the meter more polished; stylisms and sophistications are numerous. Strained integrations are not numerous, having, I suppose, been ironed out during the many centuries since the tribe was formed. There has been practically no intermarriage with the Ifugaos, who live only about ten miles distant, as the crow flies, across a high mountain range, but there have been trading relations.

THE KANKANAI VIRGIN BIRTH [NON-RITUAL VERSION]
HERO-DEITY MYTH No. 3, BRR III

a. Gatan, an unwanted son [ubiquitous Kankanai motif!] is driven by parental abuse and neglect to a lonely life in the fields.

♯ He lives in a field shack and plants pomelo [Philippine grapefruit]; the pomelo grows rapidly, producing fruit after one year. He inserts gold in a fruit and casts it into the river.

♯ Many people grab at the fruit as it rides past them on the current, but fail to catch it.

C. Finally, one of two sisters, Bangan, catches it, puts it between her skirt and her belly. When it the sisters arrive home, it is not there. They retrace their path, but fail to find it.

E. Bangan finds herself pregnant, is scolded and rejected by her father and sent with her sister to find the owner of the tree that produced the pomelo.

I. Bangan bears twin boys when they arrive at the hut, and leaves them there.

♯ "Father" recognizes sons by their golden finger-nails.

L. "Father" chugs them on the floor: they are able to sit up. Next day, he stands them up, and they are able to stand alone. He gives them a push and they are able to walk and run. On the following day, he talks with them, and they are able to talk.

♯ Gatan's mother steals the children. Gatan takes them away from her and reproaches her for her heartlessness toward himself.

♯ Gatan and sons attend a prestige feast at Sabangan. Gatan dances. Bangan comes and dances with him. The children recognize her as their mother and run to her. They follow her home, then fetch their father. Gatan and Bangan marry, become exceedingly wealthy and establish the dominant family of Sabangan.

KANKANAI SUPERNATURAL FIELD-BUILDING MYTH
[NON-RITUAL VERSION]
HERO-MYTH NO. 1, BRR III

♯ Lumauwig marries earth woman [Cf. Ifugao Myth 5].

V. Lumauwig goes to make fields, orders wife to bring his lunch, but to cough before coming in sight.

X. Wife approaches without coughing and peeps.

W. She sees that Lumauwig's penis is acting as a crowbar, his scrotum as its fulcrum, his ears as shovels.

♯ Woman returns to the coughing place and coughs.

Y. Lumauwig knows wife's disobediance, upbraids her.

♯ Next morning he sends his wife to the field ahead of him, wraps ashes in a *gabi* leaf, then comes and works with his wife in the ordinary human manner. At night he sends her home, ordering her to blow into what he wrapped in the *gabi* leaf [Cf. Ifugao Myth 15].

♯ Wife blows, is blinded [Idem].

♯ Lumauwig ascends into the Skyworld.

KANKANAI UNWANTED CHILD MYTH [OR FOLKTALE ?]

No. 39, BRR III

a. Son not wanted ...

♯ because he is a head without a body. [Main theme, reversed, of Myth 2 ? Cf. Myth 19].

d. Father fells tree on boy.

e. Boy recovers, carries tree home.

f. Father lets rock down on boy.

g. Boy carries rock home.

h. Father takes boy on long journey, "loses" him.

♯ Boy, realizing that he is not wanted, changes into a squash vine and produces fruits luxuriantly. [Cf. Myth 19].

Very few general myths are used ritually among the Kankanai, I think. They seem to exist mainly in non-ritual or folklore versions.

Affiliations with Nabaloi and Southern Kankanai. — Mr. C. R. Moss has published[4] 15 myths that are used ritually by the Nabaloi. Of these, four contain general motifs; the pages on which they are found, with the corresponding Ifugao myth indicated in parentheses, are: 307 (No. 3), 313 (No. 7), 323 (Ifugao myth recorded by me but not published); 327 (No. 22). Moss has also recorded a number of general myths that are not used ritually in his Nabaloi Tales.

Of Moss's 11 Kankanai myths, only one is built on general motifs — it is our "Iron-eather" myth. In order to show to what extent the process of shrinkage has gone among Southern Kankanai (as also among the Nabaloi), I reproduce this myth:

There were a brother and a sister, Bogan and Singan. Bogan was a woman and Singan was a man. They had children, two boys. The larger was Pintum, the smaller was Liblibian.

When they became older they did not eat. Their father gave the cooked rice from the center (of the pot) and the center of the liver, but they did not like it.

One day when their father and mother had gone to cultivate the land and had returned, they had already eaten one half of their pot. They said, "How is this? you like to eat iron pots." "Yes, iron is what we like to eat."

Then Liblibian and Pintun left together and went to the land of the Ilocano. When they arrived, they made one child of an Ilocano sick so that there would be a reason for giving them bolos to eat. The Ilokano did not know enough to give them bolos to eat, but knew of medicine only. They said, "Oh! The Ilocano do not know the prayer, so let us go to Igorot land."

They went to Igorot land and made sick one child of an Igorot. He took at once one chicken and fifteen bolos and held the ceremony *liblibian.* As soon as this was done the sickness of the child was cured at once.

The name of one of these children, Liblibian, is the name of a class of Ifugao deities [Barton, 1946, p. 65] to whom just such an offering is made.

The principal hero of Nabaloi myths is Kabigat; Balitok, his brother, is a secondary one. Among the Southern Kankanai, the hero is Kabigat, with Lumauwig and Balitok, his brothers, secondary. Among the Northern Kankanai, and the Bontok, Lumauwig is the sole hero in all the myths I have recorded. Among the Mayaoyao, Wigan is the sole hero. Among the Central Ifugao, Balitok is the principal hero, with Wigan, Lumauwig or Kabigat represented as a brother sometimes and playing a secondary role.

Affiliations with the Tinggian and Kalinga: I found only three general motifs in common with the Tinggian myths published by Cole. They are: No. 56, man-eating bird; No. 73, quarrel between Sun and Moon; No. 74, human being changes to coconut tree.

My Kalinga materials were lost during the Japanese invasion, but I remember that about all the standard motifs were present and that some myths were strikingly similar to Ifugao myths.

Affiliations in Greater Indonesia: Some of the myths recorded by Loeb[5] are of great ritual significance, but not so much for the sake of magic parallels as among the Ifugao. Rather they are used to support the exceedingly elaborate Mentawei ritual — the only one I have encountered that is more extensive than the Ifugao, as it is also more tyrannous over the lives of men and more exacting of prolonged abstinences. The Mentawei religious trend has been expansive primarily with respect to ritual, that of the Ifugaos with respect to the pantheon.

The following is a list of the motifs of the Mentawei Unwanted Child myth:

i. Woman bears septuplet boys.

a. Father says their appetite will be impossible to satisfy, puts them in a bamboo,[6] paddles out to sea, throws them overboard and anchors them.

♯ Father cuts up python, throws pieces into sea; their writhing causes waves which tear bamboo loose from its anchorage. [Strained integration: he is undoing his own work just accomplished].

b or h. Waves carry bamboo to the mouth of a river.

c. Boys are adopted by a fisherman. In the pig offered at the adoption rites, an eighth "brother" is found.

♯ Eighth brother envious because not so "adorned" as the seven and has "bad thoughts" [Tendentious, so as to accomplish, as will be seen, the ritual purpose of the myth].

a, c. Boys kill guests [instead of eating guests' "irons" as in the Ifugao myth]. Finally kill adoptive parent's brother.

d. Adoptive parent sends them up a tree, causes it by magical means to elongate, conjures up a wind. Tree drops them in a far country.

e. Boys return home, plant a garden, carry 8 bunches of bananas and eight bundles of wood home to adoptive father.

♯ Peeved because adoptive father has tried to get rid of them, boys build boat, resist their father's attempt to obstruct their departure [strained and inconsistent]. From the boat, the eighth brother, who has "bad thoughts," shouts curses of diseases and evils on humanity, while the seven others, after each curse . . .

j. shout the ritual remedies by which men can save themselves.

h. (?) Boys sail off into the sky.

♯ Are followed by wives ["faulting!"] in another boat. Father goes to live in the moon.

♯ Both boatloads become constellations, the brothers becoming the Pleiades.

Another Mentawei myth [p. 222], constructed on the motif of the marriage of a goddess (or star) to a man, has common motifs with Myth 10 of this work, but is nearer to Kankanai and Kalinga versions I have recorded than to Ifugao.

A Wyandot myth, published by Barbeau, is in all probablity a shrunken cognate.[7] Another verison of the same myth[8] is remarkably similar to a Kankanai myth I have recorded, as yet unpublished, and has elements in common with Ifugao Myth 10.

Another Wyandot myth[9] is cognate with the Virgin Birth Myth. The motifs are:

A.

♯ Girl marries a youth.

B. But finds out, when she louses him that he is a snake.

♯ Flees from husband, is rescued by Thunder and marries one of his sons [in Ifugao myth I, girl conceives from a son of Thunder], by whom she conceives.

E.

L. Child grows rapidly. Mother takes him to her village, on promising the father to take good care of him.[10]

M. Child receives a bow as a plaything.

N. Quarrels with village children.

Q. Darts out a thunderbolt.

♯ Becomes the Sun-Shower.

A Bella Coola myth is interesting because it not only contains the familiar motifs, but is also remarkably parallel to the Icarus myth.[11]

A.

♯ Woman compelled to marry a stump. Is forced to (B ?) louse him, but finds that the lice are toads. She runs away.

C. She conceives from the Sun.

♯ She descends with her child to earth along the sun's eyelashes [rays].

L. Child grows rapidly.

N. Village children taunt child with having no father.

♯ Child shoots a chain of arrows up into the sky.

♯ He begs his father to permit him to carry the "torches" through the sky. Father permits him, after instructing him to light the torches gradually.

Q. Child lights the torches all at once and scorches the world.

♯ Sun throws his son to earth, transforms him into the mink.

The similarity to the Icarus myth of the Mediterranean area is great; it is somewhat less to the Ifugao Virgin Birth in Indonesia, but still striking. Borrowing is out of the question in either case. I have found other instances of great similarity in South America and Asia.

I suggest that such similarities occur because the motifs of these ancient myths have been carried by migrations and because they tend to *cling together*. They tend to cling together because, although there is a fragmentation of the myths carried by the migrant streams during their amalgamation with other groups, the ancient association of motifs in men's minds never entirely fades. Furthermore, the fragmentation is probably not often atomistic — is rarely a dissolution into single motifs. And so, in the reconstructions, although intrusions may be admitted and some motifs dropped and others drawn from other ancient myths or even from newer ones, the possibilities of variation are limited. Sometimes, essentially the same fragments are put together again and essentially the same myths, making allowance for cultural and environmental differences, result. When one takes into consideration how little of the total body of mythology has been recorded, it seems likely that a full record would show many of these striking parallels.

Comparison of North Luzon Formulary Myths: All tribes of this area with the possible exception of the Apayao, about whom I do not know, have myths of a formulary type, more or less similar to the Ifugao "invented" myths. The literary merit of this kind of myth is higher among the Ifugaos, meager though it be, than in any other tribe except possibly the Tinggian, where the myths are of so different character that comparison is difficult. The Ifugao has succeeded in relieving their monotony by occasional imaginative touches [as, for example, the oratorical clash in 24] and by already mentioned crude, stereotyped devices of suspense, which, I suspect, were primarily introduced for the purpose of lengthening the myth. There are three types of these: 1) A hero starts out to secure something, as a loom [Myth 12], or pacifiying magic [Myth 16]. One deity sends him on to another and that one on to another and so on until he reaches the right one. 2) The hero secures a charm or power from this deity, another from another and so on, or a deity helper here, another there, another farther on, then descends with the whole snowballed-up lot against his enemies [16, 27]. 3) The hero comes into power over a deity and bargains with him [6, 11].

The formulary Mayaoyao myths are much given to the first two devices — consist of little else, in fact — but employ them more crudely than the Ifugao. I have not found any of these devices used in the other mythologies except in one Nabaloi myth [Moss, p 323, which has an exact but much fuller cognate in Ifugao], and in one Kankanai myth.

The Tinggian ritual myths, *diam*, have been developed mainly by female mediums and differ more from those of the other tribes than the latter do among themselves. They are verbose and conversational, go into great detail; they set a precedent to the patient's situation and confirm the rationale of the ritual remedy. There are enormous numbers of them. The more successful mediums are those who are most conversant with what occurs in the village and who exercise care in selecting *diams* that psychologically fit the particular case and are likely therefore to cure by suggestion. Thus if the real cause of the woman's illness be a suspicion that her husband is unfaithful, the medium will know that and will mumble a *diam* that fits the case. These Tinggian *diams* are longer than the formulary myths of any other mountain tribes except some Ifugao ones and are quite logical from a psychological standpoint.[12]

The *tulud* is a most interesting development of this regional mythology. We have mentioned its three forms among the Ifugao: 1) a form appended to the myth in which the myth hero is "pushed" or guided to the site of the rites; 2) repetitions appended to a myth, by which a power, charm or subservient deity is brought by stages to the site of the rites; 3) a form independent of a myth, which is hardly myth and hardly tulud, but both at the same time: the desired result is apparently conceived as being realized simultaneously with the recitation and yet the narrative is regarded as something that happened in the past. I do not believe that the first two forms enumerated above have been found outside the Ifugao mythology.

The Mayaoyao have the latter form and sometimes a form which begins as a myth and ends as *tulud*.

The following is a summary of a fairly typical Mayaoyao myth:[13]

Wigan and Bugan see in their dream that their food and belongings are full of worms [bewitched]. They offer sacrifices and recite myths. In the morning, Wigan and his grandfather go and look for a big tree and fell it in order to dam a river. The enemies, who presumably were responsible for the "worms" are drowned by the rising waters, along with their pigs and chickens. Wigan opens the dam and the enemies are carried downstream.

Wigan of the Skyworld looks down and tells Wigan the Ifugao to go home, offer sacrifices and recite the myths. He obeys and all goes well henceforth. [Narrative in the present tense].

According to Lambrecht, the priests sometimes switch at about midway of the recitation from Wigan the Ifugao, always the hero of these myths, to the name of the modern Ifugao on whose behalf the rites are being performed. Thus, in the myth above, after the tree is found by Wigan and his grandfather, the priest might have the modern Ifugao dam the river of his modern enemies and carry on in his name the rest of the way.

There is no interjection of *fiats* into Mayoyao myths, but there is a sort of clinching phrase at the end: "On account of this Bugan and Wigan [or the modern Ifugao and his wife, if the switch mentioned above is made] are living at — and their pigs, their chickens, their rice and their children multiply."

In the formulary myths of the Northern Kankanai, the *tulud* is historical, hence almost a myth, although the form is precisely the same as in the Ifugao *tulud* that is favored by Kiangan. The tense, however, is the historical present. The pattern is: Lumauwig, the hero-deity, makes a journey on earth, carrying some rite or observance that will benefit men. On the way, he performs miracles, stopping here to chew betels and turn the earth roundabout red with his spittle, stopping again to astound a woman by cooking for her and miraculously increasing the food. Finally he delivers the rite to somebody in one of the wards of a town. It accomplishes all and more than might reasonably be hoped for there. Then a man of the ward says, "Shall we keep it for ourselves only? Let us share its benefits with other men" and carries it to another ward, where it accomplishes its wonders again and is again generously shared with another ward, or perhaps carried to the ward of another town and so on, and on, until it reaches the site of the rites. At the end there is a clinching phrase of substantially the following formula: It always worked before, it will this time.

Thus the *tulud* purports to be a history of the rite and its dissemination and at the same time an accumulation of evidence of its effectiveness and hence infallibility.

Most of the Tinggian formulary myths are not of the nature of
tulud and do not have a clinching phrase. One type, however, according to Cole,[14] the *pala-an diam*, ends in a direct supplication and
may be a form of tulud.

I recorded very few Kalinga myths in their ritual form and do not
know how well I recorded them. I found no evidence of any sort of
tulud in them. Quite definitely the sickness rites do have a clinching
phrase:

"Ofai! Get thee hence; for why should Kabunian have taught it if
it were not effective ?"

Southern Kankanai and Nabaloi myths have no *tulud* at present,
but may have had once, for even in their degenerated form they
somehow often breathe the spirit of Ifugao myths. One can be sure
of the degeneration because of internal evidence and form. For
example, the following myth is only the tradition of a myth:

They say Kabigat of the earth did this. He was childless, no children
were born. Kabigat of the sky pitied him. He told Kabigat of the
earth to make *tapuy* [rice wine] and that if, on the third day the
tapuy was fermented, he would come down again and make the
*pasang** so that he would have children.

The *tapuy* was fermented and Kabigat of the sky came down again
and they took one jar of *tapuy* and two chickens and twenty pesos
and two blankets and made the *pasang*. For the *pasang* of the sky had
imprisoned the soul of Kabigat of the earth, and they gave the money
and other things that they might release the soul from on high.

This is perhaps an extreme case of degeneration, or perhaps the
myth was ill-recorded or secured from a poor informant, but all the
myths Moss gives us show similar stigmata.

Indeed the priests are themselves conscious that they do not know
the ritual as it used to be. For they end myth-recitations and prayers
with such phrases as the following:

You *mambunong* [priests] of the past for *sibisib* [name of the myth
just recited] come. If you pray (the injury) will be taken away
quickly as if water washed it away. There will be no pain, there will
be no swelling. [Moss, Nabaloi, p. 328]

You the *mambunong* of long ago, if there is something forgotten
which I did not say, you cause it to be done; give luck to the giver of
the *kapi*. [Ibid, p. 305]

Indeed, such phrases seem to serve as a clinching phrase for the
recitation.

An interesting relationship exists between the myth heroes of some
of the tribes or sections of tribes, which merits further investigation
and an attempt at explanation. In the table below, the hero of most

of the myths of the tribe indicated [or in some cases the hero of all
the myths] is named first. Immediately below are his brothers, or
other relative, indicated by an asterisk. These frequently appear
associated with him, or may, in other myths, themselves play the
leading or sole role. The brothers in one mythology are each princi-
pals in one or another of the other mythogies. Following this group,
there may be another hero or deity, who has a rank only secondary
to the principal hero.

Table showing Relations Between Tribal Myth-Heroes.

Ifugao	Mayaoyao	S. Kankanai	Nabaloi	N. Kankanai	Bontok

I. Balitok
  Kabigat*
  Lumauwig*
  Amtalao
  (grndfthr)
II. Wigan
Many others,
  especially in
  the invented
  myths.
	I. Wigan
	
	Amtalao
	(grndfthr)
		I. Kabigat
		  Balitok*
		  Lumauwig*
			I. Kabigat
			  Balitok*
				I. Lumauwig	I. Lumauwig

Part II
The Myths[1]

A. Poetic Recitatives in Ifugao with Line-by-Line Translation

1. GALIDU: THE VIRGIN BIRTH*

Subject: Balitok's kinship with the omen-givers. Used: in war and sorcery rites. Informant: Malingan of Bulâ. Recorded by Marco Manghe, November 9, 1923. Translated by R. F. Barton.

I

Kánadih Amtálao d Kiyángan:
Óna pánalpal-íwan,
Doládad Kiyángan.
Abúnadi kanú tatáowa ya kanádih
Wada Búgan nak Amtálao,

Doládad Kiyángan —
Dídan hintúlang ke Magápid,
An bumálubáludah,
Bumálabaláhangda,
Doládad Kiyángan.
Kánadimo kaná tatáowa
Bulalákid Kiyángan,
Kánadin kaliónda,
"Kána-attóg!" an kaliónda,
"Da Búgan ke Magápid —
An bumálabaláhanda,
An mángadadiďa,
Ónda mamílipíli tatáowa".
Abúnadimo kanú tatáowa
Natníp on natníp di ambáyug
Di bulalákid Kiyángan,
Bálen Búgan ke Magápid,

Doládad Kiyángan.
Kánadimo kanú tatáowa
Kapiánan mángad-adída,

I

Kánadih Amtálao of Kiángan:
Time pásses unnóted,
In their víllage of Kiángan.
Abúnadi kanú tatáowa ya kanádih
There is Búgan, the daúghter 'f
　　Amtálao,

In their víllage of Kiángan —
Shé and her síster, Magápid,
Álways staying yóung,
Álways unmárried,
In their víllage at Kiángan.
Kánadimo kanú tatáowa
The young mén of Kiángan,
Kánadin sáy they,
"Alás, alás!" they sáy,
"Shé and her síster, Magápid,
Stay álways unmárried,
Are álways refúsing,
Théy're too choicy, *tatáowa*".
Abúnadimo kanú tatáowa
Píle on píle are the hípbags
Of the young mén at Kiángan,
In the hoúse of Búgan and
　　Magápid,
In their víllage of Kiángan.
Kánadimo kanú tatáowa
They habítually refúse,

46

The sísters too stríctly choóse
In their village at Kiángan.

Mamílipíliday hintúlang
Doládad Kiyángan.

II

Hogpónday hintúlang baléda,
Kánadimo kanú tatáowa
Tibúnday gináko,
Óndamo mongámal,
Pagibúanday gámalda,
Iwáklinday gináko.
Kánadimoh kanú tatáowa
Balobláonday mom-ónda,
Doládad Kiyángan,
Kánadin pimmángpang an bim-
múbug.
Abúnadimuh kanú tatáowa,
Kímmalih Búgan 'd Kiyángan,
Kánadin Kalióna,
"Dimmákol di pungámalantakú".
Kánadi óh kanu díye
Guyúdon Búgan di palúngan,
Balédad Kiyángan.
Kánadimo kanú tatáowa
Lumáhon di hintúlang,

Doládad Kiyángan,
Kánadih kanú díye
Pangáyanday alángda,
Alángdad Dókyag,
Kánadi ya dumátong,
Nun-alángandad Dókyag.
Kánadi mo Búgan 'd Kiyángan,
Ibúgholnay alángda,
Alangdad Dókyag.
Kánadi kanú tatáowa Búgan,
Hogpónay alangdad Dókyag,

Kánadi kanú tatáowa
Hokónay gótob di páge,

Nun-alángandad Dókyag.
Kánadimo kanú tatáowa
Katkátonay pagéda,

II

The sísters go ínto their dwélling,
Kánadimo kanú tatáowa
Take dówn their uténsils,
And gó ahead and éat,
They fínish eáting,
Then pút things awáy.
Kánadimoh kanú tatáowa
They chéw their bétel quíds
In their víllage of Kiángan,
Túrn them réd and thick-
spíttled.
Only thát, it is said, *tatáowa*,
And Búgan spáke at Kiángan,
Kánadin remárks she,
"Our foód basket's émpty".
Kánadi óh kanu díye
Búgan draws fórth their hámpers,
In their hóuse at Kiángan.
Kánadimo kanú tatáowa
The sísters go dówn from the
hoúse,
In their víllage at Kiángan;
Kánadih kanú díye
And gó toward their gránary,
Their gránary at Dókyag;
Kánadi arríve there,
Their gránary place in Dókyag.
Kánadimo Búgan of Kiángan,
She opens their gránary,
Gránary at Dókyag.
Kánadi kanú tatáowa Búgan,
Climbs ínto their gránary at
Dókyag,
Kánadi kanú tatáowa
Résts her hánd on the úpper rice
láyer,
In their gránary at Dókyag.
Kánadimo kanú tatáowa
Takes dówn their rice búndles,

Kánadih Búgan 'd Kiyángan,
Talwánay palúngan,
Óna panalpal-íwan,
Kánadih kanú tatáowa
Idáwatnay palúngan.
Dawáton Magápid,
Ipátukna dupílak.
Kánadi hintúlang
Nun-alángandad Dókyag,
Ónda pánalpal-íwan,
An kumánukut-tú-wan,
Nun-alánganda d Dókyag.

Kánadih Búgan 'f Kiángan
Fills úp their rice báskets,
Not heéding time's pássage,
Kánadih kanú tatáowa
Hands dówn the rice báskets.
Magápid recéives them,
Séts them ón the stone páving.
Kanádi the sísters,
At their gránary place in Dókyag,
Sít, not nóting time's pássage,
Hunting líce on each óther's heads
At their gránary place in Dókyag.

III

Kanadi kanu tataowa
Wadah Maingit hi Kabunyan,

Ona panalpal-iwan,
Doladad Kabunyan.
Kanadi kanu tataowa
Ona inuhudungan di hintulang
Nun-alangandad Dokyag.
Kanadih Maingit,
Kanadin kaliona,
"Kana-attog di hintulang
Nun-alangandad Dokyag,
An nalhom di binlada,[2]
An mangadadida,
An mamilipilida,
Doladad Kiyangan".
Kanadih kanu tataowa
Maingit hi Kabunyan
Pangayana amana,
An hi Amkidul hi gaw-wana,
Kanadih ya dumatong
Ihudhudnan amana.
Kanadi kanu tataowa
Amanan hi Amkidul,
Kanadin kaliona,
"Ot dan haoy di malahin!
Ot nangamungkan unga".
Abunadi kanu tataowa ot kanadi
Mundayun ungan hi Maíngit,[3]

III

Kánadi kanu takáowa
There is Mayíngit of the Sky-
   world,[1]
He is taking his leisure,
In their village in the Skyworld.
Kánadi kanú tatáowa
He looks down on the two sisters
At their granary place at Dokyag.
Kánadih Mayíngit,
Kánadin says he,
"Alas, alas! the sisters,
At their granary place in Dókyag,
Whose beauty's profound,
They're always refusing,
Too strict in choosing,
In their village of Kiángan."
Kánadih kanú tatáowa
Mayingit of the Skyworld
Goes seeking his father,
God of Thunder, in the center.
Kánadih when arrived there
He states the case to his father
Kánadi kanú tatáowa
His father, the Thunder,
Kánadin says Thunder,
"Am I the one to marry them!
Do as you please, my son".
Abúnadi kanú tatáowa ot kanádi
His son Mayíngit goes downhill,

Kanadih kanu tataowa	*Kánadih kanú tatáowa*
Ona panalpal-iwan,	Goes not noting time's passage,
An damanayudayu,[3]	Goes rejoicing and rejoicing,
Kanádi ya pumah-ad	*Kanádi* and stops at
Balena nundada-an.	His house in the lower village.
Kanadi kanu tataowa	*Kánadi kanú tatáowa*
Maíngit hi Kabunyan,	Mayíngit of the Skyworld,
Kanádih ya tibona	*Kanádi* looks around for
Moma ya hapid hi tabako,	Betels, betel leaves and tobacco,
Kanadi kanu tataowa	*Kánadi kanú tatáowa*
Ambayuonay moma ya hapid.	Puts them into his hipbag.
Kanadih kanu tataowa	*Kánadih kanú tatáowa*
Mayingit hi Kabunyan,	Mayingit of the Skyworld,
Alanay gimbatana,	He takes down his scabbard,
Ona iko-tok-tom.	He belts it around him,
Kanadih kanu ya kanadih	*Kánadih kanú ya kánadih*
Ihanynupnay ambayugna,	He tucks on his hipbag,
Talaoiyonay gayangna	Takes spear in hand.
Kanadih kanu tataowa	*Kánadih kanú tatáowa*
Mayingit hi Kabunyan	Mayíngit of the Skyworld,
Ona danaydayu-won	Goes continually downward,
Ona panalpaliwan,	Goes not noting time's passage.
Kanadimo kanu diye	*Kánadimo kanú díye*
Mayingit hi Kabunyan	Mayíngit of the Skyworld
Kanadi kanu pumahaad	*Kánadi kanú* comes down to
Hi Ablatan hi Kabunyan.[4]	The precipice of the Skyworld,
Kanadih ya kaliona,	*Kánadih* and says he,
"Muniyatuy tago,	"The man will rest,
Te *Na*-atuy tagu".	Because the man is tired",
Abunadimoh kanu tataowa	*Abúnadimoh kanú tatáowa*
Imodmodnay gayangna.	He puts his weight on his spear.[5]
Kanadih kanu tataowa	*Kánadih kanú tatáowa*
Mayingit hi Kabunyan,	Mayíngit of the Skyworld,
Baghutonay ambayugna,	He untucks his hipbag,
Kanadih ya boloblaonay,	*Kánadih* chews betels,
Boloblaonay mimmana,	Crunches his betels,
Kanadi ya pimmangpang,	*Kánadi* turns them red,
Pimangpang an bimmubug.	Red and thick-spittled.
Kanadi kanu diye	*Kánadi kanú díye*
Mayingit hi Kabunyan,	Mayíngit of the Skyworld,
Ona anu-ahdungan,	Keeps looking downward
Bobled Kiyangan.	On the village at Kiangan.
Kanadih kanu tataowa	*Kánadih kanú tatáowa*

4 Barton

Mayingit hi Kabunian,	Mayíngit of the Skyworld,
Inuh-dungnay hintulang,	Looked down on the two sisters,
Da Bugan ke Magapid,	On Búgan and Magápid,
Nun-alangandad Dokyag.	At their granary place at Dokyag.
Kanadin kaliona,	*Kánadin* says he,
"Daya da an madikit,	"There are the pretty ones,
Da Bugan ke Magapid,	Búgan and Magápid,
An kumanut-tuwanda,	Lousing each other,
An nalhom di binlada."	They whose beauty 's profound."
Abunadimo kanu tataowa ya kanadi,	Only that, it is said and *kanadih*,
Kanadih Mayingit	*Kánadih* Mayíngit
Numpohod hi Ablatan,	Pretties himself on the steep place,
Iktomnay wanona,	Arranges his g-string,
Umat hi pango-na, balitokna.	And also his gold beads and amber.[6]
Kanadi Mayingit hi Kabunyan,	*Kánadi* Mayíngit of the Skyworld,
Biliblionad Pangagauwan,	Looks on Mount Pangagáuwan,
Kanadih ya koh-pona,	*Kánadi* descends it.
Kanadih Mayingit hi Kabunyan,	*Kánadih* Mayíngit of the Skyworld,
Kanadin kaliona,	*Kánadin* says he,
"Hituey kagalutaan."	"This is the earth world."
Abunadimo kanu ya kanadih,	Only that, it is said, and *kanádih*,
Biliblion Mayingit,	He looks all around him,
Kanadih ya mundayu,	*Kánadih* keeps descending,
Dayuwon ad Hawali,	Goes down to Hawáli,
Kanadih kanu tataowa	*Kánadih kanú tatáowa*
Aganamod Uldop,	Continues to Úldop,
Ona panalpaliwan,	Goes not noting time's passage,
Kanadih ya dumatong,	*Kanadih* arrives there,
Domatong ad Dokyag,	Arrives at Dokyag,
Nun-alangan da nak Amtalao.	At the granary-place of the Amtalao's.
Kanadih kanu tataowa	*Kánadih kanú tatáowa*
Mayingit ad Kabunyan	Mayíngit of the Skyworld
Onah bah-elon	Goes to the other side of
Nun-langanadad Dokyag.	Their granary place at Dókyag.
Kanadimoh kanu tataowa	*Kánadimoh kanú tatáowa*
Iluhadnay gayangna.	He thrusts down his spear.
Kanadih diye	*Kanadih díye*
Numbayninday hintulang,	The two sisters are startled,
An kumanuttu-wanda	Who've been lousing each other

Nun-alangandad Dokyag.
Kanadih kanu tataowa
Mayingit hi Kabunyan —
An maid bai-inna,
An maid takutna.
Kanadi ya paldangana,
Paldanganay hintulang
Hi alangdad Dokyag.
Abunadimoh kanu ya kanadi
Manuka-ukat Mayingit,
Ukatonay inultikon,

Kanadi kanu tataowa
Idawatnan Bugan,
Nun-alangandad Dokyag.
Kanadi kanu tataowa Bugan
Kauwatonay inultikan[7]
Kanadih ya mom-ona,
Pimmangpang an bimmugbug.

At their granary place in Dókyag.
Kánadih kanú tatáowa
Mayíngit of the Skyworld —
There's no shame in him,
There's in him no fear.
Kánadi he sits down alongside,
Alongside the two sisters,
At their granary at Dókyag.
Only that, it is said, and *kanádi*
Mayíngit takes out his betels,
Takes out his ready-wrapped
    quids,

Kánadi kanú tatáowa
Gives a quid to Búgan,
In their granary place at Dokyag.
Kánadi kanú tatáowa Búgan
Accepts the wrapped quid of betel
Kánadih and chews it,
Turns it red and thick-spittled.

IV

"BATDAKANA" kaliona,
Kalion Mayingit hi Kabunyan,
Abunadimo kanu tataowa
Namodwongday hintulang,
Nun-alangandad Dokyag.
Kanadih Mayingit,
Kalionah hintulang,
"Adikayu tumakut
Te tumalag-eyak
Tumalakdangak hi Kabunyan."
Kanadi bo kanu tataowa
Kanadin kalion Mayingit,
"Deket waday athidi di adolmo,
  Bugan,
Ya hi Mayingit hi Kabunyan."

Kanadi kanu tataowa Bugan,
Kanadin kaliona,
"Kanape waday athina

Hi hapitmo, Mayingit ?"

IV

"SO LET IT BE!" exclaims he,
Cries Mayíngit of the Skyworld,
Only that, it is said, *tatáowa*;
The sisters stare in amazement,
At their granary place in Dokyag.
Kánadih Mayíngit,
He tells the two sisters,
"Don't ye be afraid;
I'm going to leap upward,
I'll ascend to the Skyworld".
Kánadi bo kanú tatáowa
Kánadin says Mayíngit,
"If aught should be wrong with
  thy body, Búgan,
"Why t'will be from Mayíngit of
  the Skyworld."

Kánadi kanú tatáowa Búgan,
Kanadin says she,
"Why shouldst thou talk that
  way ?
What do thy words mean,
  Mayíngit ?"

4*

"Takon", an kalion Mayingit,
"Oddonon damdama,
Oddonon an nila-uh ?"
Kanadi mo kanu Bugan
Kanadin kaliona,
"Ondan nan numomma-anta,
Ot pimmangpang an bimmug-
      bug ?"
Kanadin timbal Mayingit,
Kanadin kaliona "Hia!"

Abunadi kanu ya kanadi
Kanadin kalion Mayingit,
"Dieket munayayamka Bugan

Adiyu ihal-lay ngadanna" —
Kanadin kalion Mayingit,
"Ingadanyu Ballitok," kaliona.

"Even so —" replies Mayingit —
"What to do now ?
What to do when it's done ?"
Kánadi mo kanú Búgan
Kánadin says she,
"Is it because we chewed betels,
Turned them red and thicks-
      pittled ?"
Kánadin answered Mayíngit,
Kánadin "That's right!" he an-
      swered.

Abúnadimo kanú ya kanádi
Kánadin continues Mayíngit,
"If thou shouldst give birth,
      Búgan,
Don't go wrong on the name." ·
Kánadin continues Mayíngit,
"Name him Balitok," he says.

V

Abunadi kanuy hintulang,
Nun-alangandad Dokyag,
Agtuonday pinage,
Nodnodondad Intanap,
Onda papalpaliwan
Dakdakondad Ambangal.
Kanadi kanuy hintulang
Dumakaldad Ambangal,
Kanadi kanu tataowa
Ipatukday pinage dupilak,

Kanadin kimmali Bugan,
Kanadin kaliona,
"Makaha-kit di potang,
Ontah mundahlup".
Kanadi kanu tataowa
Tinumbal Magapid,
Kanadin kaliona
"Ontaku ot mundahlup
Patuningontay na-adlan."
Kanadimo kanuy hintulang,
Tobladonday dinhinganda,
Kanadi kanu tataowa

V

With that, 't is said, the sisters,
At their granary place in Dókyag,
Lift to their heads their burdens,
Go down to *Intánap*,
Go not noting time's passage,
Go into the stream at Ambangal.
Kánadi kanú the sisters
Ford the stream at Ambangal,
Kánadi kanú tatáowa
Set their burdens of rice on a flat
      stone.
Kánadin spake then Búgan,
Kánadin says she,
"The sunshine's a torture,
Let's go in bathing."
Kánadi kanú tatáowa
Magápid answered,
Kánadin says she,
"Let us, indeed, go bathing,
And cool off our bodies."
Kánadimo kanú the sisters,
Strip off their loincloths,
Kánadi kanú tatáowa

Kalibugonday danum,	Have a soak in the waters,
Onda panalpal-iwan,	Not minding time's passage,
An dumanadahlupdah liting.	And sport in the waters.
Kanadi mo kanuy hintulang,	*Kánadi kanú* the sisters,
Onda nadah-lupan,	They have finished their bathing,
Kanadi ya dumakalda.	*Kánadi*, now leave the waters.
Kanadi kanu tataowa	*Kánadi kanú tatáowa*
Mamag-ananday hintulang.	And dry themselves in the sun.
Alanday dinhinganda.	They fetch their loincloths.
Kimali Bugan,	Spake Búgan,
Kanadin kaliona,	*Kánadin* says she,
"Muntubnang di dinhinganku —	"My loincloth's too little —
Numpallog di dinhinganta,	"Must be thy loincloth, Magápid."
Magapid".	
Kanadi ya tinumbal	*Kánadi* the answer,
Hi tulangnan Magapid,	Of her sisters Magápid,
Kanadin kaliona,	*Kánadin* says she,
"Uggeman numpallog —	"We haven't mixed loincloths —
Tibom! di dinhinganku,	Look — this is my loincloth,
An tinikuy kugutna."	For its hem's a little crooked."
Kanadibon kalion Magapid,	*Kánadibon* says Mágapid,
Kanadin kaliona,	*Kánadin* says she,
"Tibom di dinhinganmo —	"Look at thy loincloth —
An bimallog di kugutna!"	Its hem is even!"
Kanadibon kalion Magapid,	*Kánadibon* continues Magápid,
"Nalumantualiyadolmo, Bugan!"	"Why, thy body is swollen, Búgan!"
Abunadimoh kanu tataowa ya kanadi	*Abúnadimoh kanú tataowa ya Kanadi*
Kanadin kalion Bugan,	*Kánadin* says Bugan,
"Bumainak an kumayat	"I'm ashamed to go home
Hi dolatakud Kiyangan,	To our village at Kiangan,
Te muntubnang di dinhinganku."	For my loincloth doesn't go round."
Kanadin kalion Bugan,	*Kánadin* says Búgan,
"Kumayatka Magapid,	"Run thou up, Magápid,
Dolatakud Kiyangan,	To our village of Kiangan,
Ta onmo alan di hapen	And fetch the blanket
Amata 'n hi Amtalao,	of our father, Amtálao,
Dolatakud Kiyangan."	From our village of Kiangan."
Kanadi kanu tataowa	*Kánadi kanú tatáowa*
Magapid ya ume	Magápid goes thither
Alanay hapen amanah,	Brings the blanket of her father,

Idetongna kawadan Bugan.	Brings it back to Búgan.
Kánadimoh kanu tataowa	*Kánadimoh kanú tatáowa*
Ikalbon Bugan.	Bugan receives it.
Abunadimo kanu ya kanadih	*Abúnadimo kanú ya kanádih*
Agtuonday pinage.	They put on their heads their burdens.
Kanadi kanu Bugan,	*Kánadi kanú* Búgan,
Ilikonay dinhingana,	She winds her "skirt" around her,
Onda panalpal-iwan,	They go not noting time's passage,
Punladanday Botak.	Go up to Bótak.
Kanadi kanuy hintulang	*Kánadi kanú* the sisters
Gawaonday Wala,	Go through the center at Wála,
Dumatongdad Kiyangan,	They arrive in Kiángan,
Kanadih kanu tataowa	*Kánadi kanú tatáowa*
Idu-ulday pinage bale,	Raise to the house-floor their burdens,
Kanadih ya hogpondah.	*Kánadi* and shove them on to it.
Katkatonday pinage,	They take the rice from the baskets,
Kanadi kanu tataowa	*Kánadi kanú tatáowa*
Ibatauwilday pinage,	Place the sheaves on the fireframe poles.[8]
Gukudanday huguhug.	Pack the poles tight on the fireframe.
Kanadi kanu tataowa	*Kánadi kanú tatáowa*
	The rice fills the fireframe completely.
Nunhinidol di page.	

VI

Abunadih kanu ya kanadi	*Abúnadih kanú ya kanádih*
Kimmali Amtalao,	Then up spake Amtálao,
Doladad Kiyangan,	In their village at Kiángan,
"BATDAKANA" 'n kaliona	[*Fiat:*] "SO LET IT BE!" says he,
"Ta hinidol" an kaliona,	"Let it be well-filled," he says
"Mahinidol di kinadangyan-mi	"Well-filled out our wealthiness
Dolamid Kiyangan,	In our village of Kiángan,
Ta dakami" 'n kaliona,	So that we," he says,
"Makalkali hinu-wi	"Will speak and talk bravely
Dolamid Kiyangan."	In our village of Kiángan."

VII

Abunadimoh kanu tataowa ya kanadi	*Abúnadimoh kanú tatáowa ya kánadi*

Numotwong hi Amtalao,
Doladad Kiyangan,
Nanib-anan Bugan,
Te nabuklog moy adolna,
Nunlinongboy gitangna.

Amtálao starts with wonder,
In their village of Kiángan,
When he glances at Búgan,
At her body without waistline,
At her middle bulged out from
   the waistline.

Kanadi kanu Amtalao,
Kanadi ya kalionan Bugan,
"Adikaman kattog
Umagimayom, Bugan,
Te ondita ehlekan[9]
Bulalakid Kiyangan,
"Hina tuali kaliok,"

Kánadi kanú Amtálao,
Kánadi says he to Búgan,
"Do not thou, alas!
Sit brooding, Búgan,
Thou and I were always refusing
The young men of Kiángan.
And, I indeed, was always telling
   thee,"

An kalion Amtalao,
Doladad Kiyangan
"An adita mangadadi,
Adita mamilipili
Bulalakid Kiyangan."
Kanadi kanu tataowa
Tinumbal hi Bugan,
"Kudukdul," an kaliona,
"Maid di tinangadkon," kaliona

Goes on saying Amtálao,
In their village at Kiángan,
"Let us not be always refusing,[9]
Not be too strict in choosing.[9]
From the young men of Kiángan."
Kánadi kanú tatáowa
Búgan answered him,
"None the less", she answers,
"I've never looked up [from
   beneath him]

"Himihim di lalaki."
Kanadi kanu tataowa
Kalion amanan hi Amatalao,
Doladad Kiyangan,
Kanadin kaliona,
"Kanapey athinay adolmo?"
Kanadi ya tinumbal hi Bugan,
"Taon!" an kaliona.

At the rim of a man's haircut![10]
Kánadi kanú tatáowa
Says Amatálao her father,
In their village of Kiángan,
Kánadin says he,
"How comes thy body to be so?"
Kánadi Búgan answered,
"I don't know!" she says.

VIII

Kanadimoh kanu tataowa
Onda panalpal-iwan,
Doladad Kiyangan,
Abunadimoh kanu tataowa ya
   kanadi
Nalaoy himbulan,
Himbulan ot potlang,
Tanibtibonda Bugan —
Tanibtibon di bulalaki,

VIII

Kánadimoh kanú tatáowa
Time passes unnoted,
In their village of Kiángan.
*Abúnadimoh kanú tatáowa ya
   kanadi*
A month passes by,
A month and a half,
They keep looking at Bugan —
The young men are always staring,

Bulalakid Kiyangan,
Kanadin kalionda,
Te "On gimmayad hi Bugan,"
Te "Gimmayu Bugan,
Dolamid Kiyangan."
Kanadin kalionda,
Kalion di bulalaki
Bulalakid Kiyangan,
"Kanape bo umat hina, Bugan ?
An mangad-adi nian,
An mamailipili ni-an,

Bulalakid Kiyangan ?"
Kanadi ya timbal Bugan,
Kanadin kaliona,
"Kudukdulman an bulalaki,
An maid tinangadko
Himihim di lalaki!"
Abunadimoh kanu tataowa
  Bugan,
Pangayana kadaklan,
An e mondah-lup,
Te on munayam.

The young men of Kiángan,
Kánadin they gossip,
For "Bugan's become pregnant,"
For "Búgan with child is heavy,
In our village of Kiángan."
Kánadin say they,
Say the young men,
The young men of Kiángan,
"Why is it so with thee, Búgan ?
Who wast always before refusing,
Who wast too strict before in
  choosing
From the young men of Kiángan ?"
Kánadin answered Búgan,
Kánadin says she,
"None the less, you young fellows,
I've never looked up [from be-
  neath him]
At the rim of a man's haircut!"
Only that, it is said, and Búgan
Goes down to the river,
Goes down to bathe there,
For she's going to give birth.

IX

Kanadih kanu tataowa
Mayingit hi Kabunyan,
Panalpal-iwanah Kabunyan.

Kanadih kanu tataowa
Pangayana amanah,
Amanah hi Amkidul hi gauwana,
Kanadih ya ihudhudna,
Kanadi "Mayingit ya mondayu."

Panalpaliwanay uhdong,
Inuh-dungana Bugan,
An monhikal hi kadaklan.
Abunadimoh kanu tataowa
Mayingit hi Kabunyan,
Ona pah-adon,
Kadaklandad Kiyangan.
Kanadi kanu tataowa

IX

Kánadih kanú tataowa
Mayíngit of the Skyworld
Taking his leisure in the Sky-
  world.

Kánadih kanú tataowa
He goes to his father,
His father, Thunder, in the center,
Kánadih informs him,
Kánadi "Mayingit will go down-
  hill."

He looks at his leisure downward,
Looks down on Búgan,
Who sits by the river moping
Only that it is said, *tatáowa*
Mayíngit of the Skyworld
Goes down to her there,
To their river at Kiangan.
Kánadi kanú tatáowa

Numotwa Bugan,

Búgan looks up and sees him;

Kanadin kaliona,

Kánadin says she,

"Imali din tagu."

"That man has come."

Kanadih kanu Mayingit,

Kánadi kanú Mayíngit

Higupona tadol

Enters a thicket of bamboo,

Kanadih ya hagadona.

Kánadih and sweeps it.

Kanadin kaliona,

Kánadin says he,

"Maka-tu tuali, Bugan."

"Come hither, indeed, Búgan."

Abulotana ot hogpona.

She obeys and goes thither.

Kanadi kanu tataowa

Kánadi kanú tatáowa

Mayingit hi Kabunyan,

Mayíngit of the Skyworld,

Kanadin kaliona,

Kánadin says he,

"Munpohodka, Bugan.

"Give birth to it, Búgan.

Dao-wahom di ulpum."

Open out thy thighs."

Kanadi Bugan ya daowahona,

Kánadi Búgan, she opens them,.

Kanadi kanu tataowa

Kánadi kanú tatáowa

Nunolot hi Bugan.

Búgan makes an effort.

Kanadih ya nabab-wa-a,

Kánadih sound of something emerging

Ona inuhudungan:

She looks down to see it:[11]

Kawitan an halangon,

It is the cockbird of the omen,[12]

Kanadih ya monpitpit

Kanádih it cries "Pit-pit, pit-pit."

Tumayupnay balukna!

Flies around the village.

Kanadih Bugan, tataowa

Kánadi Búgan *tatáowa*

Ona bagaan Mayingit,

Inquires of Mayíngit,

Kanadin kaliona

Kánadin says she

"At hituy i-ay-ayamko?"

"Such things am I bearing?"

Tinumbal hi Mayingit,

Mayíngit answered,

Kanadin kaliona,

Kánadin says he,

"Kapiana," 'n kaliona,

"Usual thing," he says,

"Hinai panguluan di tago."

"Firstlings to the human!"

Kanadih bo kanu tataowa

Kánadih bo kanú tatáowa

Kalion Mayingit hi Kabunyan,

Says Mayíngit of the Skyworld,

"Mon-olotka boh Bugan."

"Exert thyself, Búgan."

Kanadi bo Bugan,

Kánadi bo Búgan,

Nun-olot bo Bugan,

Búgan makes an effort:

Nabab-wa-a ya gudgud,

Sound of emergence — it's the large owl,

Umat hi taktak hi yodyod.[13]

And the omen insect and katydid,.

Kanadi bon kalion Bugan,

Kánadi bon says Búgan,

"At hitu y i-ayamko!"

"What things I am bearing!"

Kanadih Mayingit an tinumbal,

Kánadi answered Mayíngit,

Kanadin kaliona,

Kánadin says he,

"Tagun mangudidi."
Kanadi bo kanu tataowa
Mayingit bon kaliona,
"Munolotka bo Bugan."
Kanadi kanu tataowa Bugan,
Nagagwa-a an naga ya ulog,
Umat hi gayaman ya inginggi.
Kanadi kanu Bugan,
Kumaynit an tumakot,
Te inulup di ulog di waowan,

Umat hi gayaman
Inulupnay igid di ulpuna.
Kanadin kalionan Mayingit,
"Athituboy impangih-alim!"

"Kapianan," kalion Mayingit
"Te hitui kapiana gagangayna."
Abunadi bo kanu tataowa
Kimali Mayingit an kaliona,
"Umlotka nuppe Bugan."
Kanadih kanu Bugan,
Inumlot an nuhokot.
Nagagwa-an naga ya koliog,

Umat hi gode ya nginingini.

Kanadi bon kalion Bugan,
"Napnuy putuk hi malgom!"

Kanadin kalion Mayingit,
"Kapyana danaey panguluan di
　　tagu;
Agam ot monolotka."
An kalion Mayingit.
Kanadi kanu Bugan
Numpalak an immanay!
Ta adi mippolan hi hakit.
Kanadi "Pumalakka?"
Kalion Mayingit hi Kabunyan.
"Agam ot: umlotka."
Kanadi kanu Bugan ya munolot.

"The man will come last."
Kánadi bo kanú tatáowa
Mayíngit again says,
"Make another effort, Bugan."
"*Kánadi kanú tatáowa* Búgan,
Sound of emergence—a snake falls,
And a centipede and a rat.
Kánadi kanú Búgan,
She shivers in panic,
For the snake crawls up her right
　　thigh,
And, likewise, the centipede
Crawls up her left thigh.
Kánadi says she to Mayíngit,
"Even such as these, too, thou
　　hast brought me!"
"Matter of course," says Mayíngit,
"Usual in such cases."
Only that it is said, *tatáowa*
Spake Mayíngit and says he,
Try hard now, Búgan."
Kánadi kanú Búgan
Exerts herself to the utmost.
Sound of emergence — it's the
　　Earthquake.[14]
And the Landslide and rubble that
　　follows.

Kánadi bon says Búgan,
"My belly is filled with a hodge-
　　podge."
Kánadin says Mayíngit,
"Usual thing — forerunning the
　　human;
Go on — make an effort."
These were the words of Mayíngit.
Kánadi kanú Búgan
Felt pangs and cried "Anay!"
For she couldn't bear the pain.
Kánadi "Does it rend you?"
Says Mayíngit of the Skyworld.
"Go ahead, make an effort."
Kánadi kanú Búgan makes an
　　effort.

Munpapah-lih-piy lingotna,
Palikdona gitangnay hakitna,
Kanadi kanu tataowa Bugan
Inumlot an bimmika.
Nagagagwa-an naga
Ya tinapayan Mayingit hi Kabunyan.
Kanadi kanu Bugan ya inuhdungana,
Na-imi ya nabog-ak:
"Umat hina," n kaliona,
"Ta lalakiy banayugko."
Abunadi kanu tataowa
Kanadi Mayingit,
Ona kalion ke Bugan,
"Onka munpohod mo Bugan,
Ta punbalitangngadanta Balitok."
Kanadi kanu tataowa
Puguwonday puhog di unga,
Kadaklandad Kiangan.
Kanadih kanu tataowa
On natilagan ya at-tibunalon!
Kimmali Bugan,
Kanadin kaliona,
"At-tibungalon di puhog Ballitok."
Tinumbal hi Mayingit hi Kabunyan,
"Kapyana gagangayna,
Hi naey udidihan di tagu."
Abunadimoh kanu tataowa
Alan Mayingit di hubong,
Kanadih ona idyohan,
Ona amhon hi Ballitok,
Kanadi kanu tataowa
Ona tanibtibon di unga —
Munyakuyak an munkaytin!
Kanadi kanu tataowa
Paboltanay ungan Bugan.

Kanadi kanu Mayingit,
On anululahan,

Her body is covered with sweat,
And the pains encircle her middle.
Kánadi kanú tatáowa Búgan
Tries and is strong.
Sound of emergence — it falls into
The hands of Mayíngit of the Skyworld.
Kánadi Bugan looks upon it,

Smiles and bursts into laughter:
"That's what I wanted," says she,
"For a male was born of my belly."
Abúnadi kanú tatáowa
Kánadi Mayíngit
Says he to Búgan,
"Go ahead and recover, Búgan,
For we'll put on thy right side Balitok"[15]
Kánadi kanú tatáowa
They cut off the babe's birth cord,
By the river at Kiángan.
Kánadih kanú tataowa
There glimmered the Rainbow![16]
Spake Búgan,
Kánadin says she,
"The birth cord of Balítok 's a rainbow!"
Mayíngit of the Skyworld answered,
"Usual thing in such cases,
For that's what follows the man".
Abúnadimoh kanú tatáowa
Mayíngit unstrings a jewel
Kánadih crushes it to powder,
And with it bathes Balitok,
Kánadi kanú tatáowa
Then looks the child over —
He's leaping and jumping —
Kánadi kanú tatáowa
Puts the child in the arms of Búgan.

Kánadi kanú Mayíngit
Goes ahead washing off,

On anap-apu-wahon,
Di dala hi ulpun Bugan.

Goes ahead wiping off,
The blood from the thighs of
Bugan.

Kanadi mo kanu tataowa
Nagibun na-ulahan di dala,

Kánadi mo kanú tatáowa
When he's washed all the blood
off,

Kimmali Mayingit an kaliona,
"Adi-ta anat-aton hitu, Bugan,

Spake Mayíngit and says he,
"Let's not keep on like this,
Búgan,[17]

Ta adidaka ehlekan hi piduana
Hi bulaladid Kiayangan."
Abunadimoh kanu tataowa
Baklulukon Bugan hi Ballitok,
Ta onda kumay-at
Hi doladad Kiyangan.

Not keep on refusing
The young men of Kiángan."
Abúnadimoh kanú tatáowa
Búgan carries Balítok,
And they start homeward
To their village at Kiángan.

Kanadi kanu tataowa
Ladangondad Kiyangan,
Kanadih ya dumatong,
Doladad Kiyangan.

Kánadi kanú tatáowa
They go up to Kiángan,
Kánadi arrive at
Their village of Kiángan.

Kanadi kanu Amtalao,
Doladad Kiyangan,
Kanadin kaliona,
"Waday at hina, Bugan,
Munpinhodanka kadaklan ?[8]
Ondan maid di bale ?"
Kanadih kanu tataowa
Tinumbal Mayingit,
"Takonbo," an kaliona,
"Te hidie daohona pinhodna."
Abunadimoh kanu tataowa
Panalpal-iwanda
Doladad Kiyangan.

Kánadi kanú Amtálao,
In their village at Kiángan,
Kánadin says he,
"Why didst thou choose so, Búgan
To right thyself at the river ?
And were there no houses ?"
Kánadih kanú tatáowa
Mayíngit answered,
"Never mind it," he answers,
"For that's how she wanted it."
Abúnadimoh kanú tatáowa
Time passes unnoted
In their village of Kiangan.

Kanadi ya kimmali Mayingit,
Ona kalion ke Bugan,
Doladad Kiyangan,
"Onak tumalag-e —
Onak tumalakdang
Dolamid Kabunyan.
Ta on nangamungkan" kaliona,
"Punhikalan Ballitok."
Kanadih kanu tataowa
Tumalagen tumalakdang,
Hi Mayingit hi Kabunyan.

Kánadi and spake Mayíngit,
Says he to Búgan,
In their village of Kiángan,
"I'm going to rise upward —
I'm going to leap up to
Our village in the Skyworld.
It's up to thee, now," he says
"To look out for Balítok."
Kánadih kanú tatáowa
He rises, leaps upward,
Mayíngit of the Skyworld.

Abunadimo kanu tataowa
Nuntikid Mayingit
Doladad Kabunyan,
Madaga gaw-wana,
Balen Amanan hi Amkidol.

Abúnadimo kanú tatáowa
Mayíngit goes uphill,
In their village in the Skyworld,
And stops in its center
At the house of his father the
Thunder.

Kanadin kalion Amkidol,
"Nabangadkan unga,
Ya uddi inuna ?" kaliona,
Kanadih kanu tataowa
Himumang hi Mayingit,
Kanadin kaliona,
"Numpinhodan hi Bugan,
Doladad Kiyangan."
Kanadibon kalion amana,
"Ngaday inayan Bugan,
Doladad Kiyangan ?"
Kanadih tataowa Mayingit
Ona kalion, hapiton,
"Lalakiy in-ayyam Bugan,
Doladad Kiyangan."
Kanadi bo kanu tataowa Amkidol,
Ona bo ibagay ngadana.
Kanadin kalion Mayingit,
"In-ngadankoy Ballitok."
"Umat hinan" kalion Amkidol.

Kánadin says Thunder,
"Thou 'st come back, my son,
And what about things ?" he says.
Kánadih kanú tatáowa
Up speaks Mayíngit,
Kánadin says he,
"Bugan has righted herself,
In their village of Kiángan."
Kánadibon asks his father,
"What was born unto Búgan,
In their village of Kiángan ?"
Kánadi tatáowa Mayíngit
Tells the story and answers,
"A male was born unto Búgan,
In their village of Kiángan."
Kánadi bo kanú tatáowa Thunder
Inquires the name that was given.
Kánadin answers Mayíngit,
"I named him Balítok."
"Be it so," answers Thunder.

X

Abunadimo kanu tataowa
Onda panalpal-iwan,
Doladad Kiyangan.
Kanadi kanu tataowa Amtalao,
Doladad Kiyangan,
Hanal-ha-law-wadona Ballitok
Doladad Kiyangan.
Kanadi kanu tataowa Amtalao
Tibona anagangongay unga

Muntagtag an muntagiling.
Kanadih kanu tataowa
Onda panalpal-iwan
Doladad Kiyangan,
Kanadin ya ohan algo

X

Abúnadimo kanú tatáowa
Time passes unnoted
In their village of Kiángan.
Kánadi mo kanú tatáowa Amtalao,
In their village of Kiángan,
Plays every day with Balítok
In their village of Kiángan.
Kánadi kanú tatáowa Amtálao
Observes and watches the young-
ster
Running and toddling around.
Kánadih kanú tatáowa
Time passes unnoted
In their village of Kiángan,
Kánadih and one day

Kalion Ballitok ke apuna,
Kanadin kaliona,
"Kanape dayah-dah an umum-
    bun ?
Dolamid Kiyangan ?"
Kanadih Amtalao ya timbal,
"Man adida umumbun,

Dolamid Kiyangan —
Te man uhung an bumanowbow-
    wotda."
Kanadih kanu tataowa Ballitok,
Kanadih kaliona,
"Da-an moy bow-wotmo, Apu ?"
"Neh-nay bow-wotkoy duklig,

An umlanon galiogiwon,

Bow-wotko di ka-ungak, kahi-
    nongtak."
Kanadi mo kanu Ballitok,
Doladad Kiyangan,
Uhukonay duklig
Ya alanay bow-wot apuna,

Ona ilahun hi dola.

Kanadi kanu apuna
Doladad Kiyangan,
Alanay wale,
Kanadi ya munlubid,
Kanadi mo kanu diye
Ona hulwingon.
Kanadih kanu tataowa Amtalao,
Doladad Kiangan,
Idawatnan Ballitok.
Kanadih kanu Ballitok,
I-latalat-nay bow-wotna.

Kanadi kanu tataowa
Tue da nak Ambalittayon,

Doladad Kiyangan,

Balítok asks of his grandsire,
Kánadin asks he,
"Why are those yonder just sit-
    ting
In our village of Kiángan ?"
Kánadi Amtálao makes answer,
"But they're not just sitting and
    sitting

In our village of Kiángan —
For they're watching the game of
    tops."
Kánadih kanú tatáowa Balítok,
Kánadin says he,
"Where is thy top, Grandsire ?"
"My top 's there behind the fire-
    place —
Top made of the heart of *galio-
    giwon*[19]

Top of my childhood, the same
    now as then,"
Kánadi mo kanú Balítok,
In their village of Kiángan,
Ferrets behind the fireplace,
Brings forth the top of his grand-
    sire,
And takes it down to the house-
    yard.

Kánadi kanú his grandsire,
In their village of Kiángan,
He gets strips of *wále* bark,
Kánadi spins them into a string,
Kánadi mo kanú díye
He ties an end loop to it.
Kánadih kanú tatáowa Amtálao,
In their village of Kiángan,
Gives the top to Balítok.
Kánadih kanú Balítok
Winds the string round and round
    the top.
Kánadi kanú tatáowa
Here come the sons of Ambalit-
    áyon,[20]
In their village of Kiángan,

Kanadi ya kimmali,
"Daanka Ballitok,
Ap-apun Amtalao d Kiyangan ?
Ta ontaku monbowbow-wot,
Dolatakud Kiyangan."
Kanadih kanu tataowa
Lumahon hi Ballitok,
Doladad Kiyangan,
Pangayanday aldattan an palaha.
Kanadi da nak Ambalittayon,
Palpagonday bow-wotda.
Kanadih kanu tataowa Ballitok,
Ona bliblionna lani-lih-igon,
Di bow-wot da nak Ambalittayon.
Kanadih ya top-ona "gayang-
ona!"
Kanadih kanu tataowa
Nahilhilit an nahegheget
Bow-wot danak Ambalittayon!
Kanadi kanu tataowa
Kimmali da nak Ambalittayon,
Kanadin kalionda,
"Namahig hi Ballitok
An hi nak Pudun, nak Binutag,
An maid hi amanan tinangadna."

Kanadih kanu Ballitok
An bimma-in ippolna,
Hablutonay bow-wotna
Pangayana baleda.
Kanadin kaliona,
"Kalion da nak Ambalittayon
Ha-oy di nak Pudun, nak Binu-
tag."
Kanadih kanu Amtalao,
Doladad Kiyangan,
"Adim kaya dongolon!
Teh tuak an hi amam;
Hungupka ot an unga,
Ta onta mongamal."
Kanadih kanuy unga,
Hogponay baleda
Mungammaldan hinapu.

Kánadi and said they,
"Where art thou, Balítok,
Grandson of Amtálao 'f Kiángan ?
Let us go have a top-fight
In our village of Kiángan."
Kánadih kanú tatáowa
Balítok emerges.
In their village of Kiángan,
They go to a wide level place.
Kánadi the sons of Ambalitáyon
Spin their tops in a row.
Kánadih kanú tatáowa Balítok,
Surveys glancing sidewise,
The tops of the Ambalitáyons.
Kánadih hurls his "spearer!"[21]

Kánadih kanú tatáowa
Scattered and tumbled
Are the tops of the Ambalitáyons!
Kánadi kanú tatáowa
Said the sons of Ambalitáyon,
Kánadin said they,
"His Balítok's too much!
Son of Betel Leaf and Betel Nut,
Who never had a father to look
up to."

Kánadih kanú Balítok
Is shamed and keeps silence,
Hangs his top in his top-string
And goes to their houseplace.
Kánadin says he,
"The Ambalitáyons called me
'Son of Betel Leaf and Betel
Nut.'"
Kánadih kanú Amtálao,
In their village of Kiángan,
"Don't mind their jeering!
Here am I as thy father!
Come into the house, my child,
Come, let us go eat."
Kánadih kanú the youngster,
Climbs into their dwelling
And eats with his grandsire,

Kanadi kanu tataowa	*Kánadi kanú tatáowa*
Magibudan mongammal,	And when they have eaten,
Onda pawaklinan,	They put away their utensils.
Kanadi kanu tuali	*Kánadi kanú tuáli*
Onda panalpal-iwan —	Time passes unnoted —
Nahadom di hodom adi,	It is dark, it is night-time,
Doladad Kiyangan,	In their village of Kiángan.
Onda hanuyhuypon.	They fall into slumber.
Kanadi kanu tataowa	*Kánadi kanú tatáowa*
Nabagatabat di bigat adi,	Early next morning,
Doladad Kiyangan,	In their village of Kiángan
Onda mangododon,	They pound rice for their breakfast,
Nalutuy lutu,	When their boiled rice is ready,
Kanadi kanu tataowa	*Kánadi kanú tatáowa*
Mungammalday hinapu.	They eat, child and grandsire.
Kanadi kanu tataowa	*Kánadi kanú tatáowa*
Nagibudan mungammal,	And when they have finished,
Ipalogday mom-onda,	Change to chewing betels,
Pimmangpang an bimugbug.	Turn them red and thick-spittled.
Kanadi bo kanu tataowa	*Kánadi bo kanú tatáowa*
Mangalida nak Ambalittayon,	There come the sons of Ambalittáyon
Doladad Kiyangan,	In their village of Kiángan,
"Da-anka bo Ballitok,	"Where art thou, Balítok,
Ap-apun Amtalao?	Grandson of Amtálao?
Umalika," n kalionda,	Come down," they invite him,
"Ta onta e-mundah-lup	"Let's go swimming,
Kadaklantakud Kiyangan."	In our river at Kiángan."
Kanadi Ballitok tinumbal,	*Kánadi* Balítok answers,
"Hadonak" an kaliona,	"Wait for me," says he,
"Ta onta e-mundah-lup."	"We'll all go in swimming."
Kanadih kanu tataowa	*Kánadih kanú tatáowa*
Onda umey u-unga	Forth go the children
Kanadih ya dumatong	*Kánadih* and arrive there
Kadaklandad Kiyangan.	At their river at Kiángan.
Kanadi kanu tataowa	*Kánadi kanú tatáowa*
Kalibungonday danum,	They soak in the waters,
Onda panalpaliwan,	Not noting time's passage,
An dumanahdahlup.	And play in the river.
Kanadi bo kanu tataowa	*Kánadi bo kanú tatáowa*
Onda dumakal	They quit the water
Pangidakalanday "paling."	And play "building rice-fields."

Kanadih tataowa Balitok	*Kánadi tatáowa* Balítok,
Kanadi ya biliblion di winaowan	*Kánadi* he looks on the right side
Umat hi iniggidna.	And then on the left side.
Kanadi kanu Ballitok	*Kánadi kanu* Balitok
Munappit hi winaowan	Decides on the right side.
Abunadi kanu ya kanadih	*Abúnadi kanú ya kánadih*
Onda panalpaliwan,	Time passes unnoted,
Kadaklandad Kiyangan.	At their river at Kiángan.
Kanadi kanu Ballitok	*Kánadi kanú* Balítok
Umat ke da nak Amballittayon,	And the sons of Ambalitáyon,
Onda ika-yay tagiong,	They dig out a channel, flood-race
Kanadih kanu tataowa	*Kánadih kanú tatáowa*
Onda pahiknadon,	Keep on and finish it,
Kanadi kanu diye	*Kánadih kanú diye*
Onda hanabhabuwan,	With their hands scoop water into it[22]
Hi kadaklandad Kiyangan.	At their river at Kiańgan.
Abunadi kanu tataowa	*Abúnadi kanú tatáowa*
Onda anuh-uh-dungan,	They look down on their "rice-fields,"
Onda banil bilibliyon,	Keep watching their "rice-fields" intently,
Kanadih kanu tataowa	*Kánadi kanú tatáowa*
Palingan da nak Ambalittayon	The fields of the Ambalitáyons
On timmabuy an timmabuwao-a.	Crumble and fall in ruins!
Nahukokon, napayangpang	Destroyed, swept away by the current
Di paling da nak Ambalittayon!	Are the "fields" of the Ambalitáyons.
Kanadimo kanu Ballitok,	*Kánadimo kanú* Balítok,
Kanadin kaliona,	*Kánadin* says he,
"Buwan kinanku	"A betel nut that I ate
Da nak Ambalittayon!"	Are the sons of Ambalitáyon!"
Kanadimo kanu tataowa	*Kánadimo kanú tatáowa*
Kimmali da nak Ambalittayon,	Said the sons of Ambalitáyon
Kanadin kalionda,	*Kánadin* say they,
Kanadi "Anhan! hi Ballitok	*Kanadi "Anhan!* Balítok
Way ay-ayam an hiay mangapaput."	Has an *áyam* and that's what wins for him."[23]
Abunadi kanu tataowa	*Abunadi kanu tatáowa*
Onda i-ba-ag Ballitok;	They jeer at Balítok,
Kalionda "Hia nak Pudun, nak Binutag.	Call him "Son of Betel Leaf and Betel Nut,

An maid tinangadna amana." | Who never looked up at his father."

Abunadi kanu Ballitok
Ona pubohol an punbungot
Di kinalin da nak Ambalittayon.
Kanadih kanu Ballitok
Dumakal hi kadaklan,
Tangadonay tadol,
Kanadi ya puh-ngitona.
Kanadih tuali Ballitok
Ona ikayat ni boble,
Doladad Kiyangan,
Kanadi kanu tataowa
Pa-agidnay tadol ke apuna,
Doladad Kiyangan,
Kanadi kanu apuna
La-nanlan-nunay tadol.

Kanadih kanu tataowa apuna

Idawatnay tadol ke Ballitok.
Kanadih Ballitok,
I-ayudukna da-ulon,
Doladad Kiyangan,
Kanadi kanu tataowa
Idulugna kulingda.
Kanadih kaun tataowa
Hogponda baleda;
Kanadih kanu Amtalao
Kohponay pungammalan.
Kanadi kanu tataowa
Pungammalday hinapu,
Kanadi kanu tataowa
Magibudan mungammal,
Pawaklinonday ginako.
Onda imadahan,
Pimangpang an bimmubug.
Abunadimoh kanu ya kanadih
Onda panalpal-iwan
Doladad Kiyangan.
Nahadom di hodom,
Onda hanuyhuypon,
Doladad Kiyangan.

Abúnadi kanú Balítok
Takes umbrage and rages
At the words of the Ambalitayons.
Kánadih kanú Balítok
Comes out of the river,
Looks up at the bamboo thicket,
Kánadi goes and twists a stalk off.
Kánadih tuáli Balítok
Carries it up to his grandsire,
In their village of Kiángan,
Kánadi kanú tatáowa
Asks his grandsire to sharpen it,
In their village of Kiángan.
Kánadi kanú his grandsire
Sharpens and sharpens the bamboo.

Kánadi kanú tatáowa his grandsire
Gives the stick to Balítok.
Kánadih Balítok
Takes it under their house, there,
In their village of Kiángan,
Kánadi kanú tatáowa
Puts it on the house beams.
Kánadih kanú tatáowa
They go into their dwelling;
Kánadih kanú Amtálao
Takes down the rice basket.
Kánadi kanú tatáowa
They eat, child and grandsire,
Kánadi kanú tatáowa
And when they have eaten
They put things away.
And then they chew betels,
Turn them red and thick-spittled.
Abúnadimoh kanú ya kánadi
Time passes unnoted
In their village of Kiángan.
Dark falls, it is night time —
They drop into slumber
In their village of Kiángan.

Kanadih kanu tataowa	*Kánadih kanú tatáowa*
Nabagatabat di bigat,	At the dawn of the morrow,
Kanadih hinapu	*Kánadih* child and grandsire
Halamanonday gammalda,	Eat their cooked rice together
Doladad Kiyangan.	In their village of Kiángan.
Kanadih kanu tataowa	*Kánadih kanú tatáowa*
Nagibudan mungammal,	And when they have eaten,
Pawaklinonday ginako,	They put things away,
Ipalogday mom-onda.	Change to betel chewing.
Kanadi bo kanu tataowa	*Kánadi bo kanú tatáowa*
Tue bo da nak Ambalittayon,	Come again the Ambalitáyons
Doladad Kiyangan,	In their village of Kiángan.
Kanadin kalionda,	*Kánadin* say they,
"Da-anka, Ballitok,	"Where art thou, Balítok,
Ap-apun Amtalao,	Grandson of Amtálao,
Dolamid Kiyangan ?"	In our village of Kiángan ?"
Abunadimo kanu tataowa	*Abúnadimo kanú tatáowa*
Tinumbal Ballitok,	Balítok answered,
Kanadin kaliona,	*Kánadin* says he,
"Da-anay ayantaku ?"	"Where shall we go to ?"
Kanadi ya tinumbal,	*Kánadi* and answer
Da nak Ambalittayon,	The sons of Ambalitayon,
Kanadin kalionda,	*Kánadin* say they,
"Eta-u mundahlup	"Let's bathe in the river,
Kadaklan takud Kiyangan."	Our river at Kiángan."
Kanadi kanu tataowa	*Kánadi kanú tatáowa*
Onda pangayan di kadaklan.	They go to the river.
Kanadih kanu tataowa	*Kánadih kanú tatáowa*
Onda dimmatong di kadaklan,	When arrived at the river,
Onda pumalpalingan,	They build their play rice-fields,
Onda tagingon,	They dig out a canal,
Bohwatonday dodolgan,	And then make a weir,
Kanadi diya kanu tataowa	*Kánadi diye kanú tatáowa*
Onda pahiknadon,	Bring their work to a finish,
Onda anol-olhan !	Their war cries rend the air !
Kanadibo kanu tataowa Ballitok	*Kánadibo kanú tatáowa* Balítok
Ona tanibtibon,	Keeps looking and looking,
Ona banil-biliblion.	Keeps watching and watching.
On napayangpang,	Swept away by the current,
On nakuhuku,	Swept and tumbled in ruin
Paling da nak Amballitayon !	Are the "fields" of the Ambalitá-yons !
Kanadi kanu tataowa Ballitok,	*Kánadi kanú tatáowa* Balítok,

5*

Kanadi kaliona,
"Utok da nak Amballitayon!"

Kanadi kanuda nak Ambalitayon,
Onda iba-agbo Ballitok,
Kanadin kalionda,
"Man maid hi aman Ballitok,
An hi anak Pudu, nak Binutag!"
Abunadi kanu Balitok ya kaliona,
"Kaa-attog" an kaliona,
"Pangalikalidan haoy."

Abunadimo kanu Ballitok ya
   kanadih
Ona dakalon di kadaklan,
Ilataladnay tinonwe,
Kanadi mo diye mo
Biliblionay huk-kudna nan tadol.
Kanadi mo diye kanu tataowa
Ona bilibilion,
Di gawan da nak Amballitayon.
Kanadih kanu tataowa
"Buwa" n kaliona
Dinch-nagnay ohan dida.
Kanadi kanu tataowa
On nanguhakuhag.
Hi nak Ambalittayon
On inul-luwanad Daya,
Inandayanad Lagod,
An niploy di appangolna,
An maid inilana bumalo!

XI
Abunadimo kanu tataowa
Pangayan Ballitok di baleda,
Kanadih ya dumatong
Doladad Kiyangan,
Kanadin kaliona,
Apunan hi Amatalao,
"Man ginayangko, Apu,
Ginayangko nak Ambalittayon

Kadaklan takud Kiyangan".

Kánadin says he,
Marrow, "soft the Ambalitayons!"

Kánadi kanú the Ambalitayons
Jeer again at Balitok,
Kánadin say they,
"Thou 'st no father, Balitok!
Thou'rt a son of the Betels!"
Abúnadi kanú Balítok, and says he,
"Alas, Alas!" he says,
"What things they keep saying to
   me!"

Abúnadi kanú Balítok *ya kanádih*

He comes out of the river,
Winds on his g-string,
Kánadi mo díye mo
Fetches his colstaff of bamboo,
Kánadi díye kanú tatáowa
Stares, eyes fixed on
The center of the Ambalitayons,
Kánadih kanú tatáowa
"Betel Nuts!" he calls them,
Transfixes one of them.
Kánadi kanú tatáowa
That one is instantly dead.
That son of Ambalitáyon
Falls head to the Upstream,
And feet to the Downstream,[24]
Scattered, his weapons,
He knows nothing now of fighting!

XI
Abúnadimo kanú tatáowa
Balítok goes homeward,
Kanadi arrives there,
In their village of Kiángan.
Kanadin says he
To his grandsire, Amtálao,
"I speared one of them, Grandsire,
Speared a son of the Ambali-
   táyons,
At our river in Kiángan."

Kanadih kanu tataowa Amatalao,	*Kánadih kanú tatáowa* Amtálao,
Doladad Kiyangan,	In their village at Kiángan,
"Tibom" an kaliona,	"Look thou!" says he,
"Din kinalik ke he-a?	"What did I tell thee?
An adita gumayang,	We mustn't spear,[25]
Onta na-angi,	We have no kindred,[25]
Maid tulangtaku,	We have no brothers
Dolatakud Kiyangan."	In our village of Kiangan."
Abunadi kanu ya kanadih	*Abúnadih kanú ya kánadi*
Hungup da Amtalao ya Ballitok,	Balítok and Amtálao enter their dwelling,
Kanadi ya mundakigda.	*Kánadi* fasten the door shut.
Kanadi kanu tataowa	*Kánadi kanú tatáowa*
Nahikal da nak Ambalittayon,	Headlong come the Ambalitáyons
Doladad Kiyangan,	In their village of Kiángan.
Kanadi kanu tataowa	*Kánadi kanú tatáowa*
Kayda manabtab,	As if they would chop the house down,
Kayda manuhil,	As if they would pay to pieces,
Hi balen di hin-apu.	The house of child and grandsire.
Abunadi kanu tataowa ya kanadih	*Abúnadi kanú tatáowa ya kánadih*
Kimmali Amtalao hi bohongna,	Spake Amtálao from the inside,
Kanadin kaliona,	*Kánadin* says he,
"Adi dakami," n kaliona,	"Do not ye us —," says he,
"Patayon adwani,	"Slaughter on this day,
Ta bigat ahidakamin patayon."	You'll kill us tomorrow."
Abunadi kanu tataowa	*Abúnadi kanú tatáowa*
Da nak Ambalittayon,	The sons of Ambalitáyon,
Doladad Kiyangan,	In their village of Kiángan,
Makiwil da budud,	Carry away their dead one,
Kanadi kanu diye,	*Kánadi kanú díye*
Ik-akday ginayan.	Carry away their speared one.
Kanadi kanu tataoway hinapu,	*Kánadi kanú tatáowa* child and grandsire,
Onda hanuyhuypon,	They drop into slumber
Te nahdom di hodom,	For darkness has fallen.
Kanadi kanu diye	*Kánadi kanú díye*
Alutuwonda nak Ambalittayon.	The Ambalitáyons shoulder their dead one.

XII

Hi Mayingit hi Kabunyan,
Kanadi kanu diye
Muntikid hi Mayingit,
Kanadi kanu tataowa
Ihud-hudnan amanan hi
  Amkidul,
Kanadih Amkidul,
Dolanah gawana Kabunyan.

Kanadin kalion Mayingit,
"Gimmayang hi Ballitok
Ya onak adi ume
Doladad Kiyangan."
Abunadi kanu tataowa Amkidul
Pundayyuwona Mayingit,
Kanadi kanu tataowa Mayingit,
Pah-adonay Ablatan,
Kanadi kanu diye
Bibliblionad Kiyangan,
Kanadin kaliona,
"Gimmayang peman di unga!"

Abunadi kanu Mayingit,
Pumah-ad Kiangan.
On hahilingan hi Mayingit.

Pagpagonay hinapu,

Kanadih ya kimmaliy unga,
Kanadin kaliona,
"Immalin dumatong hi Ama!"

Kanadi ya tinumbal hi Amtalao,
Kanadin kalion Amtalao,
"Gulatnay immali amam

Ya adi-ot madandani!"

Kanadi kanu Mayingit
An wada dolan dongdongolona,
Tobbalan di hinapu.

XII

Mayíngit of the Skyworld,
Kánadi kanú díye
Mayíngit climbs upward,
Kánadi kanú tatáowa
Reports to his father, the
  Thunder,
Kánadih Thunder,
In his village in the Skyworld
  Center,
Kánadin says Mayíngit,
"Balítok has been spearing,
And I'm going downhill
To their village at Kiángan."
Abúnadi kanú tatáowa Thunder
Sends Mayíngit downhill.
Kánadi kanú tatáowa Mayíngit,
He stops at the Steep Place,
Kánadi kanú díye,
Looks down on Kiángan,
Kanádin says he,
"The child, indeed, speared one
  of them!"

Abúnadi kanú Mayíngit
Déscends tó Kiańgan,
Mayíngit will spend the night
  there.

He raps the door of child and
  grandsire.

Kánadih upspeaks the youngster,
Kánadin says he,
"He's come and that's he — my
  father!"

Kánadin answers Amtálao,
Kánadin says Amtálao,
"If indeed thy father 's come to
  us,
Why — he hasn't been in a
  hurry!"

Kánadi kanú Mayíngit
Down below overheard them,
Heard the talk of child and
  grandsire.

Kanadin kalion Mayingit,
"Adim aton hina, Amtalao,
Te ugge dakayu impaya."

Abunadi kanu tataowa ya
  kanadih
Alan Amtalao di gayang,

Kanadi ya wao-wanona,
Iggidonay dakig.

Kanadih kann Amtalao
Ona buh-buwon di dakig,
Kanadih ya nabughol.
Kanadi kanu tataowa Mayingit
Malantue ya hogpona.
Kanadi kanu Ballitok
Nawalawal an immanla.
Kanadi kanu tataowa
Awalaonay apun amana.

Abunadimo kanu tataowa
Agamidon Mayingit di unga,
Kanadi ya pahyupona.

Kanadi kanu tataowa Mayíngit
Taktakonay wolwolna,
Alanaboy banuna di kodomna,

Kanadih kanu tataowa Mayingit
Ikapyanay wolwolnan Balitok,

Alanboy banuna,
Itoktoknan Ballitok.
Kanadih kanu tataowa Mayingit
Bangunonah Ballitok.
Kanadih Mayingit an kaliona,
"Da-anay pinuguyu ?"
Kanadin kalion Ballitok,
"Pinugumi d Kud-dang,
An di damayon nun-oltan
Umat hi bayukan ya gakad."
Kanadih diye Mayingit,

Kánadin says Mayíngit,
"Don't talk that way, Amtálao,
For I'm guilty of no neglect of
  you."

Abúnadi kanú tatáowa ya kánadih

Amtálao holds spear in hand
  ready,[26]

Kánadih in his right hand uplifted,
With his left takes hold of the
  door bar.

Kánadih kanú Amtálao
Jerks out the door bar,
Kánadi throws open the door.
Kánadi kanú tatáowa Mayíngit
Leaps up and enters.
Kánadi kanú Balítok
To his arms runs rejoicing.
Kánadi kanú tatáowa
His father embraces the
  grandsire.[24]

Abúnadimo kanú tatáowa
Mayíngit takes the youngster,
Kanádi makes him fall into
  slumber.

Kánadi kanú tatáowa Mayíngit
Jerks out one of his own molars,
Takes one of his stiffest brow
  bristles.

Kánadih kanú tatáowa Mayíngit
Plants the tooth in the jaw of
  Balítok,

Takes also the brow lash,
Implants it in Balítok's forehead.
Kánadih kanú tatáowa Mayíngit
Awakens Balítok.
Kánadih Mayíngit, inquires he,
"Where are your hills ?"[28]
Kánadin answers Balítok,
"Our hills are at Kúdang,
Thickgrown with trees of *damáyun*
And also *bayúkan* and *gákad*."
Kánadih díye Mayíngit

Itud-akna Ballitok.	Sends Balítok thither.
Kanadi Ballitok	*Kánadi* Balítok
Ona panal-pal-iwan,	Goes not noting time's passage,
Dumatong ad Kudang.	Comes to the hill at Kúdang.
Kanadih kanu tataowa Ballitok	*Kánadih kanú tatáowa* Balítok
Ona blibliyon,	Goes looking around him,
Ona tangtangadon.	Looking upward and upward.
Kanadih tataowa Ballitok	*Kánadih tatáowa* Balítok
Ona gihigihon,	Goes dancing as if with *pinókla*,[29]
Kanadi ya kodyamana,	*Kanádi* flashing lightning,
Kanadi kanu tataowa	*Kánadi kanú tatáowa*
Ona pupuh-itan,	Goes striking and striking,
Kanadi ya immahiduayao!	*Kánadi* withers all green things!
Kanadin kalion Ballitok,	*Kanadin* utters a *fiat*:
"Batlakana" n kaliona	"SO BE IT," says he,
"Ta onmu uk-ukulon	"So that thou imitatest;
Ta onmu angdupon mo ————,	Go thou, drop down on [name of enemy][30]
Gawanah bobled ————,	In the center of their village at————[30]
Ta mangapkaya balena,	So that his house be bewitchéd,
On naduhidun,	Crushed down like harvested rice straw,
Na-at-atuganga.	And scattered in all directions,
An nabatingalngal,	His witchcraft turns backward against him
Ikapkapyana on kababaíana,	His women folk, all bewitchèd,
Umat di imbalbalena.	And likewise his children.
Ngininginiy ihikalna,	Always worried and haunted,
On dinamunay himbulan di matana!	Meeting demons with eyes enough to make a moon!
In-dinna in dingdingngolmi,	We shall soon be hearing and hearing
On puhbakbaktadanay hongana,	That his welfare rites avail nothing[31]
Mate ta ihaludagda,	That he's dead and propped in his death chair
Ta e-da ilubok.	That they bear him unto his sepulchre,
Ta lanitlitta-onda,	Clay the stones of his sepulchre's entrance,
Hi nalaot hi dalipe,	Seal it up with the strongest of tombstones,

Ta maid inilanan
Umawing hi buholna.
Dingolmi intatao-mi
Di nunggao-way algo inakuimi!"

That now he knows nothing
Of vengeance 'gainst his foemen.
We will hear — be informed of it,
When the sun is half way we
  will pity!"[32]

XIII

Kanadi kanu tataowa
Mumbangangad hi Ballitok,
Doladad Kiyangan,
Kanadih ya dumatong.
Kanadin kalion amana,
"Uddi kaatnay impangatmo?"

Kanadin tinumbal Ballitok,
Kanadin kaliona,
"On immahiduyao" an kaliona,
"Abunay tubuna nakaan."
Kanadin kalion Mayingit,
"Adiak madinol", an kaliona,
"An manayan ke dakayun
  hin-apu."
Abunadi mo kanu ya kanadi
Agamidona Ballitok
Kanadi ya pahuypona,
Toktokolnay wolwolna,
Kanadi kanu tataowa
Itoktoknan Ballitok;
Kanadiboh Mayingit,
Kaanonay banun di kidena,
Ona itoktok bo,
Hi kiden di banin Ballitok.
Kanadih kanu Mayingit
Ona bangunon Ballitok,
Kanadih Mayingit ya kaliona,
"Da-anay pinugu yo?"
Kanadih Ballitok ya tinumbal,
"Pinugumid Inigihan
An nun-oltan di damayun
Umat hi bayukan ya balagnut."
Kanadi diye Mayingit
Ona itudak hi Ballitok,
Kanadi kanu tataowa

XIII

Kánadi kanú tatáowa
Home returns Balítok,
To their village at Kiángan,
Kánadih arrives there.
Kánadin inquires his father,
"How much wast thou able to
  do?"

Kánadin answered Balítok,
Kánadin says he,
"Everything withered," says he,
"But only the leaves stricken off."
Kánadin answers Mayíngit
"I'm not satisfied yet." he says,
"With the mana given child and
  grandsire."
Abúnadi mo kanú ya kánadi
He takes in his arms Balítok
Kanádi puts him aslumber,
Jerks out a jaw tooth,
Kánadi kanú tatáowa
Inserts it in the jaw of Balítok;
Kánadihbo Mayíngit,
Jerks out a brow bristle,
Goes ahead, inserts it, also,
Into the eyebrow of Balítok.
Kánadih kanú Mayíngit
Awakens Balítok,
Kánadih Mayíngit inquires of him,
"Where are your hills?"
Kánadih Balítok answers,
"Our hills are at Inigíhan,[33]
Thickgrown with damáyun[34]
As well as *bayúkan*,[34] *balágnut*."[34]
Kánadi diye Mayíngit
Sends Balítok thither,
Kánadi kanú tatáowa

Ume Ballitok ad Inigihan,
Balítok goes to Inigíhan,

Ona panalpal-iwan.
Goes not noting time's passage,

Kanadih kanu tataowa
Kánadih kanú tatáowa

Dumatong hi Ballitok,
Balitok arrives there,

Ona tangtangadon,
He goes looking upward,

Ona biliblion.
Goes glancing around him.

Kanadi kanu tataowa Ballitok
Kánadi kanú tatáowa Balítok,

An gihigihona,
Goes dancing as if with *pinókla*,

Kanadi ya kodyamana,
Kánadi darts out lightning,

Kanadi bo kanu tataowa
Kánadi bo kanú tatáowa

Ona pupuh-itan,
Goes striking with lightning,

Ya immahiduyao
And all things are withered

An kay nunbakagan,
As it changed into skeletons,

Nanubnub di adolna,
Sink down like a corpse in the grave cave.[35]

An maid naduda-an.
And there's left no remainder.

Kanadih kanu tataowa Ballitok,
Kanadih kanu tatáowa Balítok,

Kanadin kaliona,
Kánadin says he,

"BA-ATDAKA-NA" n kaliona,
"SO BE IT!" says he,

Ta onmu anukukulon,
"Go thou, imitating,

Ta onmu panapa-aton,
Go thou, doing likewise,

Ta angdopom hi balen ——,
And drop thou on the house of —,

Gagawana bobledad ——,
In the center of their village at —,

Ta mangapkapya balena,
So that his house be bewitchéd,

On naduhidu an na-at-atugangag,
Crushed like straw and everywhere scattered,

An nabatingalngal.
His witchcraft turns back against him.

Ikapkayanan on kababaíyana,
His womankind, all bewitchéd

Umat di imbalbalena!
And likewise his children!

Ngininginiy anat-atona,
Always worried what to do,

Ngininginiy inhikalna,
Always worried and haunted,

On dinamunay himbulanan di matana!
Meeting with eyes enough to make a moon!

In-da-innah on dingngolmi,
We will soon be hearing

Ta punbakbaktadanay hongana,
That his welfare rites avail nothing

Mate ta ihalidagda,
That he's dead and propped in his death chair

Ta eda ilobok,
That they bear him away to his sepulchre,

Ta lanitlitta-onda,
Clay the stones of his sepulchre's entrance,

Hi na-lot an dalipe.	Seal it up with the strongest of tombstones.
Ta maid inilana	So that now he knows nothing
Umawing hi buholna.	Of vengeance 'gainst his foemen.
Dingnolmin intatao-anmi	We will hear — be informed of it.
Hinunggaoga-way algo inukuymi!	When the sun is half way we will pity!
Kanadi kanu tataowa Ballitok,	*Kánadi kanú tatáowa* Balítok
Ona kayaton	Now returns home
Doladad Kiyangan,	To their village of Kiángan,
Kadadih ya dumatong,	*Kánadih* arrives there,
Doladad Kiyangan,	In their village of Kiángan,
Manbunan amanan Mayingit.	Where his father, Mayíngit, is waiting.
Kanadih kanu tataowa	*Kánadih kanú tatáowa*
Kanadin kalion Mayíngit,	*Kánadin* asks Mayíngit,
"Uddi ka-atnay impangatmo?"	"How much wast thou able to do?"
Kanadin kalion Ballitok,	*Kánadin* says Balítok,
"Nunkabagut di lamutna" n kaliona	"His roots are uprooted," he says,
An maid nakudahan."	And there's nothing whatever left."
Kanadi kanu tataowa Mayingit,	*Kánadi kanú tatáowa* Mayíngit,
Kanadin kaliona,	*Kánadin* says he,
"Madinolak," an kaliona,	"I'm satisfied now," he says,
"An manayan ke dakayun hinapnu.	With the mana given child and grandsire.
Ta onak tumalage,	And now I'll go upward,
Ta onak tumalakdang	Now I'll leap upward
Dolak hi Kabunyan,	To my village in the Skyworld.
No bigat ke," an kaliona,	But tomorrow morning," says he,
"Halamhamonyuy gammal —	"Ye must eat very early —
Ta nidalagadag key algo,	At the first gleam of sunrise
On kayu lumahun.	Come down from your dwelling.
Ta dakugonyuy lagon hinapu,	Stand back to sun, child and grandsire,
Hi dolayod Kiyangan."	In your village of Kiangan."
Abunadimoh kanu tataowa,	*Abúnadimoh kanú tatáowa*
Pangayan Mayingit di Kabunyan.	Mayíngit goes up to the Skyworld.

XIV

Kanadih kanu tataowa	*Kánadih kanú tatáowa*
Munggao-gaway algo,	The sun is half way,
Kanadi kanu diye	*Kánadi kanú díye*
Onda manangmangmangon.	They stand watching and watching.
Mahikal da nak Ambalittayon,	The sons of Ambalitáyon come rushing,
Doladad Kiyangan,	In their village of Kiángan,
Kanadih kanu tataowa	*Kánadih kanú tatáowa*
Onda dumatong	And arrive there
Hi balen di hinapu.	At the house of child and grandsire.
Immalihbuk di labbuwog,	They come raising dust clouds,
Doladad Kiyangan.	In their village of Kiángan.
Abunadimoh kanu tataowa Ballitok	*Abunadimoh kan utataowa* Balítok.
Doladad Kiyangan	In their village of Kiángan,
Kanadin limmabwat,	*Kánadin* gets ready,
Igaga-anay tulang inanah,	Calls for help to the kin of his mother,
"Ibanungolanyuy iggidko."	"Line up like beads on my left side."
Kanadi bon kaliona	*Kánadi bon* calls he,
"Daan kayun tulang ama?	"Where are ye, kin of my father?[36]
Ta ibanungolanyuy wao-wanko!"	Stand like beads on my right hand!"
Kanadih kanu tataowa Ballitok,	*Kánadih kanú tatáowa* Balítok,
Doladad Kiyangan,	In their village of Kiangan,
An kay kawitan an halangon,	Like a full-fledged cock, a red rooster,
Ona gihigihon,	Goes dancing as if with *pinókla*,
Kanadih kanu tataowa	*Kánadih kanú tatáowa*
Ona puh-itan,	Goes darting out lightning,
Ona duh-ongan,	Goes thrusting and thrusting.
Kanadih kanu tataowa	*Kánadih kanú tatáowa*
Tibona da nak Ambalittayon	He sees the sons of Ambalitáyon
Onda nunhalhaluwanni.	Tumbled heels over head.
An nunbaktadanday odonda	Their sleeping place is their weapons,
An maid nakudahan	There is left of them no remainder,
An kay nunbakagan.	They're as if to skeletons crumpled.

XV

Abunadimoh kanu tataowa	*Abúnadimoh kanú tatáowa*
Kanadih nunkabalu	*Kánadih* the new-made widows
Umat hi nunkanguhu nunka pangiyan,	And the mourning-band wearers and fasters,[37]
Onda kanu tataowa	They go, it is said, *tatáowa*
Maki-am-amuday udum	Becoming some like kindred to them,
Maki-ul-ulitaoday udum.	Becoming like uncles the others.[38]
Abunadimoh kanu tataowa	*Abúnadimoh kanú tatáowa*
Kimmali Ballitok	Said Balítok
Doladad Kiyangan	In their village of Kiangan,
"Umat hina" n kaliona	"Be it so," he said,
"Ta natalk di ginayangko,	"Lost be the slain by my weapons,
An nabugigaowan," kaliona.	Blown away like dust," he says.
Abunadimo kanu ya kanadi	*Abúnadimoh kanú ya kánadih*
Kimmalih Amtalao,	Up spake Amtálao,
Kanadin kaliona,	*Kánadin* says he,
"Ta higupontay ginayangta."	"Let's carry home our speared ones."[39]
Kanadi kanuy hinapu,	*Kánadi kanúy* child and grandsire,
Onda alan di manok.	They go and bring chickens.
Kanadimoh kanu tataowa Amtalao,	*Kánadimo kanú tatáowa* Amtálao,
Doladad Kiyangan	In their village of Kiángan,
Baga-anah tun Maknongan,	Invokes the *Maknóngan* gods,
Maknongan ad Lagod,	*Maknóngan* of the Downstream Region,
Umat tun Maknongan ad Daya.	And also of the Upstream Region.
Kanadin kaliona,	*Kánadin* says he,
"Tadulanyuy tayabban,	"Ye're offered a tayaban,[40]
Ta onyu ituddu," kaliona	So that ye keep guiding," says he,
"Kataguanmin gimmayang,	The lives of us who've been spearing,
Dolamid Kiyangan."	In our village of Kiangan."
Abunadimo kanu ya kanadi	Only that, it is said and *kánadih*
Kanadi tataowa Amtalao,	*Kánadi tatáowa* Amtálao,
Doladad Kiyangan,	In their village of Kiángan,
Kalionan Ballitok,	Says he to Balítok,
"Ontako ot monditak."	"Let us make now the *dítak*."[41]
Kanadi kanu tataowa	*Kánadi kanú tatáowa*
Ya katlun di algo,	And on the third day,
Dopapaonday babui.	They chase down their pigs

Kanadih kanu diye
Baga-andah Matungulan,
Matungulan hi Kabunyan,
Umat tun Matungulan,
Hi wadad Dalum;
Manaha-ut, hi Algo, Bulan;
Ya hantu on kalionda
Nanaddapudapun hi kinowitan.

Kánadih kanú díye
They invoke the *Matungúlan* gods,
Matungúlan of the Skyworld,
And likewise these *Matungúlan*
Who live in the Underworld;
Sun, Moon and Deceiver;
And go invoking those, also,
Who feel the way for the omen bird.[42]

Kanadi kanu tataowa
Pahiknadonday bakida,
Igagaday inib-unda
Ta pa-ulanday babui.
Kanadih kanu ya lagimanda,
Onda buyangon,
Kanadih kanu tataowa
Tibonday apgun di babuy,
Ya maphod an mayagud
An mab-gan, nunlawing.
"BAAT DAKANA" n kalionda,
"Ta anukukulonna,
Ta panah-pa-aton,
Ta kataguwanmin gimmayang,
Dolamid Kiyangan,
Ta matalak di ginayangmi,
Ta on mabugigbo."
Abunadimo kanu tataowa
Pangayanday hinapuy muyungda

Kánadi kanú catáowa
They finish their praying,
Call the sitters round to help them
In sticking the pigs.[43]
Kánadi they burn the hair off,
Open up the carcass,
Kánadih kanú catáowa
Examine the bile-sacs,
These are good and auspicious,
Well-filled and *munláwing*.
"SO LET IT BE," enjoin they,
"Let it serve as a pattern,
A parallel to follow
For the lives of us spearers,
In our village of Kiángan,
So that lost be the speared ones
Blown away like spittle."
Abúnadimo kanú catáowa
Child and grandsire go to their forest,

Kanadi kanu tataowa
On olbaonday palayon,
Onda bani-biyaowan,
Kanadimo kanu tataowa
Onda ikayat hi baleda,
Doladad Kiyangan.
Onda mangapdapla
Onda managoho,
Doladad Kiyangan.
Kanadih kanu tataowa
Nahodom di hodom,
Alanday bagabag,
Onda mangapkapya,

Kánadi kanú catáowa
And chop up an oak tree,
Gather in their arms the pieces,
Kánadimo kanú catáowa
Carry them up to their dwelling,
In their village at Kiángan.
They shout invocations,
Make rites of sorcery,
In their village of Kiángan.
Kánadih kanú catáowa
In the evening, at nightfall,
They go and bring palm leaves,
And busy themselves with making,

Mangapkapyada binukal,	With making headhunters' headgear
Umatbo balanti.	And also *balánti*.[44]
Kanadih mo kanu tataowa	*Kánadi mo kanú tatáowa*
Muntalanoy manok an gulikay,	When crows the plumed rooster,
Doladad Kiyangan,	In their village of Kiángan,
Kanadih kanu tataowa	*Kánadih kanú tatáowa*
Lumahon Ballitok,	Balítok comes down from his dwelling,
Doladad Kiyangan,	In their village in Kiángan,
Kanadi mo kanu tataowa Ballitok	*Kánadi mo kanú tatáowa* Balítok.
Ona hidhid-ipon,	Goes peeping and peeping,
Ona biliblion,	Goes searching and searching
Di balen di lumay-yung.	For the house of the wasps.[42]
Kanadih kanu tataowa	*Kánadi kanú tatáowa*
Ihablenay binanukal,	Hangs up the Panoply,
Ta pangidoldolana	To serve as an token
Tun ginangayangna.	Of them he has speared.
Kanadibon kaliona	*Kánadibon* says he
"Ihab-ledakan binanukal,	"I hang thee, Panoply,
Mo adi mihabley	But let not there be hanged up
Linawan di manok ya babuy	The souls of pigs and chickens
Umat hi linawan di u-unga,	Nor the souls of the children
Dolamid Kiyangan.	In our village of Kiángan.
Ta dakamiy makalkali,	And we shall be much spoken of
Hinuwi kinadangyang,	Who've braved our way to nobility,
Dolamid Kiyangan.	In our village of Kiangan."
BOKUN TATAOWA D KIYANGAN AN PAMUKADANMIN DAKAYU MO HITU BALEMI	IT IS NOT, INDEED, AT KIÁNGAN THAT WE ARE MYTHING YOU, BUT HERE AT OUR HOUSE.[46]

2. TULUD NUMPUTUL: THE SELF-BEHEADED

Subject: Self-Beheaded destroys enemies. Used in: war and sorcery rites. Informant: Ngidulu of Bitu. Recorded and translated by R. F. Barton.

This myth was first translated in prose form, but since for purposes of comparison it would be well to present the myth recitation of a second priest in the same form as that of the "Virgin Birth," I rewrote the translation with almost no changes or polishing aside from a few contractions, rearrangements of word order, and the substitution of phrases for words or the reverse for the sake of the meter.

SYNOPSIS

Balitok of Dalegdeg is beset by creditors and enemies who rage against him and "will hardly give him another night." He and his kindred set forth to procure strong sorcery. They arrive at the Lake of the Downstream Region, dive into it and come to a village of beings headed by Ghoul (*Angob*). After exchanging betels with these beings, the visitors state their situation and purpose in coming. Ghoul advises them to await his youngest brother, Self-Beheaded (Numputul).

Soon Self-Beheaded appears, homeward bound, his neck-stump bubbling and frothing as he dances along his way. He is a rapturously happy being, as any man, able and sufficiently heroic, would be if he should eliminate his central nervous system — provided, of course, he might still remain capable of providing for his vegetative one. He prances along, grabbing all kinds of snakes and centipedes and thrusting them down his neck-stump and the more he thrusts down, the better he feels.

On seeing Self-Beheaded approach, Balitok manifests a quite ex-cusable nervousness lest he himself be also "included," but Ghoul reassures him, giving him to understand that Self-Beheaded is just what, in his present situation, he most needs. Balitok and kindred take Self-Beheaded home with them, the monster catching snakes and centipedes along the way and thrusting them down his neck-stump. Arrived home, Balitok sacrifices a chicken, feeds the monster chopped-up pieces of it mixed with blood, and "points" him against the enemies and creditors. Self-Beheaded entirely liquidates these, [*sic*], including their boy-babes, whereupon Balitok makes peace and friendship with the rest of them [*sic*].

[The *tulud* begins]: Lumawig of Gumihad, (a village lying between Dalegdeg and Balitang, where the myth was being recorded) finds himself in a predicament similar to that which confronted Balitok in the first place. He goes to Dalegdeg, secures Self-Beheaded and brings him home. Self-Beheaded liquidates the enemies with the same despatch as in the previous instance.

Lobwag of Bahelna, (a village still nearer Balitang where the myth was being recorded), next secures Self-Beheaded and has his enemies similarly liquidated by Self-Beheaded.

Barton of Balitang (having set before Ngidulu, the informant, rice wine fortified by *nipa* gin and also, on Ngidulu's refusal to have any dealings with Self-Beheaded except on condition of being able to feed him raw-meat,[1] having provided a chicken for sacrifice) is likewise beset by enemies and creditors. Barton becomes *princeps acta* in the last *tulud* and journeys to Bahelna, secures Self-Beheaded from Lobwag and brings him home. Self-Beheaded not only liquidates Barton's enemies but continues on — automatically, it would appear — and "includes" the wooden blocks used as pillows, the firestones and the pottery in their houses.

THE MYTH

I

Kánadih Bálitok ad Dalégdeg,
Wáda n nungáowa y álgo,[2]
Tibún-nay binúhol-dad Dalégdeg,
An kón-da ngáyutngótan,
Kón-da didíyan,
Adí-da hínkugábon.
Náh'dom di hodóm adí
Monháphapitón-da n hintúlang.
Nabigát di bigát adí,
Ilkán-da pungámalan-da,
Umípa-dan mongámal ya magíbu-da.
Pawaklínon-da,
Pahublíon-da y momón-da.
Wáda n nungáowa y álgo,
Ngálan-da y hintúlang,
"Kón-tako ot umánap hi nalót hi kápia."
Monaltálipón-da,
Íh'bít-da y ambáyug-da,
Iháynub-da y dúluh-da,
Ítalawídan-da y gáyang-da,
Lumáhon-da d Dalégdeg,
Pitáowan-da y akpáowan-da d Dalégdeg,
Monuhául-da, habángon-da
Hi lúbong ad Lágod.

Kánadi díye ya tibún-da
Balinhudóngan-da gáyang ya tundón-da,
Kalibúgon-da y lúbong ya pahádon-da

I

Kánadih Balitok of Dalégdeg,
When the sun is half way,
He sees his enemies at Dalegdeg,
That they're raging against him,
Urging each other against him,
Won't give him another night.
In the darkness of night time,
The kindred confer together.[3]
On the morn of the morrow,
They take down their food basket,
Begin to eat and finish.
They put things away,
Change to betel chewing.
When the sun is half way,
Ngalan-da the kindred,
"Let us go find strong sorcery."
They pack for the journey,
Tuck on their hipbags,
Next [belt on] their bolos,
Take their spears in hand,
Descend from their houses.
They cross their outskirts at Dalegdeg,
Go downstream and arrive at
The lake of the Downstream Region.

Kánadi díye they see it,
Turn their spears around and plunge into it,
Come to the bottom and arrive at

Dóla n Ángob ke da Manúnglub,	The village of Ghoul and "Facer" (Against Enemies).
Pínigpígan ke da Lúnge,[4]	Ringed-Nose, and Drooped-Over,
Ke da Kalótkot ad Dálum.	And Sound-of-Crunched-Bones.

II	II
Kon-da kanu humigup,	They, it is said, enter,
Dahiingon-da y gayang-da,	Thrust their spears into the ground,
Monhindadauwat-da momon-da,	They give each other betels,
Kanádi ya pahláon-da.	And turn them red-spittled.
Monhapihapit da Angob ad Dalum,	Said the Ghouls of the Underworld,
"Ngaday tabina y inalian-yo	"What is the reason for your coming
Dola-mi d Dalum?"	To our village in the Underworld?"
Himapit hi Balitok ad Dalegdeg,	Spake Balitok of Dalegdeg,
"Manuke immali-kami	"The reason we have come is:
Ya didiyan dakami mombaga	Our creditors urge each other against us,
Ya binuhol-mi d Dalegdeg.	Likewise our enemies at Dalegdeg.
Ekami," kanu, "manibu,	We've come," he says, "to seek for
Hi nalot hi Kapia	Strong Sorcery,
Dulaya, Duhidu."[5]	Expulsion and Counteraction."
Himapit da Angob ad Dalum	Said Ghoul of the Underworld,
"Andunni ke," kalion-na,	"Wait a while," says he,
"Ta umanamut di udidian-mi."	"Till our youngest-born comes home."
Hindodonayan ad Dalum,	In a little while in the Underworld,
Ya himbatangan di algo,	When the sun marks mid-afternoon,
Ngalana Numpútul ad Dalum	*Ngálana* Self-Beheaded of the Underworld,
Ya monananamut.	Comes homeward bound.
Tibun-da Mompútul ad Dalum,	They see Self-Beheaded of the Underworld,
An mondayudayu,	He's rejoicing and rejoicing,
An montayutayu,	He's dancing and dancing,
An montalolok di putul-na,	His neck-stump is bubbling,
An punhagamhaman-na y kauluûgan	He goes grabbing all kinds of snakes,
Ya kagaygayamanan,	And all kinds of centipedes,

Hon ihodhod-na putul-na.

And thrusting them down his neck-stump.

Ingindan-na mondayudayu,
Ingingdan-na montayutayu.

And increasingly he rejoices,
Accelerates his dancing.

Maid te motakottakot hi Balitok,

Nothing else than that Balitok be seized with fear,

Ya himapit hi Angob,

And up spake Ghoul of the Underworld,

"Adi-ka montakotakot, Balitok,

"Don't be afraid, Balitok,

Te hinai kuyugon-yo,

For that is the one you'll take back with you,

Ya kon mo ot ligwaton, Balitok."

So get ready to go, Balitok."

III

Hindondonayan ya lumûmwa-da lubong,

Soon they rise to the top of the lake,

Kanadi lubong ad Dalum,
Dumakal-da ya monhulung-da
Maid te liolion Balitok,

The lake of the Underworld,
Leave the water and go upstream,
Nothing else than that Balitok look side-wise,

Ya ah nakayang! Numptul,
Tibun-na n mondayudayu,
Montayutayu pundalanan-da,
Panaghagaman-na
Kaululûgan, kagaygayaman-an
Kon ihudhud-na putul-na!

And *ah nakayang*! Self-Beheaded,
Is seen to be rejoicing,
Dancing along as they go,
Reaching out and grabbing
All kinds of snakes and centipedes
And thrusting them into his neck-stump!

Kanadi ya pumalpaliwan-da,
Ya umakpaowan-da d Dalegdeg.

They go not noting time's passage,
And pass through the outskirts of Dalegdeg.

Lumadang-da ya humigup-da.
Adi mahlongan Balitok,
Ya dopapon-na y budi, buludon-na,

They ascend and enter Dalegdeg.
Balitok wastes no time,
He catches a large pig and ties it,

Ya dulugon-na, gombon-na tun dinakwat,

Trammels it[6] and invokes this Obtainment[7]

Tun wa d Dalum ya pahiknadon-na.

These of the Underworld and he finishes.

Tibun-na imangmangdad-na,

He sees and "faces" [Self-Beheaded][8]

Madingdinglahon-da.
Kanadih dinakwat-na
An ilodoldong-nah binuhol-da.

And feeds him raw meat.
Kánadih his Obtainment
Is pointed against their enemies.

Mala kano Numputul, / *Mala*, it is said, Self-Beheaded,
Ya kon-na kanu nunoltan, / Gathers his strength (for an on-slaught),

Tibun-na binuhol-da d Dalegdeg, / He sees their enemies at Dalegdeg,
Ya dimdimangon-na, / Descends on both sides of their families.

Tibun-na binuhol-da d Dalegdeg, / He sees their enemies at Dalegdeg,
Ya ilagat-na gohikon-da; / And includes their boy-babes.
An kai nabakagan! An maíd na-toldad. / As if skeletonized — there's left no remainder.

Tibun-na y dinongdong ya *kanádi*, / He sees the sorcery and *kanádi*
Yimapui hibayan an nahiklib! / The eaves have grown lighter and risen![9]

An maíd kumalkali. / And there's nobody talking.
Tibun-na binuhol-nad Dalegdeg, / He (Balitok) sees his enemies at Dalegdeg,

An maki-ibiba-da y udum, / They become like kinsmen, some of them,

Maki-ululitao-da y udum, / Become like uncles the others.
An tumalak-da y mibaga, / Their debts against him are lost,
An lumaklak-da y inidaowan. / Their omens against him are broken.

Tibun-na ginayang-da d Dalegdeg, / He sees those he's speared at Dalegdeg,

Ya maid di bimudu, bimalu. / And no one comes out to avenge them.

TANABTABINADI mo d Daleg-deg, / That is the reason, in Dalegdeg,

Ilyaliyak-da mo ya momboga, / That they farm and their crops are fruitful,

Momaata, an adi maduiduyanan. / And ripen, and there's no crop-failure.

First Tulud[10]

IV / IV

Ngálana Lumáwig ad Gumíhad, / *Ngálana* Lumáwig of Gumíhad,
Himapit hi Lumawig ad Gumihad, / Spake Lumawig of Gumihad,
Kalion-na, "Kana katog da Bali-tok ad Dalegdeg, / Says he, "*Kána katóg* Balitok of Dalegdeg —
An monhindingol di dinakwat-na n mabagan." / One keeps hearing of his famous Obtainment."
Monaltalipon hi dola-na d Gumi-had, / He packs up in his village at Gumihad,

Ih'bit-na ambayugna,
Tucks on his hipbag,

Ihaynub-na y duluh-na,
Then belts on his bolo,

Talawidon-na y gayang-na,
Takes spear in hand,

Lumahon d Gumihad,
Comes down (from his house) in Gumihad,

Tibun-na ya idaowihan-na y danum ad Gumihad,
He crosses the stream at Gumihad,

Palpaiwan-na monuhaul,
Goes downstreamward not noting time's passage,

Humabang di akpaowan-da d Dalegdeg,
Arrives in the outskirts of Dalegdeg,

Monladang ya humigup,
Crosses them and enters,

Immodmod-na y gayang-na,
He thrusts down his spear,

Ihunud hi punbayuan,
Goes across to the rice mortar,

Pumbaininan da Balitok ad Dalegdeg.
Balitok of Dalegdeg looks around, startled.

Ya Lagiwa d Dalegdeg.
And Lagiwa of Dalegdeg, [says]

"Naya di mangili-mi
"There is here an other-town man

An nalhom di binla-na."
Whose handsomeness is profound."

Lumahon ya mompalpaldang-da.
They go down, and sit beside him,

Monhindadauwaton-da mommon ya tabakuan,
They exchange betels and tobacco[11]

Tiktikon-da, tuugon-da ngipayda,
They lime their betels and put them between their teeth,

Baloblaon-da ibughi-da blao-na,
Crush them and spit out the crumblings,

Bimugbug, pimanangpang
Their spittle's turned red and thick.

Monhapihapit hi Balitok,
Balitok speaks,

"An uddi di tabina hi inaliam,
"What was the reason, of thy coming,

Hitun dola-mi d Dalegdeg ?"
To this, our village of Dalegdeg ?"

Kanadih Lumawig ya himapit,
Kanadih Lumawig answers,

"Manuke limadang-ko
"The reason why I've come,

Hi dola-yo d Dalegdeg —
To your village of Dalegdeg —

Ya namahig hi dolak ad Gumihad,
It's more than I can stand in my village of Gumihad,

Te didiyan-ak hi dinongdong.[12]
For they've sicked sorcery on me.

An ngimayutnut-da y binuhol,
Mine enemies are risen 'gainst me,

Adi-ak hinkugaban."
Won't give me another night."

Himapit hi Balitok,
Said Balitok,

"An dan maíd di kapiam —
"Then hast thou no witchcraft —

Hi Dulaya, Duhidu
No Expulsion, no Counteraction ?

Hi Pokipok, hi Pigwid ?"
"Maíd," an panagali-na,
Kanadih Lumawig, "Monhapi-
  hapit-da bo —
An nunhindingdingol — nan
  dinakwat-yo."
"Ya hia," an kalion-na,
"Neh'na nan dinakwat-mi,
An inala-mi d Dalum,
An hi Numputul ad Dalum,
Ke da Angob ad Dalum,
Me da Manunglub ad Dalum,
Da Mangungahon ad Dalum,
Ke da Longwe ke da Kalotkot,

Ke da Galikum.

Deket pohom ya dakwatom."

Inabulut mo Lumawig.

No Termination, no Shunting ?"
"I have not," he answered.
Kanadih Lumawig, "They're talk-
  ing about —
And it's much heard about — your
  Obtainment."
"That's the thing!" he answers,
"There is our Obtainment
That we got in the Underworld,
Self-Beheaded of the Underworld,
And Ghoul of the Underworld,
And Facer of the Underworld,
Mangungahon of the Underworld,
Drooped-Over, Sound of Crunched
  Bones,
And Crunching Sounds When
  Eating Hard Things.
If thou like, take as thy Obtain-
  ment."
Lumawig agrees [to take them].

V

Kanadih Numputul,
Nanayongtong di algo,
Monana-anamut.
Laniklion Lumawig,
Tibun-na ya montayutayu,
Tibun-na mondayudyu,
Panaghagamhaman-na kaululu-
  gan,
Ya kagaygayamanan,
An ihonhon-na y putul-na.

Ingingdan-na n montayutayu,
Ingingdan-na mondayudayu
Maid hi Lumawig te montakota-
  kot.
Kimali Balitok ad Dalegdeg,
"Adi-ka montakotakot, Lumawig,
Te hinai ya kain di bulunum."

Lumawig ya ih-bit-na y ambayug,
Ihaynub-na dulu,

Kánadih Self-Beheaded,
When the sun's a little past noon,
Comes homeward.
Lumawig looks sideways,
Sees him dancing and dancing,
Sees him rejoicing and rejoicing,
Grabbing all kinds of snakes,

All kinds of centipedes,
Which he thrusts into his neck-
  stump.
He dances faster and faster,
Increasingly rejoices.
Nothing else than that Lumawig
  be seized with fear.
Said Balitok of Dalegdeg,
"Do not be afraid, Lumawig,
For that is whom thou must con-
  trol."
Lumawig tucks on his hipbag,
Then [belts on] his bolo,

Talawid-na gayang.	Takes spear in hand.
Nakak ak Dalegdeg.	They have set forth at Dalegdeg,
Maid te numpito akpaowan-da,	Nothing else than that, as they cross the outskirts,
Akpaowan-da d Dalegdeg,	Their outskirts at Dalegdeg,
Wingion ya montayutayu Numputul.	He glances round and Self-Beheaded is dancing.
Palpaliwan-da ya monhulung,	They go upstream, not noting time's passage,
Hungduan-da akpaowan-da d Gumihad.	Arrive at their outskirts at Gumihad.
Kanadih Lumawig	*Kánadih* Lumawig
Wahitan-na manok-na,	Throws bait for his chickens,[13]
Dopapon-na kawitan,	Catches a rooster,
Ighop-na kanu bale-na,	Takes it, they say, to his house,
Gonobnobon-na y amud-na,	Invokes his ancestors,
Italban-na y makalun,	Changes [his invocation] to the Messengers,
Gomgombon-na tun dinakwat-na,	And then invokes this, his Obtainment,
Numputul ad Dalum,	Self-Beheaded of the Underworld.
Dalaan-na y manok,	He bleeds the chicken,[14]
Lagiman ya puwikon,	Singes and opens it,[15]
Tibun-na ya ningale.	Sees that it [the bile omen] is *ningale.*
Alan-na y manok ya godaton-na,	He takes the chicken and cuts it to pieces,
Ilamulamud-na dala n di manok,	Mixes the pieces with blood,
Ya imangmangdadan-na tun dinak-wat-na,	And, "facing" this his Obtainment,
Kon-na madingdinglaon.	Feeds him raw meat.
Tibun-na ya ilildong-n abinuhol-na.	He looks and points him toward his enemies.

VI

Kanadih Numputul,	*Kánadih* Self-Beheaded,
Uhiwon-na buhol Lumawig,	He rages against Lumawig's enemies,
Tibun-na ya dimdimangon-na —	Looks and destroys them on both sides —
Maid natoldad, maid nakudaan!	None left, there's no remainder!
Inunud-na wanud-da,	He follows out the remotest roots of them,

Maíd mo kumalkali.	None are left talking.
Kanadih mo Lumawig,	*Kánadih* mo Lumawig
On-na iyuli-uli,	He adopts a course of kind treat-ment,
Dola-na d Gumihad.	In his village of Gumihad.
Kanadih nuningoho, nuninbalu,	The mourning-bands wearers and widowed
Kon-da maki-ibiba,	Become like kinsmen to him,
Maki-ululitao-da y udum.	Become like uncles the rest.
Maíd te tabinadi d Gumihad,	Nothing else than that it be the source at Gumihad,
Kataguan di babui-na, manok-na	Of the life of his pigs, his chickens
Ya ilyaliyak-na.	And of the crops that he planted.
Momboga, momaata.	The crops fruit and ripen.
Monhindingdingol bo dinakwat-na —	His Obtainment was continually heard about —
An hi Numputul ad Dalum.	Self-Beheaded of the Underworld.

SECOND TULUD

VII	VII
Ngalana Lobwag ad Bahelna:	*Ngalana* Lobwag of Bahelna:
Ngalana y tulang di ginayang-na,	The kindred of those he had slain,
Da nak Pungudan ad Bangauwan —	The sons of Pungudan at Bangauwan —
Tibun-na ya ngayotngotan-da.	He sees that they rage against him.
Nahdom di hodom adi,	In the darkness of night-time,
Lumahon hi Lobwag ad Bahelna,	Lobwag descends at Bahelna,
Alan-na y hapio ya gayang-na,	Taking his shield and spear,
Bumtik ad Bahelna.	And runs away at Bahelna.
Hindodonayan ya bigat an nun-gaowa,	In a little while it is mid-forenoon,
Ya montikid hi Lobwag ad Bahelna,	And Lobwag of Bahelna climbs upward,
Umablat ad Pukao.	And goes round the mountain at Pukao.
Imodmod di gayang ya mangbun,	He presses down his spear and sits,
Nanguhuhdungan ad Gumihad.	He looks down over Gumihad.[16]
Bahutan-na gayang ya mondayu,	He pulls up his spear, descends,
Pumahaad ad Gumihad,	And arrives at Gumihad,
Tibun-na, kanu, ya humigup,	He looks, it is said, and enters,
Imodmod-na y gayang-na,	He presses down his spear,

Ihunud-na punbayuan.
Mombainan hi Lumawig,
"Taya 'tu han mangili
An nalhom di binla-na
An mabungot ta nangamong
An balbagan di mata-na."
Lumahon ya paldangan-na
Balbalukayan-da y hapit.
"Ngaday tabina di inaliam

Hi dola-mi d Gumihad ?"
"Manuke immaliak —
On-ak nadngolan hi dinakwat-
mo;
Te namahig di dolak ad Bahelna;

Namahig-da y buhol-ko,
Da nak Pungudon ad Bangauwan.

On-ak anhan! didiyan,

Adi-ak hinkugabon!"
Monhapahapit hi Lumawig,
"Takon ot ya dakwatom

Di dinakwat-ko," an kaliona,
"An hi Numputul ad Dalum,

Ta idetongmo, tuali,
Hi dola-yo d Bahelna,
Ta yabyabyabom," an kalion-na
"Ta imangmangdadom

Pumadingdinglaom;
Ta ililildong-mo binuhol-mo d
Bahelna.
Kon man humiklig an kumana-
kin."
Inabulut mo Lobwag ad Bahelna.

Goes over to the rice mortar.[17]
Lumawig glances up, startled,
"There is here an other-townman,
Whose handsomeness is profound,
Whose rage is so great that
His eyes are inflamed."
He descends, sits beside him.
They make conversation.
"What is the reason thou'st come
to
Our village of Gumihad ?"
"The reason I've come is,
I kept hearing about thy Obtain-
ment;
For I can't endure it in my village
at Balena;
My enemies are too much for me,
The sons of Pungudon of Bangau-
wan.
They urge each other against
me —
Won't give me another night!"
Lumawig speaks,
"It will be all right for thee to
take
My Obtainment," says he,
"Self-Beheaded of the Under-
world,
Take him, indeed, home to
Thy village of Bahelna,
And thou wilt fan him," he says,[18]
"'Face' him at the edge of thy
village,
And feed him raw meat;
Point him 'gainst thine enemies at
Bahelna.
He'll indeed put aside, overcome
them."
Lobwag of Bahelna agreed.

VIII

Nanayontong di algo,
Ngalana Lumawig ad Gumahid,

VIII

The sun was a little past noon,
Ngálana Lumawig of Gumihad,

Ya ayagan-nah Numputul,
Calls Self-Beheaded,

Agi nahindodonayan,
In no time at all,

Kanadih Numputul,
Kanadi Self-Beheaded,

Kon-a kanu monanamot.
Comes, it is said, homeward.

Lanilian Lobwag,
Lobwag looks sideways,

Tibun-na ya montaytayu,
Sees that he's dancing and dancing,

Tibun-na mondaudayu,
Sees him always rejoicing,

Monuhbok di libuog ad Gumihad,
Raising dustwhirls at Gumihad.

Timakot hi Lobwag at Behalna,
Lobwag of Bahelna is frightened

"Ya kai tayaban an umilagat!"
"It's like a *tayaban* that will include me!"[19]

"Hitui nimpe kuyugom;
"That is he thou must take back with thee;

Ta bulunum ke, ta ildong-mo
So control and point him

Hi dolam ad Bahelna."
In thy village at Bahelna."

Inabulut Lobwag ad Bahelna.
Lobwag of Bahelna agreed.

"Damunadi ta mombangad-ak."
"So much for that — I'll return."

Ih'bit di ambayug, italawid di gayang,
He tucks on his hipbag, takes his spear,

Makak ad Gumihad,
Sets forth at Gumihad,

Ipiton-na akpaowan ad Gumihad,
Crosses the outskirts at Gumihad,

Wingion-na Numputul,
Looks around at Self-Beheaded,

Tibun-na kon montayutayu,
Sees him dancing and dancing,

Tibun-na mondayudayu.
Sees him rejoice and rejoice.

Tibun-na montalalok di putul-na,
Sees that his neck-stump is bubbling.

Panaghagamhan-nah dalan
As he catches on the way,

Kaululûgan, kagaygayamanan
All kinds of snakes and centipedes

Ya ihonod-nah putul-na.
And thrusts them into the neck-stump.

Palpaliwan-da ot monhulung.
They go upstream, not noting time's passage.

Kon-da kano montikid,
They climb up the mountain,

Umablat ad Pukao,
Go round its side to Pukao,

Imodmod di gayang-na ta momoma,
He presses down his spear, chews betels,

Ibughi ya bimugbug.
Blows out the red spittle.

Bahutan-na gayang-na,
He pulls up his spear,

Kon, kanu, mondayu,
Goes, it is said, downhill,

Panalpaliwan-na,
Goes, not noting time's passage,

Dumatong ad Bahelna,
Arrives at Bahelna,

Lihlion-na binuhol-na.
Looks askance at his enemies.

Konda nundalili, nundalikwa.

They slide forward, surround him.[20]

Himapit hi Lobwag ad Bahelna,
"Dakayu 'n binuhol-ko
Ya duminong-kayo nihan,"
    kaliona,

Spake Lobwag at Bahelna,
"Ye enemies of mine,
Do be quiet," he says,

"Nabigaton teyak hitu,
An daan a ayak ?" kaliona.

"I'll be here everyday.
Where would I go ?" he says.

Indinong di binuhol-na.

He has silenced his enemies.

Dumatong hi dola-na d Bahelna.

He arrives in his village at Bahelna.

Wahiton-na manok-na,

He throws bait to lure chickens.

Dopapon-na kawitan,

Catches a rooster,

Ighop-na kanu bale,

Takes it, it is said, to his house,

Alan-na pungamgan,

Brings out his war chest,

Hakmaowan-na momma hapid,

Piles on betels and betel leaves on it.

Kon-na gonobnoban di amud-na;

Invokes and invokes his ancestors;

Ganomgombon-na tun dinakwat an mabagan,

Invokes this famous Obtainment,

An da Numputul ad Dalum,

Self-Beheaded of the Underworld,

Ke da Angob ad Dalum,

And Ghoul of the Underworld,

Ke da Pinigipigan ke da Manunga-hung,

And Ringed One and Manunga-hung

Ke da Longwe ke da Kolotkot.

And Drooped-Over and Sound-of-Crunched-Bones,

Ke da Galikom ad Dalum

And Sound-of-Crunching Hard-Things.

Pahiknadon-na, dalaan-na manok,

He finishes, bleeds the chickens,

Puakon-na, tibun-na ningali.

Breaks it open, sees that it's *ningale*.

Alan-na y manok ya godaton-na,

He takes the chicken and cuts it up,

Itukmin-na dala.

Mixes the pieces with blood.

Kanadih Lobwag ad Bahelna

Kanadi Lobwag of Bahelna

Ya imangmangdalna,

"Faces" (Self-Beheaded) at the edge of the village,

Punmadmadinglaon-na,

Feeds him raw meat,

Ilodoldongna binuhol-na

"Points" him towards his enemies.

Tibun-na binuhol-na ya kanadi,

He sees his enemies *kanádi*,

Nunlinikwo, an dumalidi-da.

Crowded round and sliding toward him.

Ngalana Numputul,
An montayutayu,
An mondayudayu,
Kanadi nunoltan Numputul.
Idalana binuhol,
Panagamhaman-na,
Kon inhodhod na putul-na.
Tibun-na y binuhol-na,
Da nak Pungudan ad Bangauwan,

Ya maid natoldad —
Maid nakudaan,
Maid kumalkali.
TANABTABINA mo'di,
Dola-da d Bahelna,
Ya diminong di dinongdong
Ya iagagamida-da
Hai babui ya manok.
Matagu y manok-da, babui-da.

Ngalana Self-Beheaded,
He dances and dances,
Rejoices and rejoices,
Gathers his strength for an effort.
He roads over the enemy,
Grabs them hand over hand,
Thrusts them into his neckstump.
He (Lobwag) sees his enemies,
The sons of Pungudan of Bangau-
wan,
And there's no remainder —
There are none of them left,
There's nobody talking.
That was the reason, too, there,
In their village of Bahelna,
That the sorcery ceased,
And that they go acquiring
Pigs and chickens.
Their pigs and chickens abound
in life.

THIRD TULUD

IX

Maid te monhindingdingol

Hi dinakwat an mabagan.
Kanadi Barton ad Balitang,
An didiyan di dinongdong ya
buhol,
Hi dola-na d Balitang.
"Kon-ak e manibu
Hi nalot hi kapya."
Ya monaltalipon
Hi momma ya tabakuan-na,
Ih'bit-na y ambayug-na,
Lumahun ad Balitang,

Palpaliwan-na ya umagwat ad
Piwong,
Ya mondayu ad Kudug.
Pumahad ad Higib.
Palpaliwna-na ya madmang ad
Mongayan,

IX

Nothing else than that they heard
from each other,
About the famous Obtainment.
Kánadi Barton of Balitang,
Sorceries and his enemies beset
him,
In his village of Balitang.
"I shall go searching for
Strong sorcery."
And he packs up
His betels and tobacco,
Tucks on his hipbag,
Comes down [from his house] in
Balitang,
Crosses, not noting time's passage,
to Piwong,
And goes downhill to Kudug.
He arrives at Higib.
Takes his time and crosses to
Mongayan on the other side,

Agana ad Umiyon,

Continues on to Umiyon,

Palpaliwan ya montikid ad Ambabag,

Takes his time and climbs up to
Ambabag,

Dumatong ad Bahelna,

Arrives at Bahelna.

Tibun-na ya humigup,

He locks and enters,

Iluhad-na y gayang-na.

Thrusts down his spear.

Numotwa Lobwag ad Bahelna,

Lobwag of Bahelna notes his
presence.

"Taya han mangili
An nalhom di binla-na."

"There is here an other-townsman,
Whose handsomeness is profound."

Lumahon ot paldangan-na,

He descends and sits beside him,

Monhindadawat-dah momma,

They give each other betels,

Balbalukayon-da hapit.

They engage in conversation.

Monhapihapit hi Lobwag,

Says Lobwag,

"Impungadan-mo an tagu n
limadang,

"How wast thou named, man,
who hast come

Hi dola-mi d Bahelna ?"

To our village of Bahelna ?"

Tinumbal hi Balton,

Barton answered,

"Kon-da n mibagbaga
Balton ad Balitang.

"They call me
Barton of Balitang.

Manuke linadang-ko

The reason I have come to

Hi dola-yo d Bahelna —

Your village of Bahelna —

Ya kon-ak ngayotngotan di binuhol ko

My enemies rage against me

Hi dolak ad Balitang.

In my village of Balitang.

Monhindingdingol di dinakwat-
mo —

Thy Obtainment is much heard
about —

Podhom ke, ya dinakwat-ko."

If thou like, let it pass unto me."

Ya inabulut Lumawig

And Lumawig agreed.

X

Hindodonayan,

After a little while,

Ya ayagan-nah Numputul

He (Lobwag) calls Self-Beheaded.

Tibun-na ya monanamut hi
Numputul,

He looks and Self-Beheaded is
coming homeward,

An montayutayu,

Is dancing and dancing,

An mondayudayu,

Rejoicing and rejoicing,

Panaghagamhaman-na y
kaululûgan,

Catching all kinds of snakes

Hi kagaygayamanan,

And all kinds of centipedes,

Kon inhodhod-na putul-na,

Thrusting them into his neck-
stump,

An montalolok hi putul-na. — Which bubbles and bubbles.
Montatakot hi Balton — Barton is seized with fear.
Himapit hi Lobwag, — Said Lobwag,
"Hainai bulunom." — "Thou must control him."
Makak mo hi Balton. — Barton departs.
Aganda d Bahelna, — They pass out through Bahelna,
Wingiyon Balton, — Barton looks around,
Tibun-na Numputul, — Sees Self-Beheaded,
Ya montayutayu, — And he's dancing and dancing,
An mondayudayu, — Rejoicing and rejoicing,
An panaghagamhaman-na, — Reaching out and catching
Kaululûgan hi kagaygayamanan, — All kinds of snakes and centipedes,
Kon inhodhodna putul-na, — And thrusting them into his neck-stump,

An montalolok di putul-na. — Which is bubbling and bubbling.
Palpaliwan-da d Amduntug, — They go, not noting time's passage, to Amduntug,

Ya humauwang-da d Ambabag, — And come out at Ambabag,
Mondayu, pumahad d Mongayan, — Descend and arrive at Mongayan,
Umagwat ad Higib, — Cross the river at Higib,
Montikid ad Kudug, — Climb the steep at Kudug,
Umablat-da Piwong, — Cross over to Piwong,
Monabat-da ya umagwat ad Balitang. — Go round the mountain and ford across to Balitang.
Dumatong; adi mahlongan hi Balton, — They arrive; Barton wastes no time,
Ya wahiton-na manok-na — Throws bait for his chickens,
Ya ilablabawan-na, — Catches the biggest and fattest,
Alan-na y pungamngan-na, — He brings out his war chest,
Daplalan-na momma ya hapid, — Piles betels and betel leaves on it,
Gombon-na y amud-na, — Invokes his ancestral spirits,
Itolban-na makalun, — Changes to the messenger gods,
Gombon-na tun dinakwat-na, — He invokes this his Obtainment,
Hi Numputul ke da Angob, — Self-Beheaded and Ghoul,
Ke da Mananglub, Pinigipigan, Manungahung, — "Facer," "Ringed Nose" and Manungahung,
Ke da Longwe, Kalotkot, — Drooped-Over, Sound-of-Crunched-Bones

Ke da Galikum ad Dalum. — And Crunching-Sounds-When Eating-Hard-Things, of the Underworld.

Pahiknadon-na ya dalaan-na y manok, — He finishes and bleeds the chicken,

Lagimon-na, puwikon,	Singes and opens it,
Tibun-na ya ningali,	He sees that it [the bile-sac] is *ningali*
Alan-na y manok ya gogodon-na,	He takes the chicken and cuts it into pieces,
Ya itukmina dala.	And mixes the pieces with blood.
Imangdadan-na, pumadinglaon-na,	He "faces," feeds him raw meat,
Ilodoldong-na binuhul-na.	"Points" him 'gainst his enemies,
Ah nakayah! hi Numputul,	*Ah nakayah*! Self-Beheaded,
Ingingdan-na puntayutayuan-na,	Accelerates his dancing,
Ingingdan-na pundayudayuan-na,	Increasingly rejoices,
An dimdimangon-na y binuhol Balton,	Takes the enemies of Barton on both sides their family,
Kon-na mo dabdabudabon,	Grabs them hand over hand,
Ilagat-na y gumhikon,	Includes their little boy-babes,
Ilagatna y dalapong,	Includes the wooden blocks used as chairs,
Kolotkot-na y dalikan,	Crunches the fireplace stones,[21]
Punilagat-na y banga.	Includes the cooking pots.
Maid mo natoldad, maid naku-daan,	Nothing left, no remainders,
Maid kumalkali.	There's nobody talking.
Kanadi mo Balton,	*Kanadi mo* Barton,
Iyambayug-na mo momomma, hapid,	He pockets betels and betel leaves,
Ya dimdimangon-na y binuhol,	Goes amongst both sides his enemies' kindred,[22]
Ya kai mo kawitan,	Like a full-grown cock bird,
Ya kai binah'hihingan.	Like the fastest runner among wild boars.
Tibun-na binuhol-na ya maki-ibiba-da,	He sees that his enemies become like kinsmen,
An maki-ululitao-da y udum,	And become like uncles the others,
Mombangad mo hi Balton.	Then Barton comes home.
TABTABINAMODI, kataguan	It is the source of the life of
Di babui-na hi manok-na,	His pigs and his chickens,
Mahinupan hi buhol ya ananitu,	Of the staying far away of enemies and evil beings,
Hinui kinadangyangan-na.[23]	Of the trophies of his wealth-iness.
Ilyaliyak mo ya momboga,	He farms and his crops are fruit-ful,

Momaata, ya adi maduiduyanan,	Ripen and there's no crop failure,
Ta bumga di miliak hi umalin-duat,	And the planted things fruit in the swing of the seasons.
Ta gumikud di page,	And the rice is miraculously increased,
Ta pumalauwa di oonga,	And the children grow vigorously,
Hitun dola-mi d Balitang.	Here in our village of Balitang.
KALIDI — BUKBUKADON, DAKA KE BALTON, MU HUMIKLIG-KA TA KUMINAKIN-KA HI DINONG-, DONG YA ANANITO, TE BINUKAD DAKA HANTUN BUKAD-MI!	*KALIDI* — THOU ART MYTHED FOR BARTON, BUT LIFT UP AND UNDERDIVE THE SORCERY AND EVIL BEINGS, BECAUSE THOU HAST BEEN MYTHED THESE MYTHS OF OURS!

B. Prose Texts in Ifugao followed by Translation

3. INAMONG: KINSHIP ASSEMBLAGE

Subject: Origin of the Ifugaos and their appearance on earth. Used: in rites to cure childlessness believed to be caused by neglect of distant kindred. Informant: Buligan Bugbug, of Hingyon. Recorded in 1937 by Mr. Francisco Bugbug, graduate of a middle school, an Ifugao. Translated by Barton.

Educated Ifugaos dislike to write their own language, saying that it is easier for them to write English. This is partly pose, but still there is some basis for their attitude. There is no standard orthography for the language, and each phrase, each word in fact, presents a problem to them. Being from Hingyon, Bugbug omits many *k*'s; these I have supplied. His system of orthography follows that of Mr. Manghe. He writes as one word all that seems to him to be pronounced as one word. There is also a phonetic difference from my recordings in that Bugbug hears as *o* sounds what in many cases, appear to me to be *u* sounds.

SYNOPSIS

1. Kabigat and Bugan, deities of the Skyworld, have many children. Kabigat sends a brother and sister from among these to dig tubers on the side of a Skyworld mountain.

2. Kabigat orders a heavy rain to fall; it carries brother and sister down to the earth-world, to a "level place" in the Upstream Region (*Daiya*). The two build a temporary hut there.

3. Kabigat ties jars, dogs, chickens, pigs and cats to a house, fills a granary with rice and orders house and granary to slide down to the "level place."

4. Wigan goes hunting but cannot, on level land, overtake the quarry and therefore ponders a way in which to bring the game to bay. He goes downstream, builds a dam and then orders his house to grow as tall as a mountain. On the third day he sees that the whole land is flooded. He then goes downstream and destroys his dam. The waters sweep downward and in so doing carve the level place into mountains. He is able to overtake the game in the mountains.

5. Up to now Wigan has been observing the kinship avoidances — has been sleeping beneath the house while his sister slept above. But one night he ascends and lies with her as she sleeps.[1] Next night, Bugan puts lime on her breasts and in her navel. In the morning, seeing lime on her brother, she upbraids him. He confesses and proposes that they marry, since otherwise they will be unable to "increase." Their father and mother in the Skyworld sanction the marriage.

6. Bugan and Wigan have 4 daughters and 5 sons. Wigan complains to his wife that the children observe the kinship avoidances and do not marry; he tells her to take the girls and move to another locality, while he reamins with the boys. The girls pound rice every day by the edge of their new "village" to attract the boys' attention. Wigan sends the boys to marry the girls.[2]

7. To the fifth boy, for whom there is no sister, they give a fat pig and send him to the Downstream Region to marry. He there procreates what seem to be a number of supernatural beings, namely, Childlessness, Listlessness, Bloodlessness, Leanness, Big Belly (from enlarged spleen), Puffed Cheeks and Lazy-Sleeplessness.

After many years, this father sends his children to associate with their kindred, the descendants of his brothers and sisters in the Upstream Region. The latter become afflicted by contagion. They sacrifice to their kindred Downstream, after which they increase and multiply: the field baskets (symbol for the women) form a great pile; "the shields become enough to make the walls of a house and the spears enough to make the trunk of a betel palm."[3]

COMMENT

This myth has probably more versions than any other. See Villaverde, 1912, page 319, or the translation of Villaverde's version by Beyer, 193, page 96; another version, 111-113. In this version a slightly different reason is given for Wigan's damming the river in order to form mountains. The mountains were wanted in order that there should be echoes of the dogs' baying, which would make it easier for the hunter to follow them. The termination is also different: Bugan, overwhelmed with shame flees far into the Downstream region and seeks to be devoured by the man-eating deities there. But these comfort her and send her back to "increase" with her brother, enjoining on her and her descendants only the sacrifice to them of chickens at all rites of marriage or to cure childlessness. This termination is sometimes recited as a separate myth or tulud. As such I have published it in "Ifugao Law," 1919, page 112. The latest version is a poetization in English by Hon. Luis I. Pawid, an Ifugao, the deputy-governor of Ifugao.

See also the Benauwe versions of the myth as recorded by Beyer, 1913, page 111; and by Levi Case, same Journal, Sec. A, 1909, pages 256–260. The Kankanai and Bontok myths have several of the same motifs but the plots are quite different.

Motifs found in this myth exist all over North America embodied in plots that are quite dissimilar. A long list of such myths is found in Stith Thompson, 1929, pages, 273 following.

There are at least two reasons why the mountain folk of Northern Luzon may have gone to the mountains:

1) It was easier for them to build terraces and irrigate them than in the plains, where the permanent streams flow in deep channels that would require substantial dams, which however, would wash out at flood time, or else build very long canals, which would also wash out in floods. In the mountains small weirs suffice, likewise, until the cultivated area becomes great, short canals. Probably, too, by the methods the Ifugao uses, it is easier to build terraces in the mountains than in the lowlands, for in the former the earth can be shovelled downhill, while in the latter it must be levelled by being carried in baskets.

2) They were driven from foothills into the high mountains by malaria, in all probability. In the Philippines, this disease is carried by the *Anopheles funestus minimus**, which breeds at the edges of swift-flowing streams. It does not breed in the plains nor at altitudes higher than 2000 feet. (Russell, pp. 63–64) 1935.

Ifugao Tut

1. Ngalana kano Kabigat hi Kabunyan ke Bugan in'Kabigat. Konda montanutanud, matanudanda da Bugan ya hi Wigan. Kon kano nongaway algo, omipadan mongamal, konda pawaklinon, pahobliyunday momonda, konda bolobla-on; ibugiday bolana di mimada ya kon bimugbug an pimangpang. Himapit hi ama-da, "Konkayundi e momboka, dontug nah Kabunyan." Enabolut da Wigan ke Bugan.

Konda manaltalipon an hin tulang hi moma ya hapid, konda monokak hi akpaowandad. Ahida montikid, omablat-da dontugnad Kabunyan. Konda mangmangbon, nilingtan, nidibdiban, okatonday moma hapid, konda himpanapidon, konda himobobo-wa-on; ibugiday bolan di mimada. Himapit hi Wigan, "Damonadin," kalion-na, "konta ot momboka." Konda ganganuon.

2. Nanayungtung di algo, himapit hi amada Kabunyan, "Hea an Odan, kon ka matiyutiyuk, ta montipludka hi dalowa-it, ta konmo ibalokibok di o'onga." Kanadi odanadi, kon matiyutiyuk an mamalo-balod. Ngalanada Bugan ke Wigan an hin tulang, konda mondayu, konda ot pomahad hi nundotalanad Daya. Himapitday hin tulang, "Makakaga amata, bokonman baletakoh'tu, kalionay eta momboka ya ondita-ot imbalokibok hi dagom." Himapit hi Wigan, "Konta-ot monalung."

3. Nahdom hi hodom, ngalana Kabigat hi Kabunyan, kona hibdan di baledad Kabunyan ya bohi, kaho, manok, babuy poha ya imat hi alanghi page.

"Hea an bale, konkaman domalilid Daya, hi nundutalanad Daya ta ponbaledaka o'onga."

Kanadi kanuy bale, konda domalili, humabang ad Daya hiway nonalungan di o'onga. Konda mahuyup. Hindodonayan, timaluy olon di golgoluway, lomahunda an hintulang. Himapit hi Wigan. "Nganu'an tehto han bale? Ya maid nian adnakogab." Kondamo bilbiliblion an hintulang. Kimale kano Bugan. "Te an hitue baletako ya alangtako Kabunyan." Nabigat ya konda iyayamon an hin tulang, nabigatun konda e monayayam hi pangilnad Daya.

4. Nabigat ya kon nungaway algo ya id'idnohan di amayu, tung-tungngawona, maphod an imale katlona, imin'indi hokob hi bangi. Mongamaldan hin tulang, magiboda ya momomada, nagibo dan numoma, kimale Wigan, "Hito-ka ta konakadi monanop." Inabulot Bugan. Makak ya pangayanay pinogo, tangdonay kinawitan ya ipaliwidnay labe ya pinhodna; iyena dulwa ya hiabo, iyena katlo ya donongna. Domatong hi nundotalanad Daya. Immodmodnay gayang-na ya kon momoma ya nagibo. Lohuwanna amayu ihngolna ya nadonapan hi budu. Bimwak di amayu, punlaglagudon-na an ponday-daya-ona ya maid midumut hi bangngol ya omanamot. "Odinok an mangidonap hi inanopko?" Nungawa kanuy algo, kohponday ponga-malanda ya konda mongamal, konda magibo ya pahubliyonday moma ya ngiboda.

Lomahon hi Wigan ya monuha-ul, domatong ad Lagud, batuganay kadaklan ya pahiwalana ya lita-ona ya munhulong ad Daya. Kimale Wigan, "Hea en balemi ya mangatageka ta atogom ad Awitingan." Katlon di algo ya tibunday nundotalanad Daya an ponlitap, nal-

ting dan amin di monyayam hi luta. Mondayud Awitingan ya doma-
tung ad Lagud ya tobwangona ya tibuna ya nabunibunig di bilid.
Kimale Wigan, "Midonap manhan di inanop, te nabunig di bilid, te
maatuy bangol."

Nongaway algo ya mongamal ya manaltalipon hi moma hapid ya
makak. Pangayanay pinogoda, .itangadna kinawitan ya impalinay
labe. "Batdakana," an kaliona, ta kataguwak an mondowong ya
kataguan di panuyun di amayuk." Iduwonga ya padimdimpogonay
bangol, iyanamot nad Daya ya nahdom di hodom, omipa ya mongamal. Pawaklinonay nongamalana, pahobliyunay moma hapid, lomahun hi dola an bomala' ongana hi kahodhodom. Nanayongtong di
labe hongup hi bale ot eyutona ibana ya lomahun hi dola. Nabigat
ya makak bon monanop, padimdimpoongonay inanopna.

5. Nahdom di hodom omanamot. Mongamaldan hintulang ya lomahun hi dola Wigan ya bomala'ong hi dola. Ya apulan ibanay palag-
pagna ya pohogna. Nalok boh hinongopho Wigan ot eyutona bo
Bugan ot lomahon hi dola. Nabigat ya tinibon Bugan di apul ke ke
Wigan. Himapit hi Bugan, Te ne kon heay ogan hongop?" Himapit
hi Wigan an hi ibana. "O, tatawa, te maid odom hi tagu di malhi-
nanta, ya odinon-tan mah'lag?"

Ngalana da amada ya hi inada an konda o'hodongan dida. Himapit
hi Kabigat, "Takon," an kaliona, "ta wa odinondan mah'lag." Konda
mon montanutanud, matanudanday hiyam, an opatday binabai ya
limaday linalaki. Moya ngalana, kon kanu nongaway algo.

"Odonona, Bugan? Mangongaldaman di o'onga ot mongigidawan-
da. Emot iyid Holyadan nan binabai ta imiwekayod Holyadan."

6. Inabulot Bugan. Omey kanu Wigan ya kaponay baled Holyadan
ya konda mo kano ome hidi, nataynanda Wigan hi linalakid Daya.
Ngalanaday binabaid Holyadan, konda ingilingilig di bayu kabig-
bigatna. Himapit hi Wigan hi linalaki. "mangmangonyuke nedan
binabaid domang. Konyuman idawinon dida." Imedan lima ya mon-
hapitday opat ya konda abulotun ya nahawal di ohan hi Kabigat.

7. Ya dopoponday lablabon di babuyda igitoda tukod ya hogponday
bale ya konda mongamal. Ahida pawaklinon, pahubliyonday
moma ya konda magibu. Himapit hi Kabigat, "Inlablabawon di
babuy tako mo nangamong di kon ha donodnong takod Daya. Palpa-
liwana ya humabang ad Lowong ya omakpaowan ya ladangonand
Lowong. Ibagbagana babalontagu hi donodnonga. Himapit day tagu,
"Abuna Bugan, nak Monagad." Ya mange domatong hi balen da
Bugan ya ihibodnay babuy hi tokud, ihunod-na pombayuan mangmangbon, nilingtan, nidibdiban, hogponay bale ya monhapit da ke
Bugan; ya inabulot Bugan. Kigowan damoy a'amod Bugan, ya
ibakiday babuy, ya maphod. Ya konda humaligagod. Muntanutanuda

ya matanudanda da Bomutin, Bomahig, Omaki, Pomihat, Bomadad, Tomamong ya Homamuyu.

Ngalanaday nataynan ad Daya, nuntanuda bo. Naliyam di tawon ya nangongalday o'onga. Nabigat di bigat ya mongamal da tun wad Lowong, ya pahubliyonday momonda, nagibuda n numoma ya kimale amada. "Konkayundi monhulong ad Daya ta ikayu makiayam hi i-ibayod Daya. Ume-da moy o'onga ya amodanday tinanudan di nataynan ad Daya, ya bomotinday odom, bomahigday odom, omaki da omaki, pomihat da pomihat, bomodad da bomodad, timamongday tomamong, himamuyu da homamuyu.

Ageda nahlongan di wad Daya ya tungolanda tun nunuhaol. Tabinadimo ya nahladad Daya ya hintunop di tudong, hinga-oban di hapiyu ya hinbangihan di pahul.

(*Annotation by Bugbug.*[4]) Note: This is a story of the first person sent by God.

Hay nalpuan di namangulon duan tagun impadalili Kabigat hi Kabunyan. [The origin of the first two human beings, slid down by Kabigat of the Skyworld].

Advocated by Buligan Bugbug, iAlak.
Recorded by Francisco A. Bugbug.
Directed by Mr. R. F. Barton.

TRANSLATION

1. *Ngalana* it is said, Kabigat of the Skyworld and Bugan, wife of Kabigat. They bring forth many children, bring forth Bugan and Wigan. At mid-forenoon, it is said, they begin to eat, they finish, change to betel-chewing; they crunch together the three ingredients of betel chewing (areca nut, betel leaf and lime); they spit out the first juice of the betels and it has become red, thick red. Said their father, "Go and dig tubers on the mountain of the Skyworld." Wigan and Bugan agree. Brother and sister pack up betels and start through the outskirts [of their village] in the Skyworld. They ascend, climb the steeps of the mountain of the Skyworld. They sit down a while; when cooled off and breezed, they take out their betels, they take each a betel leaf, each a betel nut; they spit out the first juice. Said Wigan, "So much for that. Let us now dig tubers." They hurry.

2. At noon, their father in the Skyworld spake, "Thou, Rain, pour down, fill the brooks to overflowing. Carry down the children." *Kanadih* Rain, he pours down, descends like the strings of a hipbag. *Ngalanada* Bugan and Wigan, brother and sister, they are carried down and land on the level of the Upstream Region. "Alas,[5] our father! There is no house of ours here. He told us to go tuber-digging and then caused us to be carried down."

3. At night time, *ngalana* Kabigat of the Skyworld, he ties rice-wine jars, dogs, chickens, pigs, cats and likewise a granary with rice to a house in the Skyworld.

"Thou, house, slide down to the Upstream Region, to the level place of the Upstream Region."

Kanadih. it is said, the house, it slides down to the Upstream Region to the place where the children had made their shack. They were asleep. In a little while the leader of the cocks crew. Brother and sister descended. Said Wigan, "Why is there a house here? There was none yesterday." Brother and sister investigated. Said Bugan, it is said, "These here are a house of ours and a granary of ours from the Skyworld." In the morning brother and sister walk about; every day they walked about their neighborhood in the Upstream Region.

4. On the morrow it is midforenoon and he (Wigan) sacrifices for his dogs, he observes a day of ceremonial idleness, the third day came without any chicken-catching by hawks and without any falling limbs.[6] Brother and sister eat, they finish and chew betels; when the betel-chewing was finished, Wigan said, "Stay thou here, for I am going to hunt." Bugan agreed. He starts and goes to the hills, looks up at the cockbird and the bird gives a slow cry (Bad omen) and he likes it; he goes a second time and it is the same, goes a third time and it is the same. He comes to the level place of the Upstream Region. He sticks down his spear and chews betels and finishes, brings his dog and sends him on trail, and is covered with runo nettles. The dog trails the quarry, pursues it far downstream, far upstream, and the quarry is not overtaken and he goes home. "How shall I bring down my quarry?" At mid-forenoon, it is said, they take down their eating basket and they eat; they finish, change to betels and finish.

Wigan quits (the house) and goes downstream, he comes to the Downstream Region, dams the river with stones, reinforces it with timbers, plasters it with clay and then returns upstream. Said Wigan, "Thou, house, become tall so that thou reach up to Awitingan (a mountain)." On the third day they see that the level place of the Upstream Region is entirely covered and that all the things that move on the earth are drowned. They come down at Awitingan and he arrives at the Downstream Region and destroys his dam and he sees that mountains are carved out (by the rushing waters). Said Wigan, "Now indeed the game may be overtaken, for mountains have been carved out and the pigs will become tired."

At mid-forenoon he eats; finished, he packs betels and starts. He goes to their hills, he looks up at the cock-bird[7] and it gives a rapid [good] omen. "So it will be," he says, "for my life who go hunting and for the life of the leader of my dogs." He hunts and the wild pig is easily killed; he carries it home in the Upstream Region and at night he eats. He cleans up where he ate, changes to betels, descends to the place beneath the house where he has been sleeping every night. In the middle of the night, he goes up into the house and lies with his sister[8] and then returns below the house. On the morrow he goes again to hunt; he quickly kills the quarry.

5. At night he returns. Brother and sister eat and Wigan goes below the house and sleeps below. And his sister puts lime on her breast and navel. Bugan sleeps also and Wigan again ascends and lies with Bugan and then returns below. In the morning, Bugan saw the lime on Wigan. Said Bugan, "Then that was thou who once came up?" Said Wigan her brother, "Yes, indeed, because there are no other people with whom we can marry, and how [else] shall we multiply?" *Ngalana* their father and mother, they look down on them. Said Kabigat, "Let it be so," he says, "so that there be a way for them to increase."

6. And they increase and increase, they brought forth nine, who were four girls and five boys. And then, *ngalana*, it is said that Kabigat [said]: "What to do about it Bugan? The children are becoming large and they observe the kinship avoidances. Go and take the girls to Holyadan and live separately with them in Holyadan."

Bugan agreed. Wigan, it is said, goes and makes a house at Holyadan and they (mother and girls) it is said go thither, they leave Wigan and the boys in the Upstream Region. *Ngalana* the girls at Holyadan, they pound rice at the edge [of the village so as to be seen by the boys] every day. Wigan told the boys. "Look you — there are the girls on the other side. Go and take them as wives." The five of them went and four bespoke the girls and they accepted and one was left over, namely Kabigat.

7. And they catch the fattest of the pigs, they tie it to a housepost and enter the house and eat. They clean up [their leavings], change to betel-chewing and finish. Said Wigan [to Kabigat] "Thou hast taken the largest and fattest of our pigs, so it is up to thee to find the equal of us folk of the Upstream Region."[9] He goes not noting time's passage and arrives at Lowong and crosses their outskirts and enters into Lowong. He inquires of the men for his equal. The men reply, "There is only Bugan, the child of Monagad." And he goes, arrives at the house of Bugan and ties the pig to the housepost, walks over to the rice mortar, cools off, is breezed, ascends the house, speaks with Bugan, and Bugan agrees. They call together, also the fathers of Bugan and they kill the pig and it is well. And they settle permanently.[10] They bring forth children: they bring forth Bumutin, Bumahig, Umaki, Pumikat, Bumudad, Tumamong, and Humamuyu.

Ngalana these left behind in the Upstream Region, they bring forth children. After fifty [many] years their children are large. One morning those at Lowong eat and change to betels, they finish their betels and their father said, "Go ye upstream to the Upstream Region and fraternize with your kindred in the Upstream Region." They go and fraternize with the descendants of those left in the Upstream Region and some of them become childless, some of them become without semen [at all events, "childless"], the jealous become jealous, the lean become lean, the anaemic become anaemic, the puff-cheeked become puff-cheeked, the sleepy and lazy become sleepy and lazy.

They did not waste time, those of the Upstream Region, and they sacrificed to those who went downstream. That was the reason why they began multiplying in the Upstream Region, so that there was a large heap of women's field baskets, there were shields enough for a housewall and spears enough to make a betel palm trunk.[11]

4. INALALTA: THE NEGRITOS

Subject: The Negritos afflict Balitok of Kiangan. Used: In rites to cure stitch in the side. Informant: Kumiha. Recorded and translated by Barton.[1]

SYNOPSIS

1. The Negritos of the Downstream Region, Upstream Region, Skyworld and Underworld come on a visit to their kindred at Banutan. A Negrito of this last place sets out with bow and arrows to kill a wild pig so as to feast the guests. He shoots at a pig, but the arrow merely grazes its skin, flies on and sticks into a corner post of the house of Balitok of Kiangan.[2] The Negrito returns home and tells his companions, "I missed the pig but perhaps the arrow struck something — we'll wait and see."

2. Balitok is seized with a stitch in the side. His "fathers" resort to the diagnosis-stick (*agba*)[3] and the bow-users are indicated. Balitok offers sacrifices and the Negritos smell these and send him relief from his affliction.

IFUGAO TEXT

1. Ngalana di mompanapana d Lagod, inalalta d Lagod, "Hikalon-tako y iba-tako an mompanapana d Banutan." Alan-da bokangda, baguya-da d Lugod. Monhulung-da, hungduan-da Banutan.

Ngalanda Mompanapana d Daiya, inalalta d Daiya, alan-da bokang-da, baguyu-da d Daiya. Monuhaul-da d Banutan. Ngalan-da Mompanapana, inalalta d Kabunian, alan-da bokang-da, baguyu-da

d Kabunian, mondayu-da d Banutan. Ngalan da mompanapana d
Dalum, inalalta d Dalum, alan-da bokang-da, baguyu-da d Dalum.
Lumumwa-da d Banutan.

Himapit di mompanapana d Banutan, "Ngano kon-kayo neya,
Mompanapana d Lagod ya Mompanana d Daiya ya Mompanapana d
Kabunian ya Mompanapana d Dalum ?"

Kalion-da, "Hinikal-mi dola-tako d Banutan."

Himapit hi mompanapana d Banutan, "Hitui-kayo ta e-ak mamana
bangol hi duntug."

Alan-na y bokang-na, baguyu-na. Ladangan-na dotalan ad Ligauwe.
Tibun-na y bangol hi duntug-na d Akeya monulultuge. Inlimilim-na
bokang-na ya baguyu-na. Inhukhuk-na y bangol hi duntug-na d Ake,
mondaga d Kiangan, nitoltog hi bagat-da Balitok ad Kiangan.

Mabangad hi mompanapana d Banutan. Himapit da mompanapana
d Lagod ke da mompanapana d Daiya ke da mompanapana d Kabunian ke da mompanapana d Dalum, "Where is what you shot ?"

"Maid, the inuhuk-na y bangol, madaga d Kiangan ot wa bo y
nabade, hadon-tako y baiyad, ta hia igamal-tako."

2. Ngalana Balitok ad Kiangan. Umananhan di taglang-na! Dola-
na d Kiangan. Adi-da mahlongan di amud-na. Alan-da dotag,
idalutag-da hukap. Gombon-da tun mompanapana d Lagod, inalalta
d Lagod ya d Daiya, inalalta d Kabunian ya d Dalum.

Hinungul-na dida: "Tibun-tako ke bayad, ta hia igamal-tako.
Igamal-da y hintutulang. Nagibu ya momomma-da, bumugbug an
pimiang-pang.

"Daan-ka ot Bugan ?" kalion hi mompanapana d Banutan, "Guyu-
dam di bagyu-ko."

Inabulut Bugan. Pangayan-na d Kiangan. Dumatong hi bale n da
Balitok, inhiuhiwa-na baguyu ya guyudon-na. Kai naguyud di dogo-
na. Mombangad ad Banutan. Himapit hi mompanapana d Banutan,
"Kon-tako ot humapud an amin, takon-tako dumalaiyup, ta bayunga-
nantako da Balitok ad Kiangan."

Monuhaul-da mompanapana d Lagod, monhulung-da mompanapana d Daiya, tumalage-da mompanapana d Kabunian, lumublub-da
mompanapana d Dalum.

Ngalana mo Balitok, duminong di taglang-na, kai inububadan, kai
inbohwat an tubtubuan. Inyagamid-na mo manok. Matagu y manok-
da. Makidaladalan hi logadan di dalan.

Kalidi, te bokûn ad Kiangan te hitu bale-mi d Bitu.

COMMENT

The myth appears to be an invention based on a traditional memory of the Negritos.

There can be no doubt that the Negritos once inhabited Ifugao-land. In Hingyon there is a ricefield which is pointed out as having been built with the aid of Negrito labor. The Kiangan Ifugaos have a number of traditions about this people, two of which are given by Villaverde, 1912, pages 314, 341. He states that Ubing, the name of a character in two or three folktales I have recorded, is reputed to have been the progenitor of the Negritos and that Maladi, another god, is his son. Maladi, Ubing and other Negrito divinities are prayed to in Kiangan as follows: "We are Negritos, too; we are people of Banutan, too. Do not shoot us with your bows and arrows!"

Lambrecht states (1932, page 458) that the Mayawyaw have a tradition that the Negritos were unacquainted with natural birth and cut the child out of the mother's belly, thus always killing the woman. It is interesting to find among the Maori a similar belief attributed to their gods, who cut the child out with stone knives (Dixon, 1916, page 78), and among the American Indians (Lilloet) Teit, 1912, JAFL, p. 294; and by the Alab (Bontok) Igorots to the people of Naneng (Moss, E. T. C., 1932, page 47).

TRANSLATION

1. *Ngalana* the bow-users of the Downstream Region, the Inalalta[4] of the Downstream Region. "We are thinking about our companions, the bow-users of Banutan." They take their bows and arrows in the Downstream Region, go upstream and arrive at Banutan.

Ngalana the bow-users of the Upstream Region, the Inalata of the Upstream Region, they take their bows and arrows in the Upstream Region and go downstream to Banutan. *Ngalana* the bow-users of the Skyworld, they take their bows and arrows in the Skyworld and descend to Banutan, *Ngalana* the bow-users of the Underworld take bows and arrows, ascend to Banutan.

Said the bow-user at Banutan, "Why are ye here, bow-users of the Downstream Region, the Upstream Region, the Skyworld and the Underworld?"

"We were thinking about our village at Banutan," they say.

Said the bow-user at Banuta, "Stay here while I go shoot a wild pig on the mountain."

He takes his bow and arrow goes down to the level place at Ligau-we, sees a wild pig on the mountain at Ake and goes over the mountain, draws his bow and arrow, loosens the arrow. It grazed the skin of the wild pig on the mountain at Ake, fell to Kiangan, struck the corner stud [of the house] of Balitok at Kiangan.

The bow-user returns to Banutan. Said the bow-users [of the other regions] "Where is what you shot ?"

"Got nothing — only grazed the wild pig; it [the arrow] fell in Kiangan; maybe it struck something. We will await a payment [tribute] and will eat that."

2. *Ngalana* Balitok at Kiangan. Terrible — the stitch in his side, in his village at Kiangan! His "fathers" waste no time. They resort to the *agba* stick. The bow-users are indicated. They bring meat, display it in a basket, invoke these bow-users of the Downstream Region, these Aetas of the Downstream (and all the other regions...).

They [the bow-users] smell it. "Look — there is tribute for us to eat." The kindred eat, finish, chew betels, turn them red and thick-spittled.

"Where art thou, Bugan ?" says the bow-user at Banutan. "Pull out my arrow." [He sends his wife on the errand, instead of himself going].

Bugan agreed. She goes to Kiangan, arrives at the house of the Balitoks, grasps the arrow by the end and pulls it. It is as if the sickness had been pulled out; she returns to Banutan. Said the bow-user at Banutan: "Let us all blow at once, let us relieve, let us cure Balitok at Kiangan."

The bow-users of the Downstream Region go downstream; those of the Upstream Region go upstream; those of the Skyworld ascend; those of the Underworld go down.

Ngalana mo Balitok. The stitch in his side ceased as if untied. He was like leafed things crushed to earth which rise again; he acquired chickens and the chickens abounded in life. He walked the accustomed paths.

Kalidi: it is not at Kiangan, but here at our house in Bitu.

C. English Translations only, with Synopses and Notes

5. IHIK: TURNED TO STONE[1]

Subject: Ihik, turned to stone, forms a channel for passage of water. Used: in rites to cure dysentery, diarrhea. Informant: Kumiha. Recorded and translated by Barton.

SYNOPSIS

1. Wigan and Ihik at Kiangan, brothers, go far into the Upstream Region, headhunting. They lie a day in ambush, without any success,

then continue on, climbing a mountain. Ihik keeps complaining of thirst. Wigan, his elder brother, finally, in irritation, strikes a rock with his spear and water gushes forth. Ihik springs forward to quench his thirst, but Wigan reproves him, saying that they must give priority to the ancestors, and that Ihik must be the last to drink. Thereupon they invite the ancestors to drink, Wigan drinks and then calls Ihik to drink. Wigan gives Ihik a shove and he becomes a part of the rock; the water enters at his mouth and emerges at his anus. Ihik acquiesces in his lot but asks that his sister Bugan be sent to keep him company. Wigan goes back home and sends her.

2. Wigan and his brother, Balitok, are afflicted with terrible belly troubles. They sacrifice to Ihik and Bugan and recover.

COMMENT

The principal themes of this myth, the turning of persons to stone and the drawing of water from a rock, are very widespread. One is reminded of certain Biblical myths, for example. The motif of priority is found in an Angami myth:

"Of the two ancestors of the Angamis, Thevo, who emerged (out of the earth) the first was the ancestor of the Kepezoma (phratry) who are entitled by virtue of his priority to a precedence in eating over the descendants of the younger, Thekrono. The Kepepfüma (phratry) however, claim that Thekrono was really the elder of the two, but that Thevo outwitted him in the matter of precedence by arrogating to himself priority of birth and proceeding to eat first on the strength of it, without giving Thekrono an opportunity to assert his right. However this may be, a Pezoma man has the right to eat or to start eating, at any rate, before any Pepfüma man if the two are about to take a meal in company on ceremonial occasions, and on such occasions Kepepfüma await Kepezoma and do not begin eating before them." (Hutton, 1921, page 112.)

This motif of priority does not appear in the same form here, as it does in one of Villaverde's recordings [translation in Beyer, 1913, page 104] where Ihik is turned to stone because he, being the youngest tries to drink before his brothers. No such priority is observed in the present day.

The application of this myth is an excellent illustration of Ifugao thinking: he has seized on it as cure for dysentery because of the analogy of water passing through the human body. Ihik and his sister are examples of a large class of deities, whose names are usually passive forms, grammatically, who afflict men in the same way they have themselves been afflicted — "because that is their nature." [Barton, 1946, pages 95–97].

The Bontok and Kankanai Igorots have legends about two dainty thin streams, called the water of Inude that fall down a precipitous mass of rock on the western slopes of Mount Data. According to the Sagada version, the twin streams were formerly on the other side of the valley on the sides of Mount Tuad, northeast of Sagada. But the people of Titipan washed dirty clothes in their waters and threw snail shells into it. Disgusted by the human filth, the streams transferred to Mount Data, telling the Sagada people that they would come back if a red chicken and a pig with red spots should be sacrificed. A Bagnen version is similar, but has the stream transfer first to Mount Batu, overlooking Besao. There they again were disgusted with human dirt and changed to the uninhabited region on Mount Data. The Bontok version is that the falls were formerly about midway between Bontok and Tukukan, and were offended because a dog barked at them continually. An Alab version (Bontok Igorots) is entirely different: A brother and sister were sent daily to scare birds from their fields. Their mother gave the girl a good lunch to carry, but gave the boy a very bad one. The sister was as outraged by this favoritism as the boy himself, and readily accepted his suggestion that they run away from home. They wandered far up the slopes of Mount Data and changed into the falls of Inodey. [Moss, E.T.C. page 37].

The favoritism-as-respects-food motif is found in an Ifugao folktale of an entirely different character. The Ifugaos use the "waters of Inude" as a figure in their invocations: "So that we be like gold which tarnisheth not, like the plumes of the cogon and runo, like the waters of Inude . . ."

If there were any borrowing in the case, the stories would surely be much more similar than these. The disparity of versions in regions so near each other as Bontok, Alab and Sagada is remarkable.

THE MYTH

1. There are, it is said, the brothers Wigan and Ihik of Kiangan. Their chickens are many, their pigs a whole drove. They pour out rice wine and call their "sitters" (priests). They invoke the Ngilins[1] and bleed a chicken. The omen is good.

Wigan accepts:[2] "So be it! Perfectly good the life of us who go headhunting into the Upstream Region, so that we be like gold which does not tarnish, like the tail feathers of the fullgrown cock, like the waters of the river, which do not grow less."

They recite the myths. Like a bamboo harp is their mything. They finish, eat, put things away. They sleep under the house[3] at Kiangan. On the morn of the morrow, they go to their hills, listen for omens [tapping their shields with their spears or coughing so as to incite the omen bird to "talk"]. The "mouther" [omen bird] speaks well — like a bamboo harp. They return, go upstream to Dadi, continue to Tanglayan, climb up to Ahin, arrive at Mapulauwan. They build a shack without walls. They finish, trim [the eaves] to a bee-line. They bleed a chicken, open it and it [the omen] is good. They sleep.

The sun is half way. They watch the roads and cross-paths. They crouch in ambush. They wait in hiding. It is mid-afternoon and no man has passed by. They climb up to Inude. They come to the mountain top at Inude. Ihik is thirsty — keeps pestering his brother, Wigan. "Where is something to drink?" he says. "Where alas! shall we get water, for there is none on these mountains?" He keeps saying it to his brother.

Wigan gets angry. He turns his spear around, downward, and strikes a stone. Withdraws it and the water gushes forth. Ihik hastens to drink. His brother shoves him aside.

"Not thou to drink!" says he. "But wait — priority to the ancestors of Kiangan, and thou, Ihik, shalt drink last."

They give priority to their priests. Wigan drinks; he finishes; gives place for his brother. "Come, Ihik, Drink thou."

He gives Ihik a shove. "Stay thou there," he says. "Await thou the chickens, the chickens and offerings of the people of Kiangan."

The water passes through his mouth and pours out from the halved place.[4] Ihik cried out "All right," he says, "Go thou, Wigan, and send our sister Bugan."

Wigan returns and arrives at Kiangan. Bugan asks, "Where is Ihik, thy brother?"

"Not here, indeed," answers Wigan, "for he is there at Inude. Go thou upstream, also, Bugan," he says.

She puts her pack on her head, goes upstream to the Upstream Region, arrives at Langon, comes up to Inude, sees Ihik, takes her place alongside him.

2. There are Wigan and Balitok of Kiangan. Their bellies are in terrible state. They cause the diagnosis-stick to be used.[5] Ihik is indicated. They bring chickens, sacrifice to Ihik and Bugan. They recite myths. Their mything is like a bamboo harp.

Kanadi the bellies of the shorn ones [men]! They are cured, the pain is relieved, as if untied, as if mud uncurling and falling off[6], as if an unwound spindle-bob. Their pigs and chickens are as if re-established, their rice increases miraculously, the grains become as numerous as those of the sands. They walk and walk the vegetation-rotted paths at Kiangan. The enemies and evil spirits are turned aside and even the centipedes, the sharp-edged stones and the poisonous snakes. They become like the water at Inude, like gold, like the tail feathers of the full-grown cock.

It is not at Kiangan, but here in our village of Pindungan, so that ... (*Fiat* not recorded).

6. ORIGIN OF IRRIGATED RICE*

Subject: Earth-folk exchange with Sky-folk: fire for rice. Used: In rice ritual and general welfare rites. Informant: Ngidulu.

SYNOPSIS

1. Wigan and Kabigat of Kayang perform the rites preliminary to hunting [of which there is a fairly good summary].

2. They pursue the quarry into the Skyworld and kill it there; the Skyworld people accuse them of having killed a Skyworld pig, but are assured finally [according to another version, after counting their pigs] that the pig was from the earthworld. The pig is cut up and the Skyworld people are given a share. They mix the meat with blood and rice and eat the mixture uncooked. Wigan and his brother refuse to eat with them, descend to the earthworld, and cook meat and rice in bamboo joints. The children of the Skyworld people have followed them and are invited to eat; after eating they are given the left-over rice and meat and told to carry it to their parents. The Skyworld people wonder at the pleasant taste of the food, for "the rice tastes like rice and the meat tastes like meat." They call Wigan and Kabitag back so as to exchange with them for whatever it was that made the food good. They offer jewels, first, then cowpeas, but these are refused by the earthworld people. They then offer their Skyworld rice, which the earthworld folk accept since it is superior to what they already have. The earthworld folk make fire for them with a bamboo fire-saw, then depart with their rice.

3. The Skyworld people carry the fire into their house, thereby setting the house on fire. In great alarm, they call the earthworld folk back again, begging them to take the fire, since it is "eating the house up." Wigan quenches the fire and builds them a fireplace and fireplace rack, sets three stones for holding the pot, and cautions them about the use of fire, for "its whole body is mouth." They, in turn, give directions that the rice is to be planted in swampy places and wallows when the leaves shoot again. The Ifugaos do as bidden.

4. Wigan goes to make rice fields. He tells Bugan, his wife, to sit on a small hill, wrapped in her blanket, and cautions her not to move. All Wigan has to do to make a field is to stab his digging stick into the ground and pry and there comes into being a wall (the first step

in constructing a field). He lays his spade along the wall and the latter is surmounted by a dike for retaining the water, (this is the last step in building a field, but it is the second in spading one, or at least is performed at the same time as the turning of the soil); and finally, by drawing his drag across the field, the land is levelled. He makes eight such fields. Bugan moves, and he can make no more except by hard work. He stabs his stick and turns only a little soil — that is all that happens. He upbraids Bugan, but the woman comforts him saying they have enough fields for the present and that their children will add to the area. Wigan then sticks his spear into a bank above the fields and water for them gushes forth, carrying along with it the plants that grow on top of the water in Ifugao rice-fields.

5. By means of a number of rituals the crop is brought to fruiting. At harvest time, Dinipaan, blacksmith god of the Upstream Region, makes harvest knives and brings them to Wigan to exchange for chickens. The harvest is abundant, further rituals store it in the granary and carry the fields through until the next planting time.

COMMENT

In other versions the rice that the Ifugaos have is specifically stated to be upland rice. The *imbalahang* variety here mentioned is a bearded, irrigated variety.

Many myths refer to Dinipaan and his village in the Upstream Region as folk with whom products were exchanged for iron implements. The village is called Paadan or Pahadan. Villaverde considers that the name of the god is drawn from this place name. He gives a somewhat different version on pages 405–415.

THE MYTH

1. Kanadih Wigan of Kayang: The sun is halfway; his dogs are catching with their mouths. They ask Wigan again and again, "Why dost thou not hunt thy dogs, for there they are seizing the pigs?" He calls the dogs and ties them with a bamboo stick,[1] ties them to a house-post. He scatters bait for his chickens, chooses the biggest and fattest, sacrifices for his dogs. He invokes the Sit-Down-Upon gods (the Hinumbians), the Tired-Ones who are in the Upstream Region and in the Downstream Region, and the Alabat gods[2] who are in the mountains. He bleeds the chicken, burns off the feathers, opens it, sees that the omen is *nungitib*. He accepts [the omen]: "It is a-bundance of life for me who go hunting."

On the third day from that one, *mala* it is said, Wigan [says] to his brother Kabigat, "Let us go hunting." Kabigat agreed. They pack up betels and tobacco supply, slip on their backbaskets, tuck on their hipbags, and then their bolos, take their *balobog* spears and go to their hills. They look up at the cock bird [omen bird]; it is on the right side. It dips its head and cries; its cry is high-pitched. Wigan utters a fiat "We hunters will have life." They go a second time. He [the omen bird] gives "harsh talk." They go a third time.[3] It perches on the left side. "So be it," says Wigan, "so that the enemy and the evil spirits will be weak."

They go to the place above, thrust down their spears. He [Wigan] fetches dried twigs. He works the fire-saw.[4] It smokes and is fire. They turn the smudge to coals. After a little while the fire has become ashes. He brings water. He quenches the fire. "Let not the mouths of the dogs be quenched. Be quenched, though, the mouths of the snakes and the snags."

2. He unties the leader of the dogs. They enter the forest. In no time at all they are covered with runo nettles. They send forth their dogs. Wigan sics them on, yells encouragement. They go from hill to hill and to the other side of their mountains in the Upstream Region. They drive the quarry upward. It climbs up to the Skyworld. It arrives up to the Skyworld.

Said Wigan, "*Ah nakayah!* — our quarry, it has gone up into the Skyworld. Let us follow it."

The brothers go not noting time's passage, keep climbing upward to the Skyworld, see the quarry. It has hidden between the houses of Lidum and Hinumbían. Wigan arrives and spears the quarry.

Said the Hinumbian's: "*Ah nakayah*, Wigan! Thou hast destroyed one of our pigs of the Skyworld."

"It is no pig of yours! For indeed our dogs trailed it from Kayang." They carry the game, one at each end, bring it to the granary place of Lidum and Hinumbían. They spread out the *atag* mat, lay the pig on it, open it up. *Kanadih* Wigan, he shares it with the Skyworld people.

Ngalan-da Lidum of the Skyworld and Hinumbían of the Skyworld, they take their shares. They cut it up into small pieces, mix the pieces with blood, mix in rice with it.

Said Lidum and Hinumbían, "Come Wigan, let us all eat."

Said Wigan, "I will not eat with you for it is uncooked."

They put the meat of the quarry in their backbaskets, shoulder the latter, descend to Butityu in the earthworld. They see *bulu* bamboo, [where] it is growing thickly. They take off their backbaskets, draw their bolos, slash off bamboos. They take one node, and use it for cooking rice; they take another node and use it for cooking meat. They work a fire-saw; they make a fire; he brings dry bamboo for fuel. After a little while rice and meat are cooked. He skins off the

cooked rice,[5] skins off the cooked meat. He invokes the place spirits
(*pinading*).

Kaya! the children [of Lidum and Hinumbían]! They gather
around. Said Wigan.

"Come, you children, so that we will eat."

The children agreed; they eat, it is said. They finish and there is
meat and cooked rice left over. They give it to the children.

"Take it home," says Wigan, "so that Lidum and Hinumbían eat
it — for, there! you are eating your food raw."

They give it to the children. The children take it home, arrive, give
it to Lidum's and Hinumbían's. They said, it is said, "What is that
swelled-up cooked rice?" They take it and eat it. The cooked rice
tastes like cooked rice, and the meat tastes like meat.

"Where are Wigan and his brother, so that we can exchange with
them?"

They shout to Wigan: "Come on back, Wigan!"

Mala bo Wigan, he climbs back up, it is said, says to Hinumbían,
"What is it you say?"

"What did you use to swell up the meat and rice you gave us?"

"What will you exchange for it?"

"Our jewels of the Skyworld."

Said Wigan, "We have jewels, but we took them off because we
went hunting."

"What do you want?" said Hinumbían. "What about seed of our
mung beans of the Skyworld?"

Wigan replied, "Our cowpeas ripen uniformly at Kayang."[6]

"What do you want, then?" says Hinumbían. "Shall we give our
rice of the Skyworld in exchange?"

Wigan, it is said, agreed. "Your rice of the Skyworld is good, for it
is *ayuhip* of the *donaal* sort. We have rice at Kayang, but it is of the
pink 'dragon-fly' kind, which is bearded."[7]

They go to the granary. They open up (the granary), Hinumbían
enters it, takes out two bundles of seed rice, gives them to Wigan.
They put back the door-lock. He (Wigan) unpockets flint and steel.
He strikes fire, makes a fire in the houseground.

"So much for that and we will return."

He takes the seed rice. Wigan descends. They arrive at Earthworld.

3. *Mala* Hinumbían and Lidum, they carry the fire to the house,
put it on the floor. The floor caught fire. *Ngalana* Lidum, he shouts,
"Return, Wigan, and take back the fire for it is including the house."

Wigan comes back, sees water, takes it to the house and quenches
the fire. He takes up the floor [of one corner]. He brings *amugaowan*
wood, splits it, makes a fireplace. He brings more *amugaowan*, splits

it, measures it, makes mortises, builds a fireplace frame. He looks
for stones, brings up three, sets them in a triangle. He brings up fire,
builds a fire in the fireplace.

"Do like this," says Wigan, "so that the fire stays on earth, for
indeed its whole body is mouth." [The Ifugaos consider this a very
witty saying and always laugh at it].

Said Lidum and Hinumbían, "Precisely so, Wigan. Descend to your
village of Kayang. When you arrive there, store the rice in your granary.
When you see that the leaves have started again,[8] plant the rice. Look
for wallowing places (?) (swampy grounds ?), make them level. Plant
the rice in circles round and round. But it must have welfare rites!"

Wigan agreed. The kindred put it in their backbaskets and descend,
arrive at Kayang. They take the seed-rice to their granary. They eat
the quarry.

Time passes unoted. They see that the leaves have started again.
They brew rice wine, and water to it, wait one day. The kindred
gather; they, it is said, perform the *pingnil* rites. They fan the seed
rice.[9] They bleed the chicken and burn off the feathers. They break
it open and it (the bile omen) is *nungitib*. Wigan accepts: "It shows
that the planted things will be fruitful."

4. Time passes unnoted. One morning when half-way (the sun),
they cross their level place at Kayang, they see the wallows, clean
them off, make them level. They plant the seed rice in circles round
and round. Time passes unnoted. They see his rice — his rice is
"boy"-sized. He gets his axe, likewise his bolo, goes to an *amugaowan*
tree, fells it, cuts it into sections, splits it, makes a spade, also a drag
and a digging stick. In the darkness of night they sleep. *Mala* husband
and wife, next morning they cross the level place at Kayang, go, it
is said to make rice fields from wild land.

Mala it is said, Wigan [says], "Wrap thyself in thy blanket on the
small hill. See that thou move not, for I am going to make fields."

Mala it is said, Wigan takes the large digging stick, stabs [once] and
pries and [comes into being] a perpendicular wall. He lays his spade
along it and there is a straight dike. He slides his drag over [the
ground] and sees that it becomes level. He goes to another place,
stabs down his digging stick and pries and there is a perpendicular
wall. He lays his spade along it and there is its straight dike. He
slides his drag (over the ground and levels it).

He goes to another place, stabs the stick into the ground and pries;
a stone wall [appears] like grains of corn. He lays his spade along it,
drags his drag over [the ground]. Wigan works fast. After no time at
all, he sees his cultivated area; the dikes rise one above the other. He
counts and there are eight of them.

8*

Bugan moved. He stabs down the digging stick and nothing happens! He hurries to [other] wild land, stabs down the digging stick. With repeated stabbing of the digging stick he turns a small plot.

"Be it so," says Wigan. He pulls up his spear, runs to the bank [above his fields], thrusts his spear into the unstoned bank. Water gushes forth and carries out water lilies. "So much for that," he says. He goes to the low hill and says,

"How is this, Bugan? Thou promisedst not to move so that I quickly redeem the waste land. And there, thou'st moved!"

Bugan said there were enough. "There are our children and they will add to our rice fields."

5. They go down to their house-ground at Kayang. In the evening of the day, he summons a band of workers, distributes pay[10] among his neighbors who are at Kayang. He invokes the ancestral spirits, changes to the messenger deities, then to the *bagol* deities, bleeds a chicken, singes off the feathers and opens it. He sees that the bile omen is *momboga*. He accepts, "It points toward the heavy-fruitedness of the irrigated fields."

At nightfall they sleep. In the morning when half-way, the able-bodied and co-settlers go across to the rice fields, pull up the rice [from the seed beds] and plant it in scratch-work patterns. About noontime, those who have been called eat. They finish, cross again to the fields, plant again in scratch work patterns. There are more than enough seedlings; they throw away [the left overs] on the wild lands and banks. They finish the transplanting and ascend to their house-grounds at Kayang.

Wigan does not procrastinate. "Let us bring rice wine to ripeness." They add water and wait one day. He calls his "fathers," they gather and pour out the wine. They invoke the ancestral spirits, change to the messenger deities, invoke the *napalungot* gods, and the *naototbe* gods of the Skyworld and of the Underworld and the *bulul* idols. They are possessed by the deities. They bleed the chicken, singe and open it. They see that the bile omen is *binumga*. They cook and it is boiled, they display it on the cooked rice. They invoke and they eat.

They walk about at Kayang. Time passes unoted. They see that the rice is ripe, is yellowing. "Our rice is ripe," says Wigan. He calls his co-settlers. They gather. They brew rice wine. *Ngalan* the co-settlers help each other in fencing the granaries and repairing the roofs. They make ties for the bundles.

Mala Dinipaan of the Upstream Region, "The rice of my companions in Kayang is ripe." He sets up the cylinders of his bellows, takes iron, cuts it into pieces and forges them. He makes *kutiwong* knives.[11] That night he finished. He sleeps. It is half way and *mala* Dinipaan, he packs up his betels, he takes the *kutiwong* knives and puts them in his backbasket, goes to Kayang. He goes not noting time's passage, arrives in Kayang, takes out the harvest knives. "Where are you women folk? Exchange for these harvest knives; use these in harvesting the rice. For they are good," he says, "for they will increase the harvest. [Speaking to Wigan] Distribute them among the women. Assemble [things] to exchange for the knives."

He sees that the temporary baskets for carrying chickens [received in exchange for the knives] are full.

Said Wigan, "Sleep here, for we harvest in the morning."

At nightfall the people of Kayang assemble, keep coming to the house. They pay back [sacrifice to] the *matungulan* gods. The outcome is good. Time passes unnoted. On the morrow when half way (the sun), Wigan does not procrastinate, they catch pigs, tie and shackle them, spread out the *atag* mat, pour out rice wine. They invoke their ancestral spirits, change to the messenger gods, invoke the *bagol* deities, and the *naototbe*. They are possessed by the deities. They dance pouring oblations on the pigs. They finish, kill the pigs, burn off the hair, open them up, cook the meat, feed those (workers) called from the fields. They keep harvesting the rice. One after another these keep coming in the carrying poles and the carrying boards.[12] The pile of bundles spreads, reaches the eaves and the fence. When the sun is low they have finished. Wigan accepts:

"Good, indeed, this Obtainment of rice that I got in the Skyworld, for there it is increasing."

They carry it beneath the granary. Time passes. On the third day, they unpile the rice, spread it out. In the evening it is dry. They take it into the granary, stack it. The upper layer rises higher and higher.

Wigan does not procrastinate. He brews wine again. They make *tuldag* rites. The result is good. Time passes at Kayang. "*Ah nakayah* the irrigated fields — grass grown, covered with weeds! And there — our wine is strong." They pour in water, wait one day. The kindred gather, pour out wine, invoke the ancestral spirits, change to the messenger gods, invoke the *bagol* and the *naototbe* who are in the Skyworld and the Underworld, in the Upstream Region and the *Bulul*. They prayed the *uka* exhortation. They finish, bleed the chicken, singe and open it, see that it is *binumga*. Wigan accepts, "It points to the fruiting of planted things according to the swing of the seasons." They cook and it is boiled; they paddle it out and invoke, finish and eat.

Kanadih mo the womenfolk, they see their fields at Kayang, go and weed them. They build temporary dikes (where the old one has given away).

Said Wigan, "There have been landslides and here is wine already strong," and he adds water and waits one day. He calls his "fathers." They pour out the wine. "We will go and put up tied runo reeds on our fields at Kayang.[13] They invoke the ancestral spirits, change to the messenger deities, change to the bagol. They invoke those from whom rice was obtained in the Skyworld, those of the Underworld and the Upstream Region and the Bulul. They bleed the chickens, singe and open them, see that the omen is *nungitib* which is *binumga*. Wigan accepts. He spreads the chicken meat on cooked rice. They recite and recite about these hunters [i. e. this very myth] who built fields in Kayang. They finish and invoke.

It kept being the reason at Kayang that their pigs and chickens abounded in life and that their rice increased and that the rice flourished in the swing of the seasons.

`Kalidi*! It is not at Kayang, for here at the house of the children[14] at Balitang is where ye who are at Kayang are being mythed for the abundance of life of the planted things and for the fruiting of their ripening, for *lape* is what ye are being prayed.

7. NUNKOVA: THE SELF-CAUGHT

Subject: The "Self-Caught" gives granary charms and the ceremonial clapper to poor Ifugaos. Used: In rice rituals and in general welfare rites. Informant: Balogan, at Anao, 1937.

SYNOPSIS

On the way home from a drinkfest, Bugan, daughter of Nagalong of Nagubatan, drops her limetube in a swollen river and it is carried away. She is inconsolable and her father advises her to follow the limetube boldly downstream, in full confidence that it, being noble like themselves, will stop only among their own kind of folk.

2. Bugan goes downstream, constantly inquiring for the limetube and arrives at mid-forenoon in the Downstream Region. The pigs there are squealing from hunger.

3. Bulol of Namtogan goes down to the river to get water for cooking pig-feed. He sees the limetube float down the river and become caught in a fish trap. He recovers the tube. Just then Bugan comes up, they chew betels together and Bugan, seeing the limetube claims it. Bulol playfully claims it as his own for a while, then yields it and invites her to his village. A marriage proposal follows and is accepted. After many years, seven sons have been born to the couple, and have grown up, and Bugan is heavy with child but for some reason cannot give birth.

4. Bugan's father longs for his daughter and sends betel nuts and betel leaves downstream, commanding them to search her out.[1] They arrive as Bugan is washing utensils in the river; she recovers them, recognizes them as being of the kind which grow in Nagubatan, her native village. They arouse strong cravings in her for betels and salt from Nagubatan, and she believes she cannot bear her child till these cravings are satisfied. She begs her sons to go to Nagubatan for these things, but all refuse on account of the danger from enemies except Tayaban, who, being winged, can fly over the enemy. Tayaban sets forth.

5. Two brothers have put up a bat net at Hadngal, a mountain pass upstream. Tayaban flies into the net. Being set free, he promises to drive great flocks of bats into the net. He then goes to his grandfather and secures great quantities of betels and salt for his mother. The grandfather predicts that the child to be born will be a girl, and says that she must be named Inoltagon ("Clapper-ed"). Tayaban expresses a desire to help the Upstream people to prosperity. "Let us not help a wealthy village but a poverty-stricken village," says the grandfather, "for thus the renown of the thing will be greater." Tayaban decides to help the family of the two bat-netters. He drives bats into their net, then flies into it himself, makes an appointment to meet them eight days later and leave them a magic gift ["Obtainment"]. Then he flies to his mother with the betels and salt. His mother soon gives birth to a girl baby, who is named as her grandfather directed.

6. Tayaban goes to keep his appointment with the bat-netters. He takes a gold bead from them, swallows it and vomits it forth as a *buga*, a kind of granary charm. He also gets bamboo and makes a ritual clapper, *palipal*. With these Obtainments the family becomes exceedingly prosperous and the Obtainments become renowned, so that, as related in the *tulud*-recitations, they are borrowed by others and are thus finally brought to the village where the myth is being recited.

COMMENT

The myth, it would seem, embodies a tradition of intermarriage between immigrants who came into Ifugaoland over the Cordillera Central and followed the courses of the Bula River downstream, and a second immigration coming up the river. Nagubatan is a place in the upper sources of this river, and Namtogan a place near where it empties into the Magat River. The *palipal* and *buga*, as the myth relates, were received from the downstream people. The present downstream people are planters of dry rice.

The dry rice planters of northern Borneo (Dusuns) and of all, or at least many, of the Philippine districts where rice is planted by the "thumming" method, including these downstream Ifugaos, use a clapper on their planting stick. This clapper [see description and illustration of that used by the Bagobo in Cole, 1913, page 87] no doubt lessens the drudgery of the work, and sets up a rhythm, which perhaps helps to secure a better spacing and to keep all the planters on the job. I was told that the dry rice planters of the downstream region call it *pakpak*. The clapper is used as a ritual object by the wet rice planters of the upstream region in all rice and general welfare rites. It is of the same general pattern as the clapper used on the planting stick of the downstream people. Although, in the myth, Tayaban uses local bamboo to make this clapper, such is not the practice of the Ifugaos. When they want to make a new clapper, they make an expedition down the river to Namtogan or neighboring places, about two days distant, to get bamboo for this purpose — that is, to the region whence the clapper, according to the myth originated and in which it is still being used as part of the planting stick.

The *buga* is a hard stone kept by the wet-rice growing Ifugaos in their granaries, in a ritual box for the purpose of hardening the rice, keeping it from spoiling and magically increasing it. But I believe that a *genuine buga*, one of the kind here spoken of, is a *tektite*. Tektites are small globules of obsidian, evidently once molten, which are attributed by some authorities to volcanic eruptions, by others to meteoric showers. Under various specific names they have a distribution in Indo-China, Australia, West Africa, America, Moravia and the Philippines. Those of Luzon, where they are found most abundantly in the province of Rizal, just outside Manila, are called, rizalites. The rizalite is of spherical, cylindrical or sometimes dumbbell shape, usually smaller than a walnut, of smoothish but pitted surface. The surface has a characteristic "sweaty" and "fatty" appearance, and it is interesting that the myth applies this description to the *buga*; those are just the words that anybody would apply to the appearance of the surface of the rizalite.

Another interesting point in the myth is that the *buga* is transformed from gold since, among native miners the reverse process is believed to occur. After a gold panner has panned out a dab of dust in the lowland rivers, he puts this dust away in a dark place alongside a rizalite, believing that the latter causes the dust to increase. (Cf. the "breeding" stones of the Hawaiians).

Professor H. Otley Beyer, of Manila, has an enormous collection of tektites, including the largest known rizalite — about the size of a medium orange, weighing 2050 grams. He obtained this from

native gold-panners who were using it in the way mentioned above.[2]
It is to be noted that in the myth the process is reversed — the *buga*
is derived from gold.

I saw a talisman of peculiar form, all but covered over with twilled
rattan, carried by the father of Deputy-Governor Pawid, which I
believed to be a rizalite from what I could see of it. I also saw one
used as a *buga* in the ritual box of a granary, but they must be exceedingly rare, for the limit of northern distribution, so far as known
lies a good hundred kilometers to the south of Ifugaoland. They were
probably brought to this region by a stream of immigrants from the
south, the forbears of the Lamot folk. If this conjecture be correct,
they ought to be found a little more frequently among this people,
and perhaps also among the dry-rice growing Sillipanes. The fact
that they are not found in the habitat would account for the fact
that the great majority of the *buga* in the ritual boxes are pebbles
used as a substitute.

The myth of the "Self-Caught" is probably the Ifugao's favorite,
for it has a good plot with pathetic little touches, Ifugao to the very
core. It is worth reading.

THE MYTH

Ngalana Bugan, daughter of Nagalong of Nagubatan: At mid-
forenoon in their village of Nagubatan, they are talking about a
drinkfest at Gonhadan. The able-bodied (call out):

"Where art thou, Bugan ? Let us go to the drinkfest at Gonhadan!"

Bugan agreed. She takes down the eating basket ...[3] She packs
betels and descends from the house. She accompanies her "ancestors,"[4]
the able-bodied of Nagubatan, and they go into the middle of the
river and cross to the side. They arrive at Gonhadan. They play
the march tune on the *balangag* gongs. They stand along the edge
of the dancing place; they go underneath the houses, pour wine and
drink.

In the evening, their "ancestors" from Nagubatan [call out],
"Where are you, Bugan and companions ? Let us return to Nagubatan." Bugan and companions agreed. They fall into file. They
cross Gonhadan and the rain pours down. They arrive at the river.
They enter the water and they hold [help] Bugan. They come to the
center of the current and her lime tube, which is glazed like a rice-
wine jar,[5] drops down. The able-bodied grab for it, but it goes downstream. Her "ancestors" run after it but without result. "Let us go
on home to Nagubatan" [they say] and Bugan keeps exclaiming
piteously "Alas for my limetube, glazed like a *ginulitan* jar — I had
become used to it from childhood."

They arrive at Nagubatan; she sits on the rice mortar disconsolate. Said Nagalong.

"*Ah nakayah*, Bugan! What is the reason? You went to the drinkfest, and you are (now) exclaiming piteously."

And Bugan said, "Because my limetube, glazed like a *ginulitan* jar, fell, was carried by the current and went to the Downstream Region."

Her father laughed. "Let us go up into the house. You will eat and then follow it. It will not stop just anywhere, but among our equals in the Downstream Region. Folk like us at Nagubatan, noble and rich, will be the stopping place of the glazed one to whom Bugan has become accustomed."

And the ear of Bugan is pleased and she goes up into the house, takes down the eating basket and eats. She finishes and packs up betels and betel leaves, makes them into a bundle and descends at Nagubatan.

"Keep staying here, Nagalong, for I will follow my limetube."

2. Her father agreed. She crosses to the river. She goes downstream not noting time's passage. She arrives at Inlimog, arrives at Ahin. The Ahin men answer, "It passed us last night. We grabbed and grabbed for it, all of us, but it went, for it was in mid-current."

Bugan and they chew betels and she goes on downstream, arrives at Pakauwol and arrives at Ampugpug. And there are men frolicking in the river. Bugan chews betels with them and asks whether a limetube was carried past them. The able-bodied Ampugpug folk answer, "It was carried past us last night; we grabbed for it, but it went on." And Bugan continues downstream and arrives at Mongayan. She goes unconscious of time to Imbuka and arrives at Bulâ. The able-bodied are there getting water at the river and she asks whether a limetube went past. The Bulâ folk answer, "It passed last night; we reached for it but it went on."

Bugan goes downstream, arrives at Bayukan, arrives at Kaba and arrives at Pangahalan, and it is mid-forenoon in the Downstream Region and the pigs are squealing with hunger.

3. *Mala mo Bulol*, son of Mongahid at Namtogan, he is dipping out pig feed. He takes the bamboo water container under his arm, but no water comes out. He takes it under his arm, goes to the spring at Namtogan, dips it under the water, lifts it and stands it against something. He turns his eyes around and sees a limetube circling around and around in the water and it is caught in the fish trap at Namtogan. He reaches for it, opens it and there is lime in it, he takes betels and wraps them together, shakes the limetube and at this moment Bugan arrives. She notices the limetube and comes to his

side and they exchange betel nut and leaves, and he takes the limetube and they lime their quids and turn their spittle red. Said Bugan.

"That is my lime tube, a glazed *ginulitan*. I became used to it in my village at Nagubatan."

And said Bulol, "That is my lime tube, a glazed *ginulitan*, I have become used to it in my village of Namtogan."

Said Bugan, "No it's not, for it's my lime tube, which I dropped yesterday night when I came back from a drinkfest at Gonhadan and it was carried by the current."

Bulol yielded, "Probably that's right, it was caught in our fish trap at Namtogan, but do not go back right away, for it is evening. Let us go up to our village of Namtogan."

Bugan agreed and followed. They went to Namtogan, arrived there. Said Mongahid the father "*Ah nakayah*, Bulol! A handsome[6] and wealthy one, the equal of us at Namtogan, has come with him."

They enter the house and eat. They finish and chew betels. Said their father, Mongahid.

"What about it, Bugan, will you and Bulol marry ?"

Bugan spake, answers, and agrees.

"Then go across to our other house at Namtogan," says Mongahid.

Bugan agrees. She and Bulol go together and sleep. They talk about their marriage. Bugan agrees. On the morrow at mid-forenoon, *mala mo* Mongahid, he calls his ancestors in their village at Namtogan, and they gather together and sacrifice to the ancestral spirits, they pay back [sacrifice to] the *naototbe* deities and make *mukun* rites for the Inumbans. They finish, bleed the chickens and burn off the feathers, they break them open and the omen is *nungitib*. Mongahid accepts. "So let it be," he says. "It is the life of Bulol and Bugan who are marrying each other."

They cook the chicken. It boils and they take it off. They finish and chew betels. The ancestors go home and observe the ceremonial idleness. Comes the darkness of the night; there has been no catching of chickens by hawks nor falling of limbs; the day is eventless and it is night. Time passes unnoted. Comes the third day: they put sugar cane on each side of the granary door; they perform the ceremonial work at Namtogan.[7]

And after fifty years and a thousand [i.e., after many years], their children have grown up. There were born to them Binongbong, Mongahid, Tayaban, Buluhan, Yumyum and Dumakdak. And Bugan was again pregnant.

4. And her father, Nagalong, in their village at Nagubatan, said, "*Ah nakayah*! fifty years and a thousand! Probably Bugan's hair is

streaked with grey! She does not think on me in my village of the
Upstream Region."

He sees betels and leaves; he takes them to the river, wraps them
together and sends them down in the current. "Do not be undis-
criminating, betels and leaf, but find out Bugan where she lives, so
that she think on me in Nagubatan."

Betels and leaf go downstream, arrive at Namtogan and are caught
in the fishtrap; it is mid-forenoon in the Downstream Region and
Bugan spake, "*Ah nakayah*, these utensils, how dirty — look like
charcoal: I'll wash them in the river at Namtogan." And she, it is
said, goes thither. She puts the utensils in the water, scours them,
sets them on a pink stone, turns her eyes around over the scene. She
saw the betels, "*Ah nakayah*, there are betels — our betels of the
Upstream Region, for they are like fruit of the *kalauwag* tree — and
betel leaves of the kind called *loyangan*!" And she takes the betels
and goes home to Namtogan. And she craves the betels of the
Upstream Region and salt from there and the water of Naltang and
water of Inude which she bathed in when a child. And her months
are completed at last and she can hardly climb the *banutan*[8] but she
does not give birth, she craves the salt.

"Go upstream, you children to bring back salt so that Bugan can
give birth. Go thou upstream, Binongbong!"

"Not I," says Binongbong, "for the enemy have come out, and
I should be *bongbong-ed* on the way" (i.e. "blocked on my way").

Said their mother, "And thou, Hinabwakan."

"Not I," says Hinabwakan, "I should be *lobwak-ed*" (i.e. "waylaid").

"And thou, Dumakdak ?"

"Not I," says Dumakdak, "I should be dakdak-ed."[9]

"And thou, Yumyum ?"

"Indeed it is known that the enemy have gone forth and would
yumyum me[10] on the way."

Bugan said, "Thou, indeed, Tayaban,[11] suppose thou fly for a
single night — fly over the populations of the men."

Tayaban agreed. He takes down the eating basket and eats, begins
and chews betels, packs up betels and betel leaves, puts on his scabbard, then his hipbag, grasps his spear and descends. He sits on the
atul[12] at Namtogan. Tayaban turns on the fire. He passes over
Bayukan, alights at Kamalig. He turns on the fire.[13] He alights at
Daulayan. He alights at Apik, turns on the fire, he goes up the steep
at Bolog. He alights at Naklingan, turns on the fire; alights at Akang,
turns on the fire; alights at Pindungan, turns on the fire; goes up to
Huyung, alights at Numpaling, turns on the fire at Numpaling. He
alights at Punkituban at Manauha. He places his spear across the

branches untucks his hipbag, takes out betels, chews, turns them red, and then sleeps, for it is mid-forenoon.

5. *Mala mo* Pitang and Kawahan, they come home from sleeping at Nanglihan, they tell Magide, "*Ah nakayah*! the able-bodied at Ampugpug, the bats they are bringing home are the talk of the day." Said Magide, "We used to net bats at Hadngal and caught many." Said Pitang "And have we a bat net?" Their father answered affirmatively. They take down the eating basket and eat, they chew betels and pack up betels and leaves. They take out the bat net and its ropes. The brothers carry it on their backs, descend from the house. They cut down bamboos, trimmed off the branches and smoothed the nodes, carry on their shoulders, go to the river. They ascend, climb the steep to Hadngal, thrust down their spears, thrown down the bat net; they clear the pass of underbush, bring the ropes, tie them to the poles, hang the ropes, go below. They attach the bat net and pull the ropes and adjust the net to the space. They make a clapper. "Let us make a shack." They set up posts, ridgepole and rafters. They tie on a layer of runos all round at the lower edge, they tie on layers of cogon grass, bend the last layer over the ridgepole and trim the lower edge of the thatch all round, they see it and it is a straight line. They make a sleeping place and a shelf. It is the dark of the night and they sleep.

Tayaban, it is said, awakes. He chews betels. He turns on the fire at Mabaluha, he flies through the pass at Hadngal. The net is drawn tense and the clapper sounds. Said Pitang, "There's a bat!" The brothers come out, they loosen the ropes, they see that what is caught scintillates. Pitang untangles him and he stands up like a man. He brushes out his hair, he stands alongside Pitang. He takes out betels, they chew. Said Tayaban:

"What are you here for?"

Said Pitang, "For bats from the Downstream and from the Upstream."

Tayaban approved. "I will go upstream, I will scare up the bats." *Ngala* Tayaban, he walks along the rice terraces. *Mala mo* Pitang, he raises the bat net. Tayaban stumbles over a rotten stump. He picks it up and hurls it (into the net). The net is jerked and the clapper sounds. Said Pitang, "There, indeed, are the bats." He goes outside, lowers the net, sees that it is a piece of rotten wood. "The man is a fraud — says [will send] bats and here it is nothing!" He removes the rotten wood, raises the net, adjusts it to the space.

Mala mo Tayaban, he goes over the mountains and along the terraces. He turns on the fire, he alights at Dinayahan. He turns on the fire at Dinayahan, he alights at Tubu, he turns on the fire at

Tubu, alights at Ahin, turns on the fire at Ahin, alights at Nagubatan. He places his spear for his roost pole. He peeps around at Nagubatan, he sees the wide-shining fire of his grandfather, who is cooking pig-feed at night, for he has many pigs. He (the grandfather) turns his spear around, thrusts it into the yard, Tayaban comes, stands face to face with his grandfather. Said Nagalong, "That is certainly my grandson." He opens the door, Tayaban flits up, sits in the doorway. Nagalong is amazed, "What kind of a man is that? — I didn't put up the ladder, yet he enters." They take out betels; grandfather and grandson exchange betels and crush them. They did not turn them red, they spit them out and they turn red. Said Nagalong, "What is thy name, man, who hast come to our village of Nagubatan?

"I am Tayaban, descended from Bugan in our village at Nam-togan."

Said his grandfather, "And how many are you (children)?"

"We are seven," says Tayaban. But the seventh is in mother's womb; she can hardly climb the *banutan* ladder, but cannot give birth, for she is craving the salt of your village of Nagubatan."

"For, indeed," says his grandfather, "It was fifty years and a thousand that she did not think on me and I sent betels downstream. Return thou now and Bugan will give birth. And I know it will be a girl, but name her Inoltagon, for she will play with the *buga* charms and the clappers."

Tayaban assented. They call their old men in the Upstream Region. They go to gather betels and betel nuts, go to get water at Inude.

Tayaban descends from the house, he keeps visiting the bats and stirs them up. He sees that they fly like flocks of crows toward the pass at Hadngal.

Mala mo Pitang, "Capital, indeed!" he says, "for the ropes have been worn frazzled and the shelf is overflowing with bats."[14]

Nagalong's kindred come home, having fetched plenty of betels which are like *kalauwag* fruits and plenty of water of Inude. Tayaban packs up.

"I will go back now, for if I wait till morning, the dogs will bark at me,[15] but I will speak with Pitang in order that we all make gifts."

Said his grandfather, "Let us not make gifts to the affluent towns; let us give to them that have only a little, so that the renown will be great, so that I be heard of at Nagubatan and ye be heard of at Namtogan."

Said Tayaban, "They are hard up at Ampugpug."

His grandfather assented. Tayaban goes down, sits on the atul at Nagubatan. He turns on the fire, flies over Ahin to Dinayahan. He alights at Mombanong. He turns on the fire at Mombanong; he flies through the pass at Hadngal. The clapper sounds. He (Pitang) peeps out at the net and it is scintillating. "That is he who was caught yesterday, because it is just the same." He lowers the net and he [Tayaban] stands up like a man. They talk together, he and Pitang.

"Let it be thus," says Tayaban. "Tomorrow at mid-forenoon, call your co-villagers, carry home the bats for your food at Ampugpug. If you have any rice left over, brew rice wine. On the eighth day, cross to the rocks at Kapihan and wait for me so that we may make presents."

Pitang agreed. *Mala* Tayaban. He turns on the fire at Hadngal, passes over the mountains, alights at Namtogan. He sits on the *atul*. He arrives in Namtogan. Said the Bulols, "Tayaban has come, he has brought back salt and water from Inude." And his mother was delighted and she stays back by the rear door [giving birth], and in a little while they see that it is a girl.

"Precisely," says Tayaban. "Inoltagon is her name, for she will occupy herself with *buga* charms and *palipal*."

6. *Ngalana mo* Pitang, at mid-forenoon he calls his ancestors, the able-bodied at Ampugpug, and they climb up to Hadngal. They distribute the bats, go down to Ampugpug and feast on them. They take the left-over rice, they ferment it, they wait a while. The eighth day comes; they see their ripened wine and they put it into their wine jars. They call their ancestors, cross to the rock at Kapihan. They sit around and it is mid-forenoon. Said Tayaban, "Now is the appointed day, I will go upstream today." His mother assented. *Mala mo* Tayaban. He puts on his scabbard, inserts his war knife, puts his hipbag on next, grasps his spear. He sits on the atul at Namtogan, he turns on the fire at Namtogan. He flies over Kamalig and Daulayan, alights at Apik, turns on the fire at Apik, flies over Naklingan and Ake, alights at Pindungan, turns on the fire at Pindungan, flies over Numpaling, alights at Mabaluha and roosts on his spear and sits a while. He glances at the rock at Kapilan and it is dark [being covered with people]. The rock is red from betel spittle.

"What a large number to receive presents!" Said Tayaban, "Begin thou, O Rain, so that the people disperse."

In a little while the rain began and poured down like acqueducts converged from the Upstream Region. In a little while, the people were chilled. They on the rock at Kapihan said, "*Ah nakayah*, the appointment made by the sons of Magide! And here it is, cold." They return to their village of Ampugpug.

In a little while the rain ceased and it changed to sunshine and shone brightly. Tayaban glances over that way. The sons of Magide are left alone.

"So let it be," he says, "so that they alone [enjoy] the rewards of riches in their village of Ampugpug."

He takes up his spear, jumps down to the river, crosses the water and it opens before him. In a little while Magide looks, "This is the man, for he is always like that — yellowing and yellowing." Tayaban comes through and the waters are parted,[16] he comes up on the rock at Kapihan. *Mala mo* Magide, he sees his jar of wine, he pours wine out into the wooden bowl, he gives it to Tayaban and he [Tayaban] shakes his head; he points to the central bead of gold ones belonging to the sons of Magide. *Mala mo* Magide, he takes out the central gold bead, drops it in the wine, raises the bowl, gives it to Tayaban. He receives it, he drinks the wine, drinks the bead with it. Said Pitang, "Alas for our gold bead — Tayaban has drunk it with the rest."

Tayaban vomits, pukes up a *buga*. He sees that it sweats and is fatty. He gives it to Magide. Said Tayaban, "Where is your bamboo ?" "Our bamboo is at Tiking." "Where is the rest of your bamboo ?" "Our bamboo is at Lotang." Said Tayaban, "We will get the bamboo at Lotang, so as to *lotang* the souls of the chickens, the pigs and the rice."[17]

Ngalana Tayaban, he crosses to Lotang, slashes off a bamboo takes a section from its middle and cuts it off by rotating it against his knife. He returns to Kapihan and makes "eyes" for it, enlarges the side openings and splits it. He gives it to Magide.

"Take it to Ampugpug and sacrifice pigs and chickens for it and stick up *pudung* in your fields at Lotang. Pray *tulud* at its *honga*."[18]

Magide assented, Tayaban goes downstream, the sons of Magide go home, arrive at Ampugpug. At the same time the rice wine is strong; they spread a mat beneath their front door, sacrifice to the Napulungot.[19] The omen is good — *nungitib*. Magide accepts: "So let it be," he says. "It points and signifies our obtainments of *buga* and *palipal*." They go to their granary place and make a general welfare rite. The omen is good there, too. They plant *pudung* in their fields at Lotang. They recite *tulud* at the welfare rites. Heading-out time comes; they see that the rice is well-fruited, stands in rows, entirely covers the field and has not been devoured [by pests]. "Let us make *paad* rites for the deities." They sacrifice for the *napulungot* and *naototbe*. "It is well, indeed," they say, and they have that off their minds. After a month and a half, they see the rice that it is yellowing, turning yellow. "Let us brew wine for havesting our rice." They see that it is clear and strong. They add water; in the evening, they visit their cooperators,[20] they hire harvesters on both sides of the family. At night they invite their old men; they assemble, they pour out wine; they keep dipping it up in cups; they make the preliminary

harvest rites at Ampugpug. The omen is good — *nungitib*. Magide
utters a fiat, "So let it be," he says, "so that what will be harvested
tomorrow shall increase. They sleep one night. On the morrow, at
mid-forenoon, they eat. They finish and chew betels. *Mala mo* the
harvesters for hire, they swarm in files passing each other on the way.
They cross to the fields at Lotang. They cross each others' paths on
the terraces and dikes. *Mala mo* Magide, they catch pigs, carry them
to the granary place at Lotang, they spread out the mat, pour out
wine, invoke the deities, they play the drum and are possessed by the
deities. Toward noon, they bring out the clappers (*palipal*), point
them over the fields at Lotang and the fields at Tukingot, they clap
them. They finish, stick the pigs, singe them, cut the meat into small
pieces. They fire the pot, force the fire, it boils and is cooked.
They call the hired harvesters, who come to the granary place, eat,
finish...

They cross to the fields at Lotang, keep harvesting the rice. They
see the carrying boards and carrying poles one after the other [coming
into] the yard, they see the bundles spreading, reaching to the fence,
reaching from eave-trench to eave-trench. In the evening they bring
the rice under cover, pile it under the granary, they see that the space
is overfilled, they look up at the caves corners, see that they are
filled. "Well, indeed," says Magide, "was our planting *pudung* for the
buga and *palipal*." Time passes unnoted. Comes the third day and
they carry forth the rice and spread it out. After a day[21] they bring
it in and put it under cover. Then they stack it. They look where they
have stacked — it climbs to the roof angle. They observe the ceremonial idleness.[22] The omen response is good. They plant *pudung*[23] in
their fields at Ampugpug for the *buga* and *palipal*.

Ah nakayah, how what they *pudung*-ed fruited and was loaded with
fruit! The sides of the dikes were afruit and the rice was miraculously
increased. The last year's rice pressed out the sides of the granaries
and their Obtainments, the *buga* and the *palipal* became renowned,
for hardships ceased and nobody had to live by working for wages.[24]

NOTE ON THE TULUD OF THIS MYTH

The *tulud* consists of several repetitions of practically the same
recital of benefits: the charms pass from one owner to another, and
each transfer of the charms brings them nearer to the village where
the rites are being performed. Of these transfers, only the first has
anything of interest.

Pitang and Kawahan died, leaving Bugan as the only child of
Magide. Litdok, of Kamandag, came to Ampugpug, married Bugan,
but he loved to fish in the river and would take Bugan with him to the

nèglect of the fields. This angered Magide and seeing the two at the
river one day, he shouted "*Kada kada!* *gayang* (crow)" as if driving
away a crow and "*Kada kada!* *butbut!*" as if driving away a serpent
eagle, adding: "Who does not think of living at home but stays at
the brook all day." Litdok, insulted, told Bugan, "You'd better go
back to your village, and I'll go back to mine." But Bugan induced
him to return with her. However, after eating, he told Bugan.

"Well, I will go now, for my mind hurts that your father called me
a crow, when I am a rich man in my village."

Bugan decided to go with him. Magide now had no children and
all went wrong with him, his fields were not worked, and he gave the
buga and *palipal* to Kitung of Akong. From Kitung the magic bene-
factions passed to Panguhan at Dugat, thence to Pohnak at Layon,
thence to Gayun at Daligon, thence to Barton at Balitang on whose
behalf the myth was being recited at the particular time.

The complete recitation of the myth and *tulud* requires from two
to three hours, depending on the rapidity of the priest's tongue. I
wanted the informant to teach me the last step of the *tulud*, when the
charms are brought home, but he was afraid to do so unless I performed the *ubaiya* rites, which would require a pig, several chickens,
quantities of rice wine, etc. I didn't think it would be worth all that.
By adding gin to the priest's rice wine, however, and by placing an
extra *peseta* in his palm, I increased his courage to the point that he
revealed the final *duyun*, or invocation, which closes the recitation.
It is:

Thou art mythed, Self-Caught, who came from the Downstream
Region and went into the Upstream Region and who gave the
Obtainment unto the ancestors of that time, so that thou come home
unto our village of Balitang and thou art raised up now [invoked]
and art mythed so that thou cure sickness in general and our fields
at Balitang are planted with *pudung* so that the crops fruit in the
swing of the seasons; so that the fruit trees of field and village bear,
likewise the plants on the terraces; so that the tubers swell in the
ground and the leafy plants flourish; so that the pigs and chickens
multiply and the rice become miraculously increased; so that the
children grow quickly in our village of Balitang! Because thou art
being mythed, Self-Caught.

8. TULUD HINUMBAN: HALUPE DEITIES COLLECT DEBT[1]

Subject: The *halupe* (suggesting and harassing deities) are brought
to Balitang village to assist in collecting debts. Used: In rites to
collect debts. Informant: Ngidulu.

SYNOPSIS

(1) Certain harassing and convincing deities (*halupe*) of the Downstream Region, headed by Lingan (a female deity), hear the invocation of an Ifugao creditor and decide to go to his aid. At first there is objection to allowing Bolang ("Uncover") to accompany the party, but at last they take him along on condition that he side with the debtors and uncover their wealth. (2) Their route from their village of Kapungahan to Balitang, where the myth was recorded. (3) Lingan sends Bolang to side with the debtors; then the deities enter Balitang, and Lingan lays her blanket on the debt bespeaker's shoulders. (4) Invocation.

COMMENT

The title of the myth means "covered," whence, figuratively, "smothered," and is derived from the name of one of the Convincing Deities, a class of the large group of Social Relations deities. Their names are most interesting: see Barton, 1946, p. 47. For another myth used in debt collection, see Barton, 1919, p. 115.

Lingan's laying her mantle on the shoulders of the debt-bespeaker is a motif that smacks of the Near East.

THE TULUD

1. *Ngalana* Lingan at Kapungahan: the sun is half-way. Said Lingan, "*Kanadih* the Ifugaos they are calling and calling us: let us go upstream." Pinyuhan and Ngilin agreed. They take down the eating-basket, begin [to eat] and finish. They put things away. They change [from food to chewing] betels. *Ngalana* Lingan of Kapungahan, she sees [finds] her blanket, shakes it, throws the ends over each shoulder. They descend [from their houses] at Kapungahan. *Ngalana* Pinyuhan and Lingan, they take their spears.

Said Bolang (Uncover), I will go with you," he said.

Said Lingan, "Do not go with us [for] later thou wouldst *let down*[1] the invokers of the halupe deities (i.e. the creditor). [Said Bolang], "It will be all right for me to go along so that I go on the side of those who are dunned in order that I *uncover* their shrouds so that what is demanded will be quickly [collected]."

2. They set out in the Downstream Region ... They go upstream. They go to the first tributary, take their time going upstream, arrive at the second tributary. They arrive at Baliti, continue upstream to Gahalit.

They take their time, go upstream, arrive at Likyu, continue to Ulilikon, go upstream to Buhne, go not noting time's passage to Pangahalan, arrive at Kaba, continue on to Banawol; they go single file, their bodies quickly moving. They arrive at Pantal, arrive at Nunkituman ("Ligauwe Gap"), arrive at Ulnui,[2] start up the river and, "It isn't here," they say. "There at Ulnui is the source of the call." They [turn back and] go upstream at Ulnui, arrive at Bulâ, arrive at Banao. They go upstream unconscious of time's passage to Buhne, continue to Dalutadit, arrive at Pugu, continue upstream, arrive at Dulagon, arrive at Pakdal, take their time and climb upward, arrive at Balitang.

3. Ngilin says, "Thou, Bolang, go on the side of the ones to be dunned, in Anao, in order to uncover their *gamong* shrouds and properties and their pigs and chickens, so that our grandchildren will quickly [collect] and thus there will be a chicken in a temporary [carrying] coop to be sacrificed to us."

Ngilin and companions enter our village of Balitang. *Ngalana mo* Lingan, she shakes out her blanket, spreads it over the shoulders of the children[3] who will bespeak [the debt].

When the sun is half way, they enter Anao and speak to the point about what is demanded. They [the Anao folk] see that they speak rightly and give out their pigs and their shrouds. They return to this, our village at Bitu, they carry back chickens and pigs. Straightway he proceeds to make ceremonies which are not for recovery from sickness but which are welfare feasts, and to purchase property. The kindred approve and there is no bad talk.

4. *Kalidi*, so as to follow this which is our myth-recitation, and thou art pointed to that family to be dunned, but accompany me in the morning and on other[4] days when I go to the village of Ginauwaan [to call on the debtor].

9. FEUD BETWEEN BROTHERS

Subject: Brothers fight, but are forced to make peace. Used: In marriage of relatives, in peacemaking rites and in prestige feasts. Informant: Balogan of Ginay.

SYNOPSIS

1. Bumabakal of Dukligan courts Bugan of Binong and brings her to his village; the couple have two sons, Balitok and Lumawig, and a daughter, Bugan, who is their youngest. (Marriage in this and in another instance in the myth is patrilocal, whereas Ifugao marriage is usually matrilocal today).

2. The brothers do not get along together. A hunt increases the bad blood between them, for Lumawig shirks his part and finally deserts the hunt, comes home and drinks up the *hôôd* (rice wine that Ifugaos

prepare beforehand for their return from arduous work, from a journey, or a hunt). Balitok persists in the hunt, brings home the game and is enraged when he finds no hôôd to refresh him.

3. Umbumabakal makes each brother a spear and war knife by the ancient process of using cast iron. He then proposes to his wife that they divorce so as to keep the brothers from fighting. She agrees. They marry their daughter to Dúlnuwan of Gauwaan, then the mother takes Lumawig and goes back to her people in Binong, while Balitok remains with his father.

4. Lumawig, of Binong, goes headhunting and takes the head of one of his father's people.

5. Balitok retaliates by taking the head of one of his mother's people.

6. Bumabakal tells his daughter that since she is the youngest, it is up to her to make peace between her brothers and suggests that she and her husband give a prestige feast, which both brothers will attend.

7. Bugan and husband give such a feast in their village of Ginauwan; the preliminaries are described in detail. Both brothers set forth to attend. Balitok arrives first, and, when Lumawig arrives, warns the latter not to enter the village. Father and mother try in vain to reconcile the brothers; they especially take it to heart that without a reconciliation it will be impossible to sacrifice animals for the feast.

8. They invite the god Lidum to reconcile the brothers. He fails. Then they invite successively, Thunder, Earthquake, and the Strong Winds, all of whom also fail. Finally the Hinumban deities come, make the brothers half-drunk and get them into a house. One of the Hinumbans then sits on the smokehole, another in the front door, another in the rear door, and the fourth underneath the house. They smother the brothers into making peace. A period of great prosperity for all follows.

COMMENT

Apparently we have here a version of the widespread "twins" story, in which one twin is good, the other bad. It is barely possible that the myth reflects a condition of society described by Wilkin for Sumatra and other parts of Malaysia, in which ownership of the children is divided equally between the parents' clans, with an odd child clanless. He cites Van Hasselt as relating of the Rawas and Musi Ilir that in case the parents divorce, the children are divided equally between father and mother. If there be a child left over, that child is "free" and remains with the mother, except that the father, by paying the sum of eight rix dollars, obtains the right of taking it into his own family as soon as it can do without a mother's care [See Wilkin, p. 144].

Among the Philippine lowlanders, who, like all Filipinos, reckon kinship bilaterally, the odd-numbered children resulting from marriage between a slave and a free person were slaves, the even numbered were free.

THE MYTH

1. *Kanadih* Bumabakal of Dukligan: in the morning when the sun is half way he takes down his eating basket and eats. He finishes eating, puts things away, changes to betels and betel leaf, wraps them together. He descends, goes to a betel palm and climbs it. He grasps the stem of a cluster with one hand, jerks it off, descends, takes them to his granary, pulls off the nuts and puts them into his hipbag. He goes to a betel vine and picks off the choicest leaves, the hanging fruits. He descends and goes to the house, belts on his scabbard, tucks on his hipbag, slips in his bolo, takes down his spear and descends from his house.

He crosses at Paowad and goes to Binong. Bugan opens the door and puts down the ladder; he goes up into the house. He eyes Bugan and she is beautiful; her ornaments are shapely, her hair is very long. They talk together and Bugan agrees.

In the morning when the sun is half way, Bumabakal returns to Dukligan. He sends a messenger [to ask Bugan's hand]. The kindred at Binong agree, as also the kindred of Bumabakal. They tie several pigs on forked sticks and go (to Binong) and it [the omen] is good and is *nungitib*. They observe a ceremonial idleness. On the third day, they go to Dukligan and they multiply and settle (there) permanently.

2. After many (lit. "fifty") years their children were many; Balitok and Lumawig were grown up, also Bugan, the female of the generation. Balitok and Lumawig, the brothers fought [all the time]. When the sun was half way at Dukligan, their father Bumabakal said,

"Alas, indeed, the brothers, Balitok and Lumawig: you are fighting every day! Go hunting, you brothers."

Bumabakal descended. He sees his chickens, which would fill a granary; he chooses a cock, takes it into the house, offers it to the Inumban's and Alabat (Nightmares) and place spirits. He finishes, he bleeds the chicken, singes it, opens it, sees and [the omen is] *nungitib*. He fires a kettle-skillet, waters it, heats it, soon it is cooked, he takes it off, places it in cooked rice. He invokes and invokes, he finishes, he cuts it up and they eat. Eating finished, they chew betels.

They observe ritual idleness. At night they sleep. [When] the cock crows they wake up, prepare food and Bumabakal says,

"Go forth, you brothers." Balitok and Lumawig agreed.

They go below, feed their dogs, tie up the leader of the dogs, tie him to a house post. They set a pole against [the tree on which climbs] a betel vine. Balitok climbs it, jerks off the choicest leaves, the clustered fruits, goes down. He turns to betel nuts, egg-shaped, like rice heads hanging over. He climbs and reaches a "hand." He comes down, takes it up to the house. The brothers pluck off the nuts, put them in their hipbags. The brothers go into the house, put on their scabbards, take their 2-barbed *buliwot* spears from the pegs, slip their arms through their backbasket straps. They go down, take the leader of the dogs, go across, look up at the cockbird; the omen is auspicious. They go a second time and that is the same; they go a a third time. The cock bird gives brave talk. Balitok "accepts" it.

"So let it be," he says, "so will we sever the navel of the quarry."

Said Balitok, "Here is a [good] place for the *mokmok* rite. He sees the branches of an *amugaowan* tree, breaks them up, arranges them for fire.[1] He sees [finds] bamboo for fire-making,[2] he draws fire, puts it underneath. The brothers sit and sit. After a while, the fire burns to coals. He brings water. He quenches; he utters an exhortation to the Naotbe, the skydwellers, those who are in the Underworld and those who are in the Upstream Region. "Crushing is what we thus make rites for. Let not the mouth of the dogs be crushed. Be crushed the mouth of the wild boar in the mountains." They sit a while longer. Toward noon, Balitok says, "So much for this. The dogs are hungry and beginning to feel bad." Lumawig agrees. They untie the leader. The brothers enter their forest at Dukligan; they run all over a place big as a field; they are covered with runo-nettles. The dogs start up a quarry. They go over hills and valleys, chase it along a divide, drive it into the Skyworld, into Ablatan. They drive it through the middle of the Skyworld. The brothers climb [thither]. They ascend at Ablatan. Balitok shouts encouragement, he sics on the dogs, he goes through the center [of the skyworld].

Lumawig is left behind in Ablatan of the Skyworld; he cuts bushes, makes a shade in Ablatan, is indifferent to Balitok, sits and sits; a little after noon he returns home. He takes down the rice wine which was the brothers' *hôôd*,[3] spoons and spoons it up in the house.

Mala mo Balitok, he does not abandon the quarry. At evening he spears it. He opens it, removes the vitals, puts them in his backbasket, carries the game on his head, goes obliquely down Ablatan, descends, stops at Dukligan, slides the quarry off his head onto [the housefloor]. Said Balitok, "Where are you, Bumabakal? Bring down the *hôôd*."

Said his father, "There's no *hôôd* there. Lumawig got to it first and ate it."

Balitok was angry. He drew his bolo, slashed a flat stone, couldn't be made to make peace. Said Bugan,

"Even so, Balitok. Divide the meat and cook it."

Mala mo Balitok, he calls his kindred. They fire the kettle skillet, heat it up, soon it is cooked. Then it is said they take it out, put it on top of cooked rice. Balitok draws it to himself, exhorts the spirits of the places he passed through. The people eat. When finished they chew betels. They divide up the meat[4]. His kindred go home. Tomorrow when half-way [the sun], Bumabakal said,

"What about these brothers, fighting all the time, fighting day by day?"

2. He sees a cast-iron kettle-skillet. He kicks it (down from a height?). He sees that it breaks into pieces. He gathers them up, he piles them one over the other. He places them on the Ladakan shelf. He sees [finds] his *haluwan* and it is a shining war knife. He scours it, sharpens it on a whetstone. He takes it to his houseyard. He finds a *talubutug* tree, chops on the up-hill side, cuts it down and divides into sections. He splits it. He arranges it for firing, he brings down fire, he places fire under. He goes to the house, the place where he had his granaries, where he sits and waits for a while. He sees that it (the wood) is burned to coals. He brings out water and a *talaka* basket, he quenches, gathers [the charcoal], puts it in the basket, takes it to the granary place, he puts it on the under-granary shelf. He finds his blower cylinders and smith's blower. He sets them up. He makes a tube for it, plasters it up. He takes the blower, pumps air through it, sees that a current passes through. He brings down fire, covers it with charcoal, blows it, he sees it glow, enters his house, gets the cast iron pieces, he takes them down, puts them into the fire, blows up the fire. In a little while he sees them come to white heat; he grasps them with his tongs, takes them out, hammers them flat, goes on shaping, finishes. He sees and they are two spears and two knives; he scours them on the whetstone; he fans the spears with a betel leaf.[5] He finishes and twills scabbards, fastens on two scabbard belts, tempers the two double-edged war knives. He finishes and scours them, gives each one a scabbard, puts together the two scabbards. He climbs up to Amlinuhadan, ascends the Ablatan, sticks up the two spears, hangs on the two scabbards.

He goes down to Dukligan. Bumabakal arrives and tells the brothers,

"Go ye, indeed, and share between ye the two spears and war-knife outfits at Ablatan at Amlinhudan."

Mala. Balitok and Lumawig, they simultaneously jump up, run across the rice dikes, climb the two steeps together, climb upward together. They take each a spear. The brothers laugh, they laugh with open mouths; they descend and arrive. Said their father,

"What can be done about these two brothers?" Said their father, "Look ye! The *humang*[6] on the other side is in flame, and the *witawit*, which is the gathering place of the birds. Go, ye brothers and bring."

Up they leap together, they race, the brothers. They arrive at the other side they climb over the greasy precipice, they climb the steep simultaneously; each takes of the *humang* and *witawit*; they return to Dukligan. Said their father [to his wife]:

"What to do about these brothers? They keep fighting and fighting. Let us divorce, Bugan, and Balitok and I will stay here, and let us separate, Bugan, so that Balitok and Lumawig will make peace.

Bugan agreed. They [Bugan and Lumawig] change residence to Binong and they settle. They engage Bugan, their womanchild along with Balitok and Lumawig, in marriage; they take Dulnuwan at Gauwaan as son-in-law.

"Let it be so," says their father, "and thou wilt settle at Gauwaan."

4. And Lumawig bethought him at Binong: he would go head-hunting, he decided. He leaves his house, calls his co-settlers. They gather at Binong. They take down the sorcery box. They invoke their ancestors. They change to the messenger gods and the gods of the Downstream Region and of the Upstream region, those at Duntug and those in the Skyworld, those who are in the Underworld, and the adjacent ones in the Downstream Region and the Gayun's. They finish, bleed the chickens, singe them, break them open. They see and it is *nungitib*. Lumawig accepts.

It is the life of me, here in my village of Binong, who go headhunting, in order to strengthen our winnings and riches in our village of Binong.

They fire a pot, they fire it furiously, it boils and is cooked. They take it off, they spread [the meat] on rice. They invoke [the gods]. Finished and they eat, chew betels. They observe a ceremonial idleness; night falls — no event of chicken catching or falling of branches,[7] it is quiet and darkness comes. They sleep. Morning of the morrow, they chew betels, pound rice [for the expedition] they prepare betels and betel leaves, they burn lime.[8] At dark they sleep under the house. On the morning, which was the third day, Lumawig said, "We go forth today. Finished the ceremonial idleness [before observing the augurs]. His old men agreed. They take their food basket and eat. After that they chew betels, they put on their scabbards, then their hipbags, grasp their spears.

The kindred cross and look upward for the cock-bird. It speaks a good omen, a rapid and continuous cry, flies and perches on a dead branch. Lumawig "accepts."

"It is the life of me who go headhunting to the village of Balitok of Dukligan." They go upstream without sensing the passage of time, arrive at Dukligan, spear a kinsman [or clansman ?] of Balitok.

At evening, Balitok comes home.

"Alas, alas! the kinsman (clansman ?) of father, slain by Lumawig. I will go headhunting also, to Binong."

5. Bumabakal agreed. *Ngalana mo* Balitok, he calls his co-settlers. They assemble at Dukligan. They take down their sorcery box. They invoke the deities. They observe the ceremonial idleness. The days are finished, it has come the third day. Said Balitok, "We also go headhunting to Binong." Midway the sun — and Balitok's party ate. Finished that, and they chew betels. The kindred go up, go across at Dukligan. They look upward for the cock-bird, in their hills at Dukligan. The omen resounds. They wait for a slow omen [bad]; none came forth. They go to a second one, they go to a third one. It gives "harsh talk." [Good, as a third omen, as referring to the victim and foretelling his death, but "harsh talk" would be bad on the first or second, as referring to party itself].

Balitok accepts, "So let it be," he says, "so that it be the sobbing of the widowed and the wearers of mourning bands at their village of Binong."

They go downstream to Kituman. They come to Inhumangob, arrive at Bayukan, go downstream to Kaba, arrive at Yangyangan, arrive at Binong. They spear a kinsman of Lumawig. In the evening of the day they return to Dukligan. Said Bumabakal,

"Didst thou spear a kinsman of Lumawig ?"

Balitok answered in the affirmative. They celebrate. Midforenoon of one day, his father said.

"What to do about these brothers ? They go hating and fighting, day by day, every day. Where are ye, Bugan and Dulnuwan, in your village at Gauwaan ? Go ahead and make a drinkfest, make a prestige feast, so that Balitok and Lumawig will have reason to make peace, so that ye be go-betweens, for thou (Bugan) art the last born of the children of Bumabakal."

Bugan agreed. She returns to Gauwaan, calls her co-settlers. They gather and gather. They bring down fermentable rice, strip it from the straw and pound [thresh] it, winnow and separate the threshed from the unthreshed, carry it to the house, and cook it. When cooked, they paddle it out, cool it, spread it out [in flat baskets] and sprinkle on yeast. They leave it alone [lit. "forget it"]. When the third day has come, they put it into jars, leave it to ferment. When the fifth day has come, they call their old men. The old men at Gauwaan gather and gather. They pour out wine, drink, pray for taking rice out of the granary, are possessed by the gods. They finish, bleed the chickens, singe them, break them open and the omen is *nungitib*. They bring a cock and consult it as oracle, ask omens of the *naototbe*: "A drinkfest is what we are praying for." It was good; [the cock] was still. They take down the cock. They bring up chickens, bleed and singe them, break them open and it is *nungitib*. Bumabakal[9] "accepts," "It is the life of us who give a drinkfest in their village of Gauwaan."

They observe a ceremonial idleness. Darkness fell without any event of chicken-catching, or falling branches. It remained quiet till night. They sleep. At midforenoon of the morrow, they call their old men. They gather at Gauwaan. They beat their *balangag*[10] gongs. They play the gongs on the way to cut *bultik* wood. They cut down [trees] cut·them into sections and distribute [the wood]. They carry it to the village. They help each other split it up.[11] They catch pigs. They take them to the house. They sing the *alim* for the drinkfest.[12] They sacrifice to the *na-ototbe*. They finish. They stick the pig, singe it and open it. They fire a kettle-skillet, put in the meat, heat it furiously. It boils and is cooked. They see it and take it off; they spread the meat on cooked rice; they invoke and recite myths; they cut up the meat and eat. That finished, they chew betels, they disperse. They put in the whole day [preparing for] the wine. They roast and cook [the rice]. In the evening it is cooled off. They carry the yeast from house to house. At nightfall they [begin to] observe the ritual prohibitions, they play the gongs (and dance). On the eighth day, Dulnuwan spoke, "We will bring the [materials for] sugar cane presses today." They beat the *balangag* gongs, gonging the *bultik* trees, they cut down [the trees] and trim off the limbs, carry them to the village. They help each other. They dig a hole for the end post of the sugar cane press.[13] They set the press block. They make the tongue, they insert the long pole. The omen is good. They "branch" their feast (i.e. sing both "branches" of the *alim* for it) They catch pigs, take them to the house, invoke the *matungulan* gods. They finish, they cut up the meat. They cook it. Soon it is cooked and they take it off. The able-bodied men eat. When they have finished, they disperse. They spend the day [working on] the sugar-cane presses; they work into the night. At mid-forenoon of the morrow, Dulnuwan says. "We will get sugar-cane today." They play gongs for the sugar-cane. They cut it down and tie it [into bundles], carry it to Gauwaan. They "branch" their drinkfest (i.e. make the other "branch" of the

preliminary ceremonies). After that the able-bodied men of Gauwaan
eat. They disperse. At night they sleep. When the cock crows, they
send their servants and servants[14] and these make invitation trips.
They invite Lumawig at Binong, they invite Balitok at Dukligan.
At night the folk of Gauwaan assemble. Balitok comes, but Lumawig
is not there. They pour out rice wine, they hold wassail. It is after
midnight, they are unconscious of the passage of time. At midforenoon,
they bring down the gongs and dance.

Midforenoon — *mala* Lumawig at Binong, he eats at his village
at Binong, finishes and chews betels. He puts himself at the head of
his co-settlers, they set forth at Binong. They go upstream to Yang-
yangen, go on the level at Kaba, arrive at Benawol, take their leisure
at Buyukon, arrive at Inhumangob, go over the ridge at Kituman,
arrive at Gauwaan.

Said Balitok, "Do not enter, Lumawig."

Said their father, Bumabakal, "What to do about these brothers?
We ought to be ashamed before our guests, the kindred on both
sides."

Said Balitok, "Do not enter, Lumawig, because thou hast killed
our father's kindred, but I killed the kinsman of our mother."

Said their mother, Bugan, "Go ahead and make peace."

Said Lumawig, "I will not make peace. I am ferocious at Binong.[15]

Said Balitok, "I will not make peace. I am ferocious at Dukligan."

Said their father, "If that is the case, we shall not be able to kill
the animals for the feast."

They invite Lidum. *Mala* Lidum of the Skyworld, he packs [for
his journey] in the Skyworld, betels and betel leaves and tobacco
supply, girds on his scabbard, then his hipbag, grasps his spear,
comes diagonally down the steep place, sticks up his spear. Like a
leaf-blade, like a runo plume,[16] he ungirds the hipbag, takes out betels,
puts the ingredients together, tosses them between his teeth, crushes
them, they turn red, have turned thick red. He pulls up his spear
and descends, stops at Gauwaan, confers intimately with Lumawig
and Balitok. "Let us now make peace." Balitok spoke and would not
make peace, slashed a flat stone with his bolo. Lumawig did the same.
Said their father, Bumabakal at Dukligan:

"I don't know what to do about these brothers. A shame for us
before the guests and kindred on both sides."

They invite Kidul (the Thunder) of the Skyworld. Kidul bethinks
himself and descends diagonally across to the Ablatan and thunder-
bolts Ablatan in his village in the Skyworld. And the drinkfest guests
perished [of thirst?] at Gauwaan. And Kidul arrives. Balitok and
Lumawig laugh. Said Balitok,

"Thou hast come, Kidul, to our village at Gauwaan, but we will not make peace in our village of Gauwaan. See," says Balitok, "the drinkfest guests have perished. We brothers, Balitok and Lumawig, are bereft."

Kidul moves not nor speaks. *Mala* Bumabakal, he invites Kaliog (the Earthquaker) of the Underworld. Kaliog bethinks himself in the Underworld and the earth shakes at his journeying. He arrives at Gauwaan and takes a big bowl [of wine]. He confers intimately with Balitok and Lumawig. Said Lumawig, "I will not make peace. I am ferocious and that's all there is to it at my village in Binong. Everybody has heard of the winnings from bravery (?) at Binong. I am the brave one, I am the *kadangyan* there at our village at Binong." Said Balitok, "It is the same with me at my village of Dukligan." Said their father, "What to do about these brothers ? They continue hating, continue quarreling. How shall we feast together ? I don't know how we will kill the animals for the feast at our village of Gauwaan. Let us invite the Puok (Wind Gods)." And they invite the Puok.

It is midforenoon in the Upstream Region and the Puok bethink themselves. They start out from the Upstream Region and beat down all the fruited plants and fruited trees on their pathway. They arrive at Gauwaan. They arrive and take rice wine and confer intimately with Balitok and Lumawig. "Let us now make peace."

Said Balitok, "I will not make peace. I am ferocious and that's all there is to it in our village at Dukligan. Lumawig went headhunting to Dukligan and killed a kinsman of father and I went headhunting to Binong and killed a kinsman of mother."

Said their father, "If it's like that," he said, "don't know what to do about you [two] here in our village of Gauwaan. How shall we kill the animals ? We will invite Inumban of the Downstream Region, Inumban of the Skyworld, Inumban of the Upstream Region and Inumban of the Downstream Region."

And they meet at Gauwaan. And they meet and gather all around over the house. They bring rice wine and pour it into a large bowl. They call Balitok and Lumawig. They confer over the rice wine. "Let us make peace." Lumawig became angry. He slashed a boulder. His knife struck fire on a flat stone. Balitok did the same.

"I am ferocious and that's all there is to it in my village of Dukligan; I am like a full-fledged cock, like a young cock in my village of Dukligan. I went headhunting to Binong and took a kinsman of mother, and thou camest headhunting to Dukligan and took a kinsman of our father. I will not make peace, I am like a cock, like a young cock."

Said their mother, Bugan, "What to do about Balitok and Lumawig? As things are, don't know how we'll kill the animals in our village of Gauwaan." *Mala* the Inumban of the Downstream Region, they give the wine cup continuously and [they are] drunk, and half-drunk the brothers. They ascend the house and *mala* the Inumbans of the Downstream Region, they sit in the front doorway, and *mala* the Inumbans of the Skyworld, they sit in the smoke hole and *mala* the Inumbans of the Underworld, they sit underneath the house. They enclose Balitok and Lumawig tightly, And after a while Balitok and Lumawig are gasping for breath.

Said the brothers, "*Ah nakayang!*" It is said that they said, "Are ye going to kill us! Open, indeed, and we will make peace so that you can kill the animals at Gauwaan." And the Inumbans of the Downstream Region, the Upstream Region, the Skyworld and the Underworld open. And they descend to the houseground and make peace. They bring wine and pour it into a large bowl. They see betels, betel leaves, *humang*, and tobacco, *witawit* and *uldiu*. They put them together in a basket, they invoke the ancestors and the messenger gods, the *na-ototbe* and the gods of the four regions, the hidit gods of the Downstream, the Upstream, the Skyworld and the Underworld and those who are at Duntug, that assemblage of all these hidit gods which are the *humang* and *buliklik* and *witawit* and gold ornament, spear and parroquet, *bidut*,[17] and *ididalo*.

"Be it so," says Lumawig, "so that we make peace now, so that we make peace with our enemies and creditors and those with whom we might quarrel, so as to make peace for (?) the betels and betel leaves and tobacco, rice wine and cooked rice. Let us become companions (?), let us fraternize, so that we may acquire chickens and pigs in our village of Dukligan, so that we live, so that what we plant will be productive, so that there will be no crop failure, so that the children will grow fast, so that the enemies and evil spirits will be turned aside from our village of Dukligan."

It is not at Dukligan, because it is at this village of Balitang here. It is not for Balitok that I call thee, because it is for Mr. Barton, so that it — (that is, the magic force invoked) reckons thee [Barton] a companion along with the Government among the Ifugaos, and it will be well. Because a custom of the Ifugaos.[18]

10. KINGGAOWAN: THE DIVIDED CHILD*

Subject: Goddess marries Ifugao; their divorce and division of child. Used: In rites to cure sickness. Also, (with different ending) in war and sorcery rites. Informant: Ngidulu. Recorded and translated by Barton and Bugbug.

Synopsis

1. Kinggaowan, of Kiangan, attends a feast given by his kindred but is snubbed in that they do not share meat with him, do not treat him as a kinsman. He goes up on Mount Pangagauwan, which towers over Kiangan, and there builds himself a shack, after which he works industriously at building pitfalls, going naked, the while.

2. Bugan, daughter of Hinumbian, of the Skyworld, sees the lone man working everyday on his pitfalls and comes down to cook for him. He comes home, smells the rice steaming hot, but is ashamed to come into the house on account of his nakedness. Bugan tosses him her skirt girdle to wear as a g-string. The two marry, have a child. Kinggaowan's traps are highly successful and the people of Kiangan come in crowds to get their share. But they eat ginger, vegetables. and prohibited foods with the game, wherefore Kinggaowan and his family are afflicted with *gulid* (skin eruptions). Kinggaowan takes his family to Kiangan to live, hoping that the change of residence will cure the skin eruptions. But that only makes the situation worse, for the people of Kiangan pound ginger and throw it on the walls and roof of Kinggaowan's house. Bugan proposes a return to their house on the mountain and they act on this suggestion. But the Kiangan people follow them up and plaster ginger and garlic on the walls of the house.

3. Bugan proposes that they transfer their residence to her village in the Skyworld. They set out, but Kinggaowan is unable to make the ascent, wherefore they decide each to go his way and to divide the child. Bugan took the upper half and gave Kinggaowan the lower half with the injunction to equip it with head and arms and vitalize it.

Kinggaowan is unable to do this and the flesh rots, giving off a stench which reaches Bugan. Bugan thereupon descends, scolds. Kinggaowan for his neglect and tries, herself to revitalize the part and to join a head and arms to it, but the corruption has gone too far. She therefore makes *lubug* [creatures and objects that give omen] out of the mass: certain birds, insects, the rainbow, landslide, etc.. She declares that these will afflict the Kiangan people.

4. They do, but the Ifugaos perform the proper sacrifices, and recover.

Comment

The divided child motif is intrusive. It is widespread in Asia and America. The Pawnee myth of Feather Woman and Her Celestial Lover is similar [Alexander, vol X, p. 94]. A Russian example is given by D. K. Zelenin [No. 13], "The Babylonian Crown."

Cognate myths are found among the Cherentes of Brazil [Alexander, vol. XI, p. 307], also among the Eastern Timbira [Nimuendaju, p. 245.

The similarity to cosmogonical myths of the Wyandot and the Mentawei Islanders has already been pointed out. All the mountain tribes of Northern Luzon have cognates — see especially, Beyer, 1913, p. 105; also p. 110, fn. 59; also the Japanese [Harris, p. 39.]

THE MYTH

1. *Ngalanda* Bugan and her son at Kiangan. The sun is half way at Kiangan. *Kanadih diye* spake Kinggaowan [the son],

"Where art thou, mother, Bugan? *Ngalana diye*, knowest thou that our kindred are giving a feast?"

Ngalana diye spake Bugan, "True they are our kindred, but distant ones."[1]

Kanadih Kinggaowan, he goes through their center at Kiangan. The people of Kiangan gather together. *Ngalana* the people of Kiangan, they assemble and catch pigs at Kiangan. They bring wine, pour it out, invoke the ancestral spirits, change to the messenger gods, invoke the *Naátob*[2] who are in the Skyworld, the Underworld, the Downstream Region, the Upstream Region, and they are possessed by the deities. They finish and kill the pig. They singe and open it, take out its liver, cut it up. *Ngalana diye*, they distribute the the pieces to the children. [The pieces] do not suffice to reach Kinggaowan. The children wipe the grease of them on Kinggaowan. They then cook the meat, force the fire, at the second boiling, they take the meat off, they recite myths, finish, invoke the gods.

They finish and then cut up the meat. *Kanadih diye*, they distribute it to the people of Kiangan, bring cooked rice and eat. There was no share for Kinggaowan. He returns to their houseground in Kiangan, tells his mother,

"Thou saidst, Mother, that they who gave the feast were our kindred. But, there, they gave me nothing!" *Kanadih diye*, "I thought they were kindred, but [it seems] they are not!"

Kanadih Kinggaowan, he enters the house, prepares food and cooks it, dries the cooked rice by the fire. *Kanadih diye* and Kinggaowan, he paddles out the rice. *Ngalana diye*, he takes down the eating basket, eats, finishes, puts things away, chews betels, spits, and they are red and thick-spittled.

Kanadih Kinggaowan, at night he sleeps. *Kanadih* after a little while the cocks crow, he awakes and prepares food, cooks, pours off the excess water and puts the pot by the fire to roast and dry. He eats, finishes, puts things away, changes to betels and divides a betel nut, spits all around. When the sun is half way, *ngalana* Kinggaowan, he takes down his spear, tucks on his hipbag, then his knife, goes down from the house, crosses their outskirts at Kiangan, climbs up at Malatiti, turns to Duyugan. *Kanadih diye*, after a little while he comes on top to the pass at Pangagauwan.[3]

He scrutinizes the pass at Pangagauwan, sees the level place at Pangagauwan. *Kanadih diye*, *ngalana* Kinggaowan, he cuts away the brush and sees a *bultik* tree, chops it down, carries it out of the forest and sets up the posts, puts on the ridge pole and runo reeds to tie the thatch to. He thatches with grass and trims. He sees that it [the lower edge of the roof] is like a bee-line.

Ngalana Kinggaowan, "I will descend, I will change residence now."

Ngalana Kinggaowan, he descends and arrives at their center in Kiangan. He enters the house and takes down his eating basket and begins to eat, finishes, changes to betels and divides (one).

Kanadih Kinggaowan, he talks [to his mother], "Thou, Mother, Bugan, stay in the center at Kiangan, for I am going to change residence to the mountain Pangagauwan."

His mother agreed. He takes his things and packs them up, takes down his spear crosses the outskirts and ascends to Malatiti, turns to Duyugan. After a little while, *kanadih diye*, Kinggaowan arrives at his shack at Pangagauwan. *Kanadih* he enters prepares food, cooks, dries out the cooked rice by the fire, paddles it out and eats.

He changes to betels, divides one, descends and goes to the pass at Pangagauwan. He looks for a place to make a pitfall and pulls up the grass. He returns after a little while and at night he sleeps. When the wild cock crows he prepares food, cooks it, pours off the excess water, dries it by the fire. After a little while he paddles out the rice, begins and eats, finishes and changes to betels, divides one.

Kanadih Kinggaowan, he takes his knives, goes to the pass at Pangagauwan and clears away grass for four [pits]. Time passes unnoted on the mountain at Pangagauwan as he makes pitfalls. At noon, he goes home to his shack ... [cooks, chews betels, etc.] ... After a while he comes out of the shack, *ngalana* Kinggaowan goes to Pangagauwan, takes his time making pitfalls. After a while it is night, he goes to his shack, takes down the eating basket ... sleeps. By and by the wild cock crows, he arises ..., (prepares food, etc.) goes out to his house-yard at Panggauwan, goes to his pits and makes pitfalls. Everyday he works alone on his pits at Pangagauwan.

2. *Ngalana* Bugan, daughter of Hinumbian of the Skyworld, she comes out on their high place and sits and sits. She turns her eyes downstreamward and turns her eyes upstreamward, rests her eyes on the mountain at Pangagauwan. *Kanadih diye mo.*

"Why! There is a man on the mountain at Pangagauwan. Everyday he works alone on his pits at Pangagauwan." *Ngalana diye* Bugan and "I will jump down in order to cook for him."

And she jumps down and stops and enters the shack. And she prepares food, cooks, pours off the excess water, dries it by the fire, paddles it out.

Kanadih Kinggaowan, at midday, *ngalana diye* he goes home to his shack. And he arrives and peeps from behind cover. "Why is there somebody here ? What she has cooked is still steaming."

Kinggaowan ran away. "Why, Kinggaowan, dost thou not enter the shack?"

Said Kinggaowan, "Because I am ashamed."[4]

Ngalana diye Bugan, she takes off the girdle of her skirt, tosses it to Kinggaowan. He takes it and enters; they eat, finish, change to betels and Kinggaowan leaves and goes to his pitfalls on Pangagauwan.

Kanadih Kinggaowan, daily he makes pitfalls every day. He sees his pits on Pangagauwan and he has layed off [begun] eight of them. In the evening of the day he cuts down wood and covers the pits. After a while *ngalana* Kinggaowan, he finishes. At night he enters the shack, takes down the eating basket and they eat, finish and change to betels ... They sleep.

The darkness lessens, Kinggaowan awakens, goes outside, goes to his pits on Pangagauwan, goes to visit his pits for the first time. He sees that there are holes in the "roofs" (of the coverings) of two of them. He takes out [the game] and carries it to his shack at Pangagauwan. When morning comes, at midday, he opens up the wild pigs, cooks the belly-fats, boils them and takes them off, spreads on cooked rice, invokes the place spirits, finishes, cuts the meat into small pieces and they eat. They finish.... Time passes without noting on their mountain at Pangagauwan.

At nightfall they sleep. At about midnight he listens intently [for sounds from] his pitfalls at Pangagauwan. He hears sounds of falling one after the other. After a while, in the morning, *kanadih* Kinggaowan, he goes to his pitfalls at Pangagauwan, sees his pitfalls at Pangagauwan. *Ngalana* his pitfalls, all eight are pierced through. He sees the wild pigs, takes out the wild pigs.

Kanadih bo the people of Kiangan, they hear about what Kinggaowan has caught in his pitfalls; every day they come in crowds for the meat and carry it down to Kiangan.

Kanadih mo the people of Kiangan, they ginger the meat, eat climbing plants with it.[5] *Kanadih* Kinggaowan and family are terribly afflicted with *gulid*. Said Kinggaowan, "Let us change residence to our village at Kiangan."

Kanadih diye, ngalana bo the Kinggaowans, they take their effects, leave the house at Pangagauwan and go downhill, arrive at Kiangan.

Ngalana the people of Kiangan, they get ginger and pound it up and take it to the center at Kiangan, throw it on the roof and walls [of Kinggaowan's house].

3. Said Bugan, "Where art thou, Kinggaowan? Let us return to our lone house at Pangagauwan. For why are thy kinsfolk like this at Kiangan — disgusting us with ginger?"

Kinggaowan agrees. *Kanadih* the Kinggaowans, they take their packs and go back to their lone house at Pangagauwan. *Ngaladay* people at Kiangan, they follow them and bring up ginger and garlic and plaster it on the walls.

Said Bugan, "And why is it thus in our village of Pangagauwan? We will get *gulid*! Let us move to our village in the Skyworld." Kinggaowan agreed. They take their packs and go outside. They climb the steep place, they go up the steep. *Kanadih* Kinggaowan, he is exhausted with climbing. *Ngalana* Bugan, she takes him by the arm, helps him upward, she sees, too, that Kinggaowan becomes very heavy. Bugan comes back. *Kanadih* Bugan,

"What shall we do, Kinggaowan? If thou like, let us divide the child and thou wilt take half of it and vitalize it in Kiangan, and I will take half of it and vitalize it in the Skyworld."

Kanadih Bugan, she cuts the child in halves: "Take thou the legs-part, put head and arms on it." Kinggaowan agreed. He takes the half of the child and descends.

After a while, *ngalana* Kinggaowan, he arrives at their center in Kiangan and enters the house, puts it on the house-shelf. Time passes at Kiangan. On the third day *kanadih* the half of the child stinks, and Bugan daughter of Hinumbian smells it in the Skyworld. Said Bugan,

"Why is it like this — a stench of the dead?"

Ngala mo Bugan, she goes outside, comes to the top-place and drops down to Kiangan. She arrives and enters, searches out with her eyes where to find the half of the child. *Ngalana* Bugan, she says, "Why Kinggaowan? Why art thou sitting around in sorrow? Thou'st done this to the child! Thou'st not endowed him with life!"

She draws forth the half of the child, she is going to endow it with life but it can't be vitalized. She puts the parts together and sees that they fly apart. And she makes then the *lubug*."[6]

"I do thus," says Bugan, "so that if, indeed, the people of Kiangan should be afflicted, sacrifice ye a cock."

4. *Kanadih* Bugan, she ascends to the Skyworld. *Kanadih* the people of Kiangan, the *lubug* affliction is severe, their sickness is severe. They sacrifice chickens, there is no result and they resort to the *agba* (divining stick). The sources of the *lubug* are indicated.

10*

The people of Kiangan do not delay. They bring chickens and invoke their ancestral spirits, change to the messenger gods, invoke the sources of the omen beings, Kinggaowan at Pangagauwan and Bugan, daughter of Hinumbian, Mayingit of the Skyworld and Amtalao at Kiangan.[7] They bleed the chicken, burn off the feathers, open it, see [the bile-sac] and it is *ningali*.

They put a pot on the fire, *Kanadih diye*, they put in water, put in the chicken, force the fire, it boils and is cooked, they take it off, put it on cooked rice. *Ngalana diye mo*, the people of Kiangan, they recite myths. They finish, invoke and finish. Kinggaowan, Bugan daughter of Hinumbian, Mayingit of the Skyworld and Amtalao at Kiangan smell it. They send back a cure and good bodily condition.

That was the reason, too, that at Kiangan the sickness ceased and was quickly cured, got well. They keep acquiring chickens and pigs. *Ngalana diye*, too, the people of Kiangan, they begin field work and [the crops] ripen and are productive and there are no crop failures. They travel and travel the accustomed paths. *Ngalana diye* too, the people of Kiangan; their enemies and the evil spirits stay far away from them.[8]

11. AMMOTINGAN: MAN IMPRISONS GODS*

Subject: Origin of a talisman. Used: In war and sorcery rites. Informant: Himingale of Habian in the Kiangan Region; in 1913.

SYNOPSIS

1. Certain wind gods destroy the fruit trees of Ammotingan of Lamot. He sets out to be avenged and follows the trail of the wind gods till he comes to their cave. He builds a stockade to seal the wind gods in and then yells to them to escape it they can.

2. The wind gods puff and the stockade is scattered all over the hill side. The priest in a fiat invokes a like scattering and destruction of his enemies. Ammotingan rebuilds his stockade, making it stronger and tighter than before by means of wax and gums. He again yells to the wind gods to get out if they are able. The wind gods puff, but the stockade, though it yields, does not give way.

The wind gods begin to bargain for their release. Finally Ammotingan sets them free in return for the gift of their talisman.

3. Ammotingan returns to his home. After a short time, Ammotingan and his kindred find that their chickens have greatly increased, and this signifies to them that it is time to go headhunting. They go into the Upstream region, lie in ambush there and spear a passerby. They return home and observe all the headfeast rites.

· 4. The priest clinches the magic and invokes terrible destruction on his enemies.

COMMENT

The contents of the myth are evidently "invented;" such bargaining as that of the wind gods for their freedom is an element frequently repeated in the myths.

However there may be in this myth a tradition of the origin of some particular talisman. Talismans, valuable jars and gongs often have myths to explain or relate their origins. The myths sometimes come to be attached to other talismans, each owner claiming his own possession to be the original of the myth. Finally the myths come to be used, as this one is, for activating *any* talisman. Such I suspect to have been the history of this myth.

THE MYTH

1. There was, it is said, Ammotingan of Lamot: his bananas and the fruits of his trees were heard about and heard about. Puok (Wind God) of Nalamban and Puok of Ambatu heard about them. Said Puok of Ambatu to Puok of Nalamban: "Where art thou, Puok of Nalamban?" he says. "Let us go eat the bananas of Ammotingan of Lamot and his betels and the fruits of his trees."

They roar as they go. They come to Dukligan, set out (again) at Dukligan, arrive at Lamot, at the house of Ammotingan. They exert their strength as they roar and the granary and house of Ammotingan at Lamot are tumbled, his bananas and fruit trees are bent over. The wind gods return to their homes, their homes at Ambatau and Nalamban. Their homes are moss-grown.

Ammotingan wakes up and is angry. He cooks, *tutuwa*. And then, indeed, he eats. He finishes eating, untucks his hipbag, takes out betels and betel leaves, inserts [the quid] in his mouth, turns them red, red and thick-spittled. He takes his spear in hand, belts on his scabbard, sets forth from his house at Lamot.

He goes and carries his spear on his shoulder and trails the path of the Puok of Nalamban and Puok of Ambatu.

"*Nakayang!*" he says, "the path of Puok of Nalamban and Puok of Ambatu — a swath is (left) where they travelled to Dukligan."

Ammotingan follows and arrives at Dukligan. He passes the night there.

The cocks crow. He sets his pot on the firestones. At the second boiling, he eats, *tutuwa*. He finishes, sets out at Dukligan, goes through the fields, continues to Wala, goes on the Kumadangyan, arrives at Nalamban.

Kana katog! the wind gods — they're roaring like thunder below. He sees trees, cuts down trees, carries them on his shoulder, arrives, sharpens the trees, puts them down. He finds vines, slashes them off, trims them. He sets the stakes in the ground, arranges a stockade, ties them together, finishes.

He says: "Go ahead and puff, thou, there!"

2. The wind-god puffs and the stakes are thrown helter skelter, like disjointed skeleton bones, scattered over their stumps, scattered all over the jungle!

FIAT: [The priest blows and flourishes his bolo in the direction of the enemy region]: Let it follow so that it be so with the kindred of Buyagaowan there and the people of Bangbang there,[1] and the people of Kultib, there. Their houses are bewitched, vine-covered and moss-covered. It [his sorcery] returns to their house and has bewitched his own body and continues on to his children and women folk, his kindred and ancestors on both sides. They are carried into the Skyworld. The bridge across the chasm is removed. They exclaim, *"Inuy, inuy!"*

Says the Skyworld dweller, "How shall I kill them." He thinks. He gets a large Chinese kettle-skillet, puts in water, forces the fire under it. It boils. They catch the kindred of Buyagaowan on both sides with their women folk and cook them. They die. Distorted and twisted, there is no one to avenge them.

Says Ammotingan, "Where is something to shut them in with so that it can't be uprooted ?" He sees *balagnut* trees, fells them, trims off the branches, carries them on his shoulder, comes out (of the forest), puts them down. He sees *palatut* vines, slashes them off, carries armfuls of them out of the forest, puts them down. He chops up his trees, sharpens, sets the stakes, ties them together with the vines. He sees gum and takes it. He gets beeswax. He gums and beeswaxes [the stockade]. Said Ammotingan, says he,

"Go ahead, Puok of Ambatu and Puok of Nalamban: blow ye, and throw down the woods." They blow down below, and it (the wind) does not come out. It [the stockade] sways, but it does not come out for it is gummed. Said the wind-gods,

"Take it down, *tutuwa*, and we will teach thee."

Said Ammotingan, "What will ye teach ?"

Spake the wind-god and says he, "Will teach thee the planting of mongo peas."

Said Ammotingan, "There are mongos left unharvested there at Lamot."

Said the wind-god again, "Take it away, so that we can show thee."

Said Ammotingan, "Wilt show what ?"

Said he, "Our jewels at Ambatu and Nalamban."

Said Ammotingan, "There are jewels of mine at Lamot."

Said the wind-god again, "Take it away, *tutuwa*, and we'll show (something) good."

Said Ammotingan, "Wilt show what ?"

Said the wind-god, "Our talisman (*kiwil*) at Ambatu and at Nalamban."

The ear of Ammotingan was convinced. He takes it away. The wind-gods leaped up from below and were men. The wind-god takes out the talisman (from his hipbag), gives it to Ammotingan.

Said the wind-god, "It will turn aside thy enemies. It will not turn aside the souls of the chickens and pigs and children. It will turn aside the sorceries of the enemy, the evil spirits of the Downstream Region and curses and witchcraft."

3. Ammotingan returns to Lamot. The breezes are quiet. He arrives at Dukligan, passes night. On the morrow, he arrives at Wala; goes through the fields, arrives at Lamot. He eats, finishes, assembles his "fathers." They see chickens. They invoke the prayables at Dukligan, also those at Mapantal. They also invoke Damuki and Tukgian. They cut the throats [of the chickens], singe and open them, see the biles; they are *nihumwit*. Ammotingan utters a *fiat*: "It is abundance of life for me who brought back the *kiwil*; it brought back fifties of chickens and pigs and rice bundles."

They walk about at Lamot. A month and a half passes. They see their chickens — their chickens have become many below the granaries. They invoke the prayables again; they are going headhunting. They go a short distance and build a shack. They take a chicken and invoke the omen-givers and omen birds: "Do not shout us away who go headhunting into the Upstream Region — shout away him whom we shall have speared." The wearer of the plume[2] arises in the night and "torches" the men (inspects by means of a torch); none are swollen. He torches their scabbards and these are slanting (properly) with the bodies of the owners.

The sun is half-way. They cook. They get a chicken, cut it up, distribute the pieces to the men. There were some pieces left over. Ammotingan utters a *fiat*.

They set forth, go through the rice fields, arrive at Ulu, arrive in the Upstream Region. They see a path and go into ambush. Night falls. They sleep. The cock crows. They cook. The sun is half-way. They eat. They set forth. They carry their spears on the alert.

A man of the Upstream Region sets out on a journey. He comes even with them there. Ammotingan and his men spear him. They shove the spears [through him] into the earth and lean on them. They cut off the head, put it into a backbasket, shoulder their backbasket and shout in concert. They go through the rice fields, arrive at Ulu, cook. At the second boiling they take the pot off, paddle out the cooked rice and eat. They set forth. They shout in concert. They arrive at Lamot. The pretty ones (women) beat loom-sticks for them. They come into the village, get a chicken and recite the *higup* ("entrance") ceremony. At night they bring *balanti*, set it in the yard, fix the head on it. They dance.

On the morrow, the sun is half-way and they assemble their "fathers." They pray the *lopad* ceremony. "Let not the souls of the pigs and the chickens be *lopad*-ed: be *lopad*-ed the loss of the speared man." They singe the chicken, inspect the bile-sac. It is well. On the third day, he calls his kinsmen. They catch a pig, tie it up, carry it to the yard. They invoke their prayables. They pour oblations on the pig, brandish their spears over the pig. They spear the pig. They invoke with a spear in the ear of the pig: they shout, "Whoo-OOO-OOOO-oooo! Come down, Bugan, wife of Deceiver (Manahaut)! Come down to our village of Pindungan.[3] Take the pig, also the sorcery-box, the betels and betel leaves. Carry it up into Skyworld. Descend into the Upstream Region. Assemble the kindred of Buyagaowan, those at Kultib, there. Wrap them up and carry them into the Skyworld. Take to the bridged place (in the Skyworld). They exclaim *"Inuy, inuy!"* They forget everything there, get a kettle-skillet, set it on the firestones. At the second boiling, take the kindred of Buyagaowan and stuff them into it."

Skin peeling from their bodies, they are distorted and twisted! There is no one to return their vengeance. Their houses are covered over with raspberry vines and with *tabuwang* vines.[4]

They carry their pig (to the fire), singe it, take it under the house, cut it up. They see the bile-sac. It is *nalauwing*.[5] They set the kettle-skillet on the firestones, force the fire. When it has boiled twice, they take it off, take out the meat, spread it on cooked rice. One of them performs the blowing rite:

"Thou art blown, Steam of Meat and Cooked Rice. Go in a stream and arrive at Bangbang, there and Kultib, there. Will smell thee the kindred of Buyagaowan, there. Will taste thee, Odor of Meat and Cooked Rice. They will think it their own witchcraft, but it will be our witchcraft."

They invoke their prayables, finish, take their bolos and myth. They myth the Talisman of Ambatu, Puok of Ambatu, Puok of Nalamban. They finish mything; eat and finish. They take out betels and betel leaves (and chew).

They take the juice of the meat (soup). They go to the fire and quench it, saying,

"Be not quenched the souls of the chickens and pigs and children. Be quenched the witchcraft of the kindred of Buyagaowan, there, and of Kultib, there."

They take the sorcery-box, they take blood and smear it on the sorcery box and *hulihil* wood. "Be not *hulihil*-ed the souls of the chickens and pigs and children. Let not the sorcery box presently become white. In the middle of the night it will be the arriving place of the prayables who are at Dukligan,[6] the prayables who are at Hunduan, of Lagiwe at Mapantal, Full-Grown Cock and Hardstone of Hunduan. They are strong and come."

They invoke the ancestral spirits, the knowing ones of former times. "As it was in the first times, so are we invoking you. Ye ancestors are exhorted to uphold us."

4. It is not at Lamot, for it is here at our house in Pindungan, here, and you prayables are pointed toward Kultib there and Bangbang there, at the houses of the kindred of Buyagaowan, so as to bewitch their houses. They return to their house and the bodies of the kindred are bewitched and their womenfolk on both sides. The Pests of the Downstream Region and of the Upstream Region come forth and sit down upon them. They swell up and their coagulated ("like egg in hot water") tongues protrude. They set them in their death chairs when the sun is half way, put new g-strings on them. Their womenfolk and kindred on both sides assemble and bewail them. They wall them up (in their sepulchres) with a strong tombstone. Their houses are covered with raspberry vines and spider-webbed, covered with *tabuwang* vines. We brothers together and fathers and sons will hear about it and pity them when the sun is half-way.

Follow thou [addressing the talisman], but be strong, be ferocious, and turn aside the evil spirits that arrive from the Downstream Region and the Upstream Region, but dive under [the sorcery of the other party] and arrive [at them] so that it follow, for there, thou hast been mythed, Kiwil of Lamot.

12. KINULHUDAN: WEAVERS' MYTH*

Subject: Acquisition of an improved loom; affliction of weavers with sleepiness and tired eyes. Used: In rites to cure loom sickness. Informant: Ngidulu. Recorded & translated by Barton and Kababu-lan.

SYNOPSIS

1. Bugan of Kiangan finds her present process of weaving very slow and is discontented. She takes a blanket to the Upstream Region to trade it for salt. She watches the women of that place weaving and

notes that they are weaving on a kind of loom that is much faster than her own. Having exchanged her blanket for salt, she returns home and tells Balitok, her husband, of the marvelous loom she has seen.

2. Balitok goes upstream on the morrow to procure a loom if he find it feasible. The folk of the Upstream Region advise him to go on into the Skyworld since that is where they obtained their looms. Balitok arrives at the house of Lidum, who takes him to the granary where his womenfolk are weaving. Balitok is convinced of the superiority of the Skyworld loom and asks for one. He is given it with the injunction that if the women of the Earth-world should become afflicted while using it, a sacrifice to the "source" of it — that is, the group of Skyworld gods who gave it — will be needed to secure relief.

3. Balitok takes the loom home and it is a great success: the women turn out their work much faster than on the old loom. But they become afflicted with redness of the eyes and with stripes before the eyes. Then Balitok remembers Lidum's injunction about sacrifices. The Kiangan people offer these, the gods send a cure, and a period of great welfare ensues. The priest invokes a similar result for the present occasion.

COMMENT

This myth probably is based on good history. The downstream people probably got the improved loom from the Upstream folk; the people of the eastern foothills are not much given to weaving even now and import a good part of their fabrics from upstream. As we have said they are still a people of ruder culture than the upstream folk. They made considerable use of tree-bark cloth only 25 years ago. Even the people of Central Ifugao used bark fiber in some of their weaving only a few generations ago, and the Kambulu people still do. Possibly the Upstream people received the loom originally from the Kankanai of Lepanto; it may be that these are the "Skyworld" people of the myth.

THE MYTH

1. *Kanadi* Bugan of Kiangan, she makes g-strings and shrouds all the time in Kiangan; she works all day at her loom. The loom is very slow —makes Bugan angry.

Said Bugan, "I'm going to go exchange a *kintug* blanket."

Said Balitok, "What wilt thou exchange it for ?"

Said Bugan, "I'll exchange it for salt."

Bugan packs up. She puts the blanket on her shoulder, descends from the house at Kiangan, crosses their outskirts, goes upstream, arrives at Litan ... [goes over the route to the Upstream Region] ... looked up at their village in the Upstream Region, climbs up to their village in the Upstream Region. The women looked up.

"Is that thou, Bugan wife of Balitok at Kiangan ? Hast come to our village in the Upstream Region ?"

Bugan, it is said answered, "I am exchanging this *kintug* blanket."

The women of the Upstream Region, it is said, answered, "What dost thou want in exchange ?"

"I want to exchange for salt."

She watches the women of the Upstream Region. They are passing the warp around the upper end-stick and their lower loom of the Upstream Region. They go back and forth, passing each other the ball of yarn.[1] Bugan watches from the corner of her eyes. She notes their weaving in the Upstream Region. In no time at all g-strings and hipbags are hanging all around. *Kanadi* Bugan, she exchanges the *kintug* blanket, exchanges it for salt, hangs the salt on a carrying pole. "So much for that — I will return," said Bugan. Time passes unnoted on her way; she arrives at Bayukon, goes downstreamward ... arrives at Kiangan, goes up, enters the center at Kiangan.

Balitok looks up. "Bugan is here," he says, "back from exchanging for baskets of salt."

She puts down, it is said, the salt baskets. Balitok comes down from the house, sits beside her; they give each other betels.

"Where didst thou go to exchange ?"

"I made the exchange in the Upstream Region."

They go up, it is said, into the house. At night they are sleeping, she is telling Balitok, "Why! when I went to trade in the Upstream Region, I saw the women weaving. They were like spiders; I sat only a little while in the Upstream Region, and I saw them finish (one piece), go on and weave another. During the little while I sat in the Upstream Region, I saw g-strings and sometimes hipbags hanging all around. They work very quickly."

"Wait till morning and I will go upstream and have a look."

After a while it is morning, they prepare food, cook, pour off excess water set by the fire to dry. They paddle it out of the pot, cool it, eat, put things away, change to betel chewing, spit it out and it is red.

2. "So much for that," says Balitok, I will go upstream to the Upstream Region in order to see what Bugan saw." He packs up betels, tucks on his hipbag, then (girds on) his knife, takes his spear in hand, crosses the outskirts, continues upstreamward. ... He crosses, it is said, their outskirts in the Upstream Region, enters their center, goes to the house, sticks up his spear, brushes off the rice mortar and sits.

Wigan of the Upstream Region comes down from his house.

"Yes," said Balitok, "I have come hither because of the looms of the women here which Bugan saw at your house when she came to exchange her *kintug* blanket."

They chew, it is said, betels, spit and turn them red. Said Balitok, "How didst thou get the loom?"

Wigan, it is said, answered, "We got it in the Skyworld at the house of the Weavers. Wilt thou go to the Skyworld?"

Balitok answered affirmatively. "So long! I will climb the steep to the Skyworld."

He tucks on his hipbag, pulls up his spear; time passes unnoted [as] he climbs. He arrives at Humadol, continues and climbs, comes to the top of their top-place in the Skyworld. He thrusts down his spear, chews, it is said, betels, spits all around on their top-place in the Skyworld. Balitok sweats out (cools off). He tucks on his hipbag and enters the village of Lidum of the Skyworld. He thrusts down his spear, turns to the rice mortar. Lidum of the Skyworld glances around.

"There is Balitok," he says. "Hast come up to our village in the Skyworld?"

Balitok answers affirmatively. (Lidum) comes down and sits alongside, they give each other betels and tobacco, they remove the husks of the betel nuts and have a talk. Said Lidum, "Why didst thou come up?"

Said Balitok, "The reason I came to your village in the Skyworld is that I heard about your loom and your weaving in the Skyworld. The work of weaving done by the women is quick in your village in the Skyworld."

Lidum of the Skyworld, it is said, answered. "That's a fact," he says. "Come, let us go to our granaries in the Skyworld. My descendants in the Skyworld, the Striped One of the Skyworld and the Weaver's helper of the Skyworld are there."

Balitok stands to go. They pass, cross their granary place in the Skyworld. They indeed see the women, Lidum's descendants in the Skyworld: all around there are g-strings, there are hipbags, skirts, *inladang* and *bayaong* blankets and shrouds. Balitok watches; the little while he sits there, they are changing what they weave all the time; they finish it, remove it from the loom.

"So much for that," says Lidum. "Let us return to the houseground where we were before."

They follow the path, go, it is said, to the house, sit a while. "Wilt thou eat?" says Lidum.

"What I ate in my village of Kiangan isn't used up yet; but about your looms — give me one," he (Balitok) answered, "to be Bugan's loom at our house."

Lidum agreed. "All right," he says, "Take this loom down, take it to your village in Kiangan to be the loomsticks of the women in weaving g-strings, shrouds and sometimes *bayaong* blankets, but if they should string the looms up quickly and if something should be wrong with the (long)-haired ones' (women's) eyes, so that if Bugan's eyes should become awfully sick in your village, then you must give us an exchange."[2]

3. Balitok agreed. "Enough, now, I'll go downhill." He tucks on his hipbag, pulls up his spear, picks up the loom. Time passes, he descends, arrives at Humadol ... Time passes and he comes up into his center at Kiangan. Bugan looks up.

"Balitok has arrived, yah! Didst bring indeed one of their looms from the Upstream Region?" He gives her the loom, she puts it on the inner house shelf.

Said Balitok, "I got nothing in the Upstream Region, so I went into the Skyworld for it, to the house of Lidum of the Skyworld. It's the loom of the Monkalabe of the Skyworld. And if it should happen that thou workest quickly with it making g-strings and shrouds and *inladang* and *bayaong* blankets with patterns such that (even) Monkulabe[3] of the Skyworld becomes envious, [then we must], he says, 'sacrifice chickens, for it will be good and they', he says, 'will share in the lives of our pigs and chickens and thou wilt make things quickly.'"

Bugan agreed. At night they sleep, in the morning they eat, put things away, change to betels, Bugan goes down, calls her women neighbors; they take down the loom and yarn and the basket in which the ball of yarn is carried when the loom is being set up and the rump belt [of the loom] and everything. They arrange the upper end-stick and the loom, unwind the thread. They finish. They put in the *toltog* stick, it is said, and they weave.

Time passes. At evening they see their weaving place; all around are hung g-strings and hipbags and *binudbûdan* and figured pieces.[4]

Said Bugan, "Excellent indeed is the loom of the Skyworld folk that Balitok brought. There! how quickly we have worked."

Every day they assembled in their village at Kiangan. The women have many looms, they praise Bugan, wife of Balitok at Kiangan. They keep acquiring pigs and chickens, forget those in the Skyworld from whom they had acquired the loom.

Then they [the givers of the loom] afflict the eyes of the (long)-haired ones. *Anhan*! what a redness of the eyes. Said Balitok, "That is what the man said when I went to the Skyworld: 'If something should be wrong with the eyes', he says, 'make an exchange payment to Monkalabe of the Skyworld.'"

Balitok does not waste time, he calls together his fathers; they assemble, invoke the ancestral spirits, change to the messenger deities, invoke these descendants of Lidum of the Skyworld. They bleed the chicken, singe and open it. They see that it (the bile-sac) is *hinumga*. They fire a pot, put in the chicken, force the fire. It cooks and they take it off, spread it on cooked rice, myth and myth Monkalabe of the Skyworld — Monkalabe and Kinulhudan and Mongadang and Ulde ... (and the rest). They finish. They invoke. They finish (invoking) and eat. They finish and put things away. They change to betels. They put the betels together and throw them between their teeth; they chew and spit out the juice, see that it is red.

These descendants of Lidum in the Skyworld smell (the sacrifices).

"They did not delay," say these Skyworld dwellers. They relieve Bugan, the wife of Balitok at Kiangan.

That was the reason that the eyes of the haired one ceased [being sick], were cured, became normal. She thinks about her loom work again. Her work is quick.

And that was the reason, too, for the abundant life of the pigs and chickens and for the miraculous increase of the rice, the abundant life of the children, for the shunting aside of enemies and evil spirits.

Kalidi — it is not at Kiangan but at the house of the father, the Barton. But let it be that the loom work of Ngidulu's household[5] proceed rapidly so that there will be something to exchange for pigs and chickens, things to give in exchange, to serve for the purchase of rice fields and wine jars and gold beads and *pango* beads so that he live [abundantly] and the enemies and evil spirits be turned aside, for thou hast been mythed, this [group of] descendants of Lidum in the Skyworld. For a myth not motivated by sickness is what ye are being prayed.

13. THE TOOTH OF THUNDER*

Subject: Ifugaos secure mana from Thunder. Used: In rites of war and sorcery. Informant: Ngidulu.

SYNOPSIS

1. Lumawig and Lagiwa, brothers, of Mapantal, are beset by enemies and insistent creditors who urge each other on against them. They flee into the forest. It rains and Thunder peals. A thunderbird sitting in a thicket of wild abaca (Manila hemp) mocks Thunder, whereupon the latter strikes the thicket but his teeth and body

become entangled in the fibers of the abaca, so that he is helpless. He sees the brothers sitting nearby and opens conversation with them. They tell him about their troubles, whereupon he offers to endow them with mana if they will set him free. They cut him loose from the abaca fibers. He then louses and puts them to sleep, after which he inserts in their jaws one of his own teeth and some hair from his body. Awakening them, he points to a tree and tells them to try out their powers. They strike at it, but nothing happens. He again puts them to sleep, and this time he inserts two of his tusks into their jaws and bristles from his eyebrows. Again they try their powers, and when they strike the tree is shattered to smithereens and nothing is left of it. He gives them further advice and they return home.

2. They find enemies and creditors awaiting them but, assuring these that they will not run away, they propose postponing the fight till morning. The enemies and creditors sleep around the yard fence the rest of the night. Next morning, when the sun is half way, the brothers descend, stand back to the sun and shout at their foes, destroying them utterly. After that they offer sacrifices to Thunder.

3. Henceforth all was well with the brothers. The priest invokes a similar happy ending to the present situation.

COMMENT

All but one of the elements of this myth have already been encountered in the myth of the Virgin Birth and that of Self-Beheaded (1,2). What is here new is the association of Thunder with the thunderbird (called *kidkidalu*: a word evidently derived from *Kidul*, Thunder, and probably signifying, "thunders all around"), who arouses Thunder's anger by mocking him. The cult of the thunderbird is frequently found in Polynesia and nearly everywhere in North America.

THE MYTH

1. Lumawig and Magiwa, brothers, in their village of Mapantal: exceedingly many are their enemies and creditors, who rage against them every day. Said the brothers:

"Let us flee into the forest, for they are about to take us, these creditors."

The brothers flee. In the morning they are sitting on a mountain and it rains hard. Thunder crashes. *Ngalana* the thunderbird, he speaks and speaks in a clump of abaca, imitating the speech of Thunder. *Ngalana* Thunder of the Skyworld, he strikes the abaca and the abaca is shattered; it holds him by the teeth and is wound round his body. He growls in the base of the [abaca] clump.

The brothers are peeping. Thunder sees them. "Ye brothers, why are you here?"

"Yes," they said, "we have taken to the runo thicket: our enemies are too many, our creditors about to take us!"

Said Thunder, "Cut me free, untangle me, and I will teach you. Have ye no *kiwil* charm?"

"None whatever," they say.

Mala the brothers, they draw their knives and cut him free, untangle his teeth and what is twisted around his body. Thunder stands up straight. They go to a hill. He louses the brothers. After a little while he makes them sleep. When they are asleep, he takes out [his own] teeth and tooths them, it is said. He hairs them with his body hair. Then, it is said, he awakens them. "You see the *balagnut* tree on the other side," [he says].

Ngala mo Lagiwa and his brother, they walk. They start a thunderclap to hit the *balagnut* tree. They see that nothing happens. They return. He puts them to sleep again. The brothers are asleep again. He changes for his tusks, inserts his eye bristles, awakens the brothers, points again to the *balagnut* tree.

Ngala da bo the brothers, they start a thunderclap, strike, it is said. They see the *balagnut* — it is shattered and thrown away. There is no remainder, nothing left of it. They go back to Thunder.

"Return ye to Mapantal. When the sun is halfway, descend from your house, turn your back to the corona of the sun. When the enemies and the creditors have gathered, begin ye brothers, and shout ye those spears of yours, and after shouting, they will have been turned aside and nothing will be left of them.

2. The brothers assented. In the middle of the night, they return home, arrive and go up into their house. They prepare their food.

Ah nakayah! their enemies and the creditors — they are calling on each other to cooperate: "Here they are — come home, the brothers — let us take them."

Said the brothers, "Ye creditors and enemies of ours, whither should we go away? Don't take us now, please — wait till morning when the sun is half way."

The enemies and creditors agreed, they slept around the fence. After a while it is morning and the sun is half way. The brothers descend, take down their spears, stand, backs to the corona of the sun.

Ah nakayah! the creditors and their enemies — everyone trying to be the one to catch them, to make them exclaim "*Anhan!*" The brothers start up; they, it is said, raise their voices, shout, start the thunderclaps to hit; they, it is said, strike. They see their enemies —

they are (lying) head to foot and foot to head, and others are head to head. They are all stiff and distorted — there is nothing left, no remainder of them. The brothers listen for sounds from their enemies. None of them are talking.

3. *Ah nakayah!* the brothers — they take a cock up into their house, invoke the one from whom they obtained the *kiwil* (talisman). They bleed [the chicken], singe, open it, see that its "seed" (bilesac) is *nakiwil* ("turned aside"). "It points, indeed, to the turning aside of these, our enemies." They fire a pot, cook the chicken; when it is cooked, they take it off, spread it on cooked rice. They myth and myth the *kiwil* talismans and finish. They change to betel chewing.

It keeps being the reason in their village of Mapantal that they keep turning and turning aside and diving under.[1] They go walking from village to village also. *Ngalana mo* their enemies, the wearers of the mourning bands and the widowed, they become like brethren, become like uncles. It is the reason at Mapantal that they keep acquiring chickens, that the chickens and pigs live. They turn their attention to planting: their crops fruit and ripen. They shunt aside enemies and evil spirits.

Kalidi, for thou art being mythed this myth of ours, thou who art in Mapantal. Do not play false, but turn thou aside; turn aside the sorcery and evil spirits, so that we abound in life, so that the pigs and chickens live, the children grow rapidly, for thou hast been mythed this here *kiwil* talisman of cours.

14. THE IRON-EATER*

Subject: Lumawig, an iron-eater, establishes a village of "raweaters." Used: In sorcery against enemies and creditors. Informant: Ngidulu.

Synopsis

1. Lumawig, son of Hinumbían, a rain god of the Skyworld, eats the spearheads and knives of his father's guests. Hinumbían, shamed before his guests and "tired of that boy," turns on a heavy rain which washes the child [cf. opening of the myth no. 3] down into the houseyard of Bihang and Bugan in the Upstream Region.

2. Bihang and Bugan adopt the boy, but his appetite for iron again brings him into disrepute and Bihang "kills" him by felling a tree on him. The boy recovers, carries the tree home and cuts it up for firewood.

3. Bihang "kills" the boy again by treacherously letting a cliff drop on him. The cliff dams a river at the same time. The boy comes to

life, tips the cliff back to place and floats down the river on the released flood.

4. He stops at a swamp where he produces eight "raw-eaters" from tossed bamboo nodes.

5. In the course of time, Bihang finds himself beset by creditors and enemies who "will not give him another day," and sends Bugan to beg the help of Lumawig and his raw-eaters. Lumawig considers himself a member of Bihang's family and comes to the rescue. The monsters he brings along, which seem to be some sort of queer ducks (no humor intended), liquidate the enemies and creditors in short order. Bihang soon becomes prosperous himself, and an arrogant creditor.

6. The priest faces these raw-eaters against his enemies and invokes on the latter such calamities as will make even himself "pity them."

COMMENT

This myth is usually cosmogonical, but has no such nature here. The creation from bamboo nodes and the appetite for iron are intrusive (cf. the Southern Kankanai myth]. A Tongan myth, "Origin of the Magellan Clouds" (Gifford, 1924, p. 103] contains a ducklike monster and throws doubt on my remarks. I let these stand, however, as they may as well refer to utilization of existing motifs as to invention of new ones. The Unwanted Child motif is found among the Eastern Timbira [Nimuendaju, p. 246].

In 1909 I recorded a myth in Kiangan in which the plot element of the "unkillable child" appeared, the name of the child being, as here, Lumawig. In this version the child is finally burned to ashes by his father, but the mother throws the ashes into water, whence eight young men emerge. The myth was ill-recorded, from hearing it told in the Ifugao language, no native text being written down, and there are lapses in it. But it evidently relates incidents of the feud related in myth 9.

Cf. Ralston, W.R.S. "Russian Fairy Tales," *The Smith and the Demon, The Priest with the Greedy Eyes.*

A close parallel to the unkillable-child element is found in a Bella Coola myth: "The Sun tests his Son-in-law" (Boas, Jessup North Pacific Expedition, Vol. 1, p. 73).

Creation from bamboo nodes is paralled in a myth found in Solomon Islands and New Britain: a woman is created from a node of sugar cane. (Dixon, p. 110). Creation of human or divine beings by throwing things is a rather frequent motif in Melanesia.

The Myth

1. Hinumbian of the Skyworld: there were guests of Hinumbian; they gathered and gathered. Everywhere there were *gayang* and *balabog* spears sticking in the ground; everywhere scabbards were hanging. And Lumawig, son of Hinumbian, goes down from the house, passes along eyeing the spearheads and bolos greedily, grabs them, twists them up and stuffs them into his mouth. They see that he devours them.

Says Hinumbian, "There is that boy — eating spears! He makes me tired of him."

He, it is said, turned the rain on strong. It catches the child, slides him along, carries him with it,[1] and he fell into the yard of Bihang of the Upstream Region and his wife, Bugan.

Says she, "What child is that who came with the rain and fell into our yard?"

She takes down her loom, goes straight to the yard, takes the child in her arms, goes to the house with him. "Who art thou, child, that came with the rain?"

"I am Lumawig, the son of Hinumbian of the Skyworld. They got tired of me."

2. At night, they went into the house in the Upstream Region, took down the eating-basket and ate. They put things away, changed to chewing betels and, it is said, stayed around home in their village in the Upstream Region. When the sun was half-way, the other-townsmen of the Upstream Region kept gathering. Their *gayang* and *balabog* spears were stuck up in rows, their scabbards and bolos hung everywhere. Nothing else than that Lumawig should go down, look at them from the corners of his eyes, and going from one iron to another, break them to pieces, bite off chunks and eat them. They saw that he devoured them. He included the scabbard belts and bolos. They saw that he laughed.

"That child causes me great shame," said Bihang, "he is driving my friends and allies away from me."

They are walking about in their village in the Upstream Region. The sun is half-way. Said Bihang, "Let us [dual] fetch wood." Lumawig agrees. They tuck on their hipbags, take down their spears, take their axes, enter their forest. *Kanadih* Bihang, he looks at an *amugaowan* tree, a long trunk in the place below the village. He sees how the trees ought to be felled [i.e. in what direction], sticks down his spear, goes to the base of the tree, clears away on the uphill side, notches it on each side and the tree sways and starts to fall. Said Bihang,

"What a pity! My spear will be crushed by the tree."

11*

The child rushed [under], caught the spear by the ferrule. The tree fell. He (Bihang) sees that [the child] is dead. He pulls out his spear and goes up to his village in the Upstream Region. Said Bugan, the wife of Bihang.

"What about the child?"

"No more, because crushed by the tree."

"What a pity for the child!" said Bugan.

After a little while the child recovers, he shoulders the tree, including the treetop, carries it up into the village in the Upstream Region. The house eaves are damaged [by the treetop dragged between them]. The people of the Upstream Region exclaim, "*Inoi, inoi*! Why, here is Lumawig carrying the full length of the whole tree, including the very leaves through our village in the Upstream Region." They saw that the tree reached all the way through the village ... He takes an axe, his body moves up and down as he chops [the tree] across. Then, it is said, he splits it into large pieces. He continues, it is said, to split it up fine. He finishes, carries it up, stores it on the *huguhug* rack. They are walking about in their village of the Upstream Region.[2]

3. In the morning, when [the sun] was half way, nothing else than that Lumawig, said, "Let us catch fish [by damming and bailing] in the river at Nambulan." Lumawig agrees, they put on their scabbards, tuck on their hipbags, grasp their spears, cross the river at Nambulan. They see a by-channel [of the river], dam the upper end; (with stones). Bihang stops the water [completes the dam] while the child says "I will bring clay." They plaster up the dam (making it water tight) and bail [a pool] with their hands. Said Bihang, "There are no *udingan* minnows here; this cliff has eaten them."[3] *Kanadih* Lumawig, he draws his bolo, goes to a *bultik* tree, cuts it down, slashes off the top, shoulders it and carries it back; they put a stone under it [for a fulcrum] they see that [the cliff] is lifted. Bihang, it is said, holds down the lever, the child goes under. *Ah nakayah*! how the minnows splash. He grabs a double-handsfull runs out with them, puts them into the fishbasket, gets and puts again in the fishbasket. The third time he went back to catch them, he (Bihang) lets go the lever; the child is crushed.

Said Bihang, "What a pity for the child, for there he is crushed by the stone." He pulls up his spear, ascends to their village in the Upstream Region. Said Bugan, "Why, where is the child?" "No more," says Bihang. "Smashed by the rock at Nambulan. What a pity for the child — so deft and competent in our village in the Upstream Region!"

Nothing else than that after a little while, *ah nakayah*, the child

recovers, tips over the rock at Nambulan, the water is dammed at
Nambulan, it ceases [its rippling]. After a little while, he sees that
the leaves are drowned at Nambulan. He releases the water at
Nambulan [by pushing away the stone]. He sees that he goes
downstream, goes downstream like a duck. Soon he arrives at the
Swamp of the Downstream Region.[4] He sees the base of the *palutan*
bamboos at the Swamp of the Downstream Region.

4. He draws his bolo, goes to the base of the bamboo clump,
slashes off a bamboo. He cuts off a two-node piece, throws it end over
end to the Underworld, sees that they have become larger as they
went to the Underworld. He cuts off a two-node piece, throws it end
over end to the Skyworld, sees that they have become larger as they
went to the Skyworld. He cuts off a two-node piece, throws it end
over end to the Downstream Region. He sees that they have become
large as they went to the Downstream Region. He cuts off a two-
piece, returns it to the Upstream Region. He takes the bamboo top,
shakes it (over?) the swamp of the Downstream Region. He sees that
they are floating; he sees that they are eight.

"What are your names?" he says.

They spoke: "We are Tayaban-Carried-by-the-Waist, Tayaban-
Carried-in-a-Backbasket, Tayaban-with-a-Feather-Plume and Taya-
ban-Wearer-of-the-Headhunters'-Headdress, Cut-off-Banana-"Hand",
Wilting, Sound-of-Crunched-Bones and Galikon (?)."[5]

"You are eight" was his answer. "I have increased in the Swamp
of the Downstream Region."

Their scabbards were pointed. They all make the noises that a
drake makes when he meets a hen duck; they are all raw-eaters with
mouths covered with blood. They tarry in their village in the Downstream Region.

5. *Ah nakayah!* Bihang of the Upstream Region — his enemies have
become aggressive, likewise his creditors. It is as if they wouldn't
wait a single day, as if they would eat him up. Said Bugan.

"Hadst thou only not gotten tired of the child! Would it then be
like this in our village in the Upstream Region?"

Said Bihang, "Suppose thou follow after him and bring him
back?"

Bugan agreed. She packs betels, carries them in her blanket, goes
downstream. Lumawig looks up and notices her. "Why is my mother
Bugan, wife of Bihang of the Upstream Region here?" Bugan, it is
said, answered,

"I have followed thee, indeed, to the Downstream Region."

Lumawig leaves the water,[6] sits alongside, they exchange betels ...
Said Lumawig,

"What is the reason for thy having come to my village in the Downstream Region?"

Bugan, it is said, answered, "The reason that I came is that our enemies, likewise our creditors, are aggressive; it is as if they wouldn't give us another day, as if they would terribly eat us." Lumawig, it is said, answered,

"If only thou hadst not gotten tired of me, thinkest thou it would be like that in your village in the Upstream Region?"

Said Bugan, "Where are thy descendants in the Swamp of the Downstream Region?"

"There they are — there are eight of them."

"Then call them so that we go upstream to our villages."

Lumawig agreed. He goes to the base of the bamboo clump, he shakes the bamboo. He sees that they float on the Swamp of the Downstream Region. After a little while they appear and they are eight. Their scabbards are pointed, their mouths are bloody and they all make sounds like a drake meeting a hen. Bugan exclaimed "Inoy!"

"It seems as if they would eat (me)!"

"Dost think they would eat *thee*?," he answered. "Those are thy grandchildren! Let us be going upstream."

They set out in the Downstream Region, go upstream, their heads nodding like ducks. They arrive in their village in the Upstream Region, go up and enter." "So ye have returned?" says Bihang. Bugan answered, it is said, affirmatively, Bihang wastes no time. He catches a pig, takes down his sorcery box, covers it with betel nuts, betel leaves. He invokes his ancestral spirts, changes to the messenger deities, invokes and invokes these Obtainments that were given, sticks the pig, singes it and cuts it up, takes the blood, takes the meat, gets cooked rice. He mixes them with the blood, he takes them [Lumawig and his descendants] to the edge of the village. He feeds them the raw meat, points them toward his enemies, likewise his creditors. The Lumawigs gather their strength. They annihilate the enemies and their kindred on both sides, they turn their attention to the creditors, they crunch [them on one side] and then go to the other side [of the family]. They clean them up utterly. They include the little children, include the bones, crunching is the way they eat; they crunch the places under the houses and the yards. There is nothing left, no remainder, they take all, on both sides, and none are left talking.

That is the reason, in their village in the Upstream Region that he flourishes on both sides of his family; it inspired him with ferocity, he effectively declares the debts owed him; the debts are easily collected, slide quickly from the hands [of his debtors]. It is the reason that his pigs and chickens have increased in their village in the Upstream Region, their rice has increased and the enemies and evil spirits have been shunted aside.

6. *Kalidi* — ye are pointed against the houses of the enemy at Humalapap, but face so that thou go underneath the sorcery of these enemies of ours so as to bewitch his house and when thou hast entered it, stay there so that thou turn aside his sorcery and bite it off and crunch it, so that he be restless in his house, so that he brush off the spider webs [from his heirlooms to sell them in order to secure animals for sacrifice] and be deserted by his women folk; so that he leave his house and thou cause him to meet a handful of eyes [of his ambushing enemies] so that they hurl [a volley of spears]. His heart is all body, so that he lies belly down on his things [that he carries], so that he can't open his hands[7] so that he knows nothing of returning his vengeance, so that they tie him tight (in the death chair) with a g-string, so that he presses down his death chair [as an inanimate object] so that his children mourn him, so that his [female] kin shout to him, so that his kindred pity him, so that they seal him [in the sepulchre] with a strong flat [tomb] stone, so that his house be covered with wild raspberry vines, covered with *tabauwang* vines, so we will pity him, because there ye are mythed, ye eight prayable beings of ours.

15. SUN AND MOON QUARREL

Subject: A quarrel between Sun and Moon. Used: In war and sorcery rites. Informant: Himingale, at Kiangan, 1912.

SYNOPSIS

1. Sun brews rice wine and gives a drinkfest which Moon and his children, certain Stars, attend. Sun boasts of his ferocity and Moon of his. Sun hangs a bag containing lime over a path in the Skyworld and dares Moon to punch a hole in the bag. Moon takes the dare and the lime falls into his eye, blinding him. His children come to his help and wash out his eye, which becomes like gold.

2. Moon gives a drinkfest, which is attended by Sun and his children, certain stars. The quarrel is renewed and Moon sets a spear-trap across the path and dares Sun to kick it. Sun takes the dare, kicks the trap and is impaled. His children find that the crows have picked his flesh from the bones and have dropped it into a whirlpool.

3. The stars gather up the pieces, burn them in a fire made of heartwood, throw the ashes into water, whereupon Sun regains his body in youthful form.

COMMENT

The myth is cosmogonical in character and among some peoples explains the moon's dark phases and the eclipse of the sun, though the Ifugaos now recognize the former, at least, as natural phenomena.

Rejuvenation by fire is a frequent motif in Ifugao myths. Cf. the belief of certain cults in India that he who immolates himself attains divinity. The trapping of the sun has its parallel in the snaring of the sun all over Central Polynesia (Williamson, p. 111–113) and in many North American (Thompson, p. 290) and South American myths (Nimuendajú, pp. 243–4).

THE MYTH

1. Sun (Umalgo) brews rice wine. He puts the malt into jars. He adds sugar cane (juice). Moon (Umbulan) and his sons attend. They pour out rice wine. They drink and become tipsy. They boast quarrelsomely.

"I am fierce," says Sun. "I am the one who takes men so that they die."

"It is the same with me," says Moon. "I am fierce — I do not back down."

He climbs up Habiatan (the Precipice of the Skyworld) and burns shells [to make lime]. He puts the lime in a banana leaf cornucopia and hangs it over the path. He returns [to the drinkfest].

"Thou, Moon," he says. "Climb up Habiatan. Sayest thou art fierce? Swing thy spear on what I have hung up."

Moon agrees. He takes his spear, climbs Habiatan and spears it. His eye becomes white. He cries "Ah kao!" He shouts for his children.

"Where are ye, sons of Moon?" shout the people. "Go and get your father for he is dead."

They [the stars] move in their places. They arrive at Habiatan. They carry Moon on their backs, carry him to their village. They bring water, wash out his eyes, wash out the lime. His eyes come to resemble gold.

FIAT: It was so in order that it follow, so that we "brothers" be like gold which doth not tarnish, like the waters of the river which do not cease flowing, like the tail feathers of the Full-Grown Cock, like the plumes of the runo canes. We talk and talk straight; we speak and strike fear into the eyes of the enemy. We scatter throughout the hills of Pugao. We flourish like the giant bamboo, like the *baliti* tree (*Ficus religiosus*).

2. Moon recovers. He brews rice wine. It becomes strong. He puts it into jars. He adds sugar cane [juice]. Sun and his sons attend. They pour out rice wine. They become tipsy and maudlin. They shout

loud in the Skyworld. They bite pieces out of the coconut drinking-cups.[1]

"I am the one who is brave. I am the one who is fierce," says Moon.

"It is the same with me," says Sun. "I do not back down."

Moon takes his bolo and scabbard, also his spear. He climbs up Habiatan. He arrives. He makes a spear trap, sets it, returns to his village.

Sun climbs up Habiatan, kicks the spear trap. The spear trap springs, impales him. He struggles, he vomits, he sweats, he hiccoughs, he flounders, he bites the dirt ... The earth is his sleeping board.

FIAT: It was so in order that it follow so with our enemies ...[2]

3. The *pauwit* and *hital* [stars] the sons of Sun heard the cries. They climb up the steeps at Habiatan, go looking for Sun. They see him: [he has been] pecked to pieces by crows and the pieces scattered and dropped into whirlpools, his roots pulled up and his irrigation ditches dried!

FIAT: It was so in order that it be so with our enemies ...

The sons of Sun collect the pieces. They chop down an *amugaowan* tree, hew out its heartwood, split it into pieces. They strike fire and burn the pieces of Sun to ashes. They sprinkle the ashes with water. They are transformed into Sun. He regains his body. His youth is renewed. They go home. They shout on the way.

"Thou seest," says Sun, "thou canst not come it over me, for I am fierce. I am like a full-grown cock, like Cobra of Mabula, like Hardstone of Hunduan [Myth 26]. I cannot be overcome under the half-way sun."

FIAT: It is not in Habiatan but here at our village of Pindungan in order that we brothers and fathers and sons be likewise. We will travel the vegetation-rotted paths of Baay here and Tupplak here and Ambabag here and Longa,[3] and from our paths will be turning aside the enemies and evil spirits, sickness, famine, sorceries, and even the poisonous snakes, the centipedes and the sharp spear sticks [*huga*][4]; we will speak and strike fear into the eyes of the enemies, ask for what we want and get it. Our bodies will not spoil or bloat. We will scatter throughout the hills of Pugâ — a myriad of spears (*men*) and a multitude of hill-farm carrying-baskets (women). For there ye have been mythed, Sun and Moon.

16. TINIKMAN: TIED-UP

Subject: Ifugao obtains a pacifying magic. Used: In preliminaries of prestige feasts. Informant: Ngidulu.

SYNOPSIS

1. Balitok of Kiangan finds himself in such prosperous circumstances that he feels compelled to relieve the inflation by giving a prestige feast. He summons his co-settlers and they begin the preliminary rites.

2. They consult a cock; it promises a peaceful feast.

3. They also perform the "tying" magic in order to control the appetites of guests.

4. Just before the drinkfest day, however, Balitok feels misgivings and decides to further fortify their magic by seeking a *hupol* or pacifying magic. He goes first to the Upstream Region. The folk there send him on to the Skyworld. There one god sends him to another until he arrives at the village of Wigan of the Farthest Side (*Hudokna*). Wigan gives him bamboo and the wood of his betel trees, which was used for spear handles in the days when men made spears with wooden or bamboo heads. Wigan also advises him to visit certain deities on his road back and to beg of them antiquated iron weapons such as were turned out by the first makers. He does as directed.

5. Arrived home, Balitok sacrifices, dulls all the weapons and ties them into a bundle along with the charms used for controlling the appetites of the guests.

6. His prestige feast, after these precautions, passes without untoward incident; the guests sing improvised songs, occupy themselves with concluding pacts of trading partnership and agreements for the marriage of their children and in the end they become helplessly but happily drunk and are carried home by their women folk and children in the evening, leaving Balitok and his kindred standing alone, "like the heartwood of a (rotting) tree."

COMMENT

The myth is obviously of the "invented" type, serving to confirm and activate certain magic practices, but it contains also a traditional element in the relations with the Upstream people and "Skyworld" people.

The use of antiquated forms of weapons to pacify the more effective modern ones is interesting.

Prestige feasts are exceedingly dangerous occasions, as is graphically revealed by Bugan nak Manghe in her autobiography in Barton,

1938 (*passim*). Hence the need of every possible "pacifying" measure
is a very real one.

The myth contains very interesting material on the theo-geography
of the Skyworld.

THE MYTH

1. Balitok of Kiangan: his pigs have grown long fangs, his chickens,
long spurs.

"How shall we use them as sacrifices ? Let us give a prestige feast."

He calls together his co-settlers. They assemble in Kiangan. He
gets fermentable rice. They lower it [from house or granary], pound
it, winnow it and sway it [to separate the threshed from the unthreshed grains]. They boil it, dry it, take it out of the pot, cool it,
spread yeast on it and brew it.

They take their leisure in Kiangan. Their rice-wine is becoming
strong. They put it in a jar and add water.[1] They wait a day for its
further strength. He calls his old men [priests]. They assemble, pour
out the wine, invoke and invoke the ancestral souls and the suggesting
deities. They change to the *Matungulan* and the *Na-ototbe*, Deceivers,
Sun and Moon. They take the chickens and bleed them, singe off the
feathers and open them. They inspect the bile-sacs and it is *mingale*.
They fire the *huladon* pot; they put in the chickens.

2. They bring a cock, stand it on the floor; they consult it [as an
oracle]. They invoke for their life who are giving a prestige feast.
They see that it remains quiet.[2] They take off the pot [of cooking
chickens]. They name [deities and ancestral names — inviting them
to participate]. They eat, finish eating. They change to betel-chewing;
they turn them thickspittled (?). Time passes unnoted.

3. They gather coconut sheath "matting"[3] and *liya* leaves, also
the *tikom*. They get *kamulitilit* vine. They spread these on the floor.
They pray to the Na-ototbe gods, also the gods of the Downstream
Region. They tie up the eating baskets of these who will assemble
[guests], so that the kindred on both sides will gather, but the knives
will be firmly fixed and the rocks and fence-stakes will remain quiet,[4]
so that the bodies of the gong-players[5] will be unharmed; they will
be gentle with each other.

That is all and at evening they go home; they finish at Kiangan.
In the darkness of night they sleep. Dawn of the morrow and they
take their backbaskets, go to the forest and fell a tree. They cut it
into sections, distribute [the burdens] carry it to Kiangan. They split
it up. They catch a small pig and sacrifice it (*tungul* — pay back, pay
tribute to) to those who are in the Skyworld, the Underworld, the
Upstream Region and the Deceivers. They kill it, burn off the hair,

cook it and it is cooked. The woodcutters eat. That is the reason that
they observe a ceremonial idleness in Kiangan.

They brew rice wine. When their wine had become strong, they
danced every night for their wine at Kiangan. They see their kindred
on both sides — every day their shields make walls [like house-walls];
their sooted ones [old spears sooty from hanging over the fireplace]
are like a flock of rice birds. Every day their kindred on both sides
come to visit them.

4. Said Balitok, "What to do ?" says he. I am going to seek a *hupol*
to pacify the spears of the drinkfest guests."[6]

Then Balitok of Kiangan packs betels and tobocco supply, comes
down the outskirts, continues and goes upstream, arrives at Mongayan.
He goes upstream not noting time's passage, arrives at Ampugpug.
He continues upstream, arrives at Bangut; soon he arrives at Pakawol;
passes on to Bayukon, arrives in the Upstream Region. He ascends
to the center of the village. He goes to a house and sticks his spear
into the ground. Wigan is startled.

"Is that thou, Balitok ?"

He descends and sits alongside him.

They exchange betels. "Wherefore hast thou come to my village
in the Upstream Region ?"

Balitok, it is said, answered, "Yes," was his way of answering. "I
go to find *hupol*, for we do not know how to make the ceremonies
preliminary to the prestige feast."

Wigan, it is said, answered, "What then ?" he said. "Climb up to
the Skyworld and go ask Lidum. It's up to whomsoever has a *hupol*."

Balitok agreed. He tucks on his hipbag, pulls up his spear. He
passes by (?) the house of Humidhid of the Upstream Region and
Dinipaaan of the Upstream Region. He passes the house of Ampuhudol in the Upstream Region. He continues and climbs upward,
turns to Adadaiyu, goes to the house of Lidum of the Skyworld. He
sees and comes up. He sticks down his spear and turns to the rice
mortar. Lidum of the Skyworld looks around.

"*Ah nakayah!*" says he. "Why, there is Balitok. Hast come to my
village in the Skyworld ?"

He descends and sits alongside. They exchange betels. They talk a
while.

"Wherefore hast thou come to our village in the Skyworld ?"

"The reason I have come — they say that thou carriest a *hupol*."

Lidum, it is said, answers. "Not so, though. Go to the house of
Punholdayan."

He pulls up his spear, goes up to the house of Punholdayan. He
asks who carries a *hupol*. Said the Punholdayans:

"We have no *hupol*. Go to the house of Hinumbian."

He pulls up his spear, goes not noting time's passage, arrives at the house of Hinumbian, sees it and enters. He thrusts down his spear, turns to the rice-mortar. Hinumbian is startled.

"Why, there is Balitok. Hast come up to my village in the Sky-world?".

They sit side by side and exchange betels. They talk together. Said Balitok,

"Have you here *hupol*?"

"None," he said. "Go up to the house of Monalûtût of the Sky-world."

... (Follows above). Said Balitok, "What about it, Monalutut? I am seeking *hupol*."

Monalutut replied, "Go then," says he, "to the house of Agudum-dum of the Skyworld."

... Agudumdum replied, "Go up to the house of Ampual of the Skyworld and follow his instructions."

... Said Ampual, "None," he says. "There is *hupol*, but get it in the Farther Side of the Skyworld, at the house Wigan of the Farther Side."

Balitok agreed. He pulls up his spear. He sees and goes upward, passes by the house of the Amtalaos, passes the house of the Am-balitians, continues climbing. He passes the house of Intukbon of the Skyworld. Time passes. He keep inquiring. He is directed to the Farther Side of the Skyworld. He continues, it is said, climbing upward. He arrives at the Farther Side of the Skyworld, to the house of Wigan of the Skyworld. He enters sticks down his spear, surveys with his eyes. Wigan of the Farther Side turns around, "*Ah nakayah!*" said Wigan of the Farther Side, "Why, there is Balitok. Hast come up to my village in the Farther Side of the Skyworld?"

Balitok replied, "Because thy *hupol* is renowned. There is a drink-fest at Kiangan. Everyday the spears make a wall and the sooted ones [spears] make a flock of rice birds."

"And hast thou no *hupol*?" says Wigan. Balitok replies affirma-tively [i.e. Yes, I have not].

Mala mo Wigan of the Skyworld. He takes of his planted bamboo, gives it to Balitok.

"There it is," says he. "Take it back for thy *hupol*: it will keep pacifying. And when thou returnest, take a by-path to the house of Thunder (Kidul) of the Skyworld so as to get his betel wood of the Skyworld, for it has served as handles and as stick-spears and will serve you as a pacifier of all kinds of spears. So it will be very good," he says. "The irons of your kindred on both sides will be very weak."

"So much for that, and I will return."

"Come up and eat."

"What I ate in Kiangan is not used up."

He tucks on his hipbag, pulls up his spear, goes and descends. Time passes unnoted. He comes down to the house of Agudumdum. "Already! Balitok?" "Yes," he answers. "I tarried in the Farther Side of the Skyworld." He continues downhill. He comes to the house of Ampual. Time passes unnoted. He descends. He takes a by-path to the house of Thunder, of the Skyworld. He sees it and arrives. He goes up. Thunder is startled. They talk a while.

"Why hast thou come to our village in the Skyworld?"

Balitok answered, "Yes," he says, "They say thou art the one who planted the betels of the Skyworld."

Thunder answered affirmatively". "What wilt thou do with the betels?"

Balitok answered, "We are making a *hupol* for the spears of the drinkfest guests."

Thunder answered affirmatively. "A strong *hupol*, indeed." He sees his betels of the Skyworld. He splits off some of the tree, gives it to Balitok. He plucks off betel nuts, picks pepper vine leaves, combines them with the nuts.

"These leaves and betel nuts will also, indeed, serve you as *hupol*, will act also as suggesters to the drinkfest guests. They will keep quiet, will keep gentle." Balitok answered affirmatively. He (Thunder) takes down also his barbless spear.

"Take this back, too. I do not give you my barbed spear because by and by if there should be a drinkfest, what would I carry when I went to it?"

Balitok agreed again. He accepts them, tucks on his hipbag and continues going downhill. He passes the house of Hinumbian, passes the house of Punholdayan. He goes on descending. He comes to the house of Lidum. Time passes unnoted. He goes downhill. In a little while he descends to Adadaiyu, descends to the Upstream Region. He passes the house of Ampuhudol of the Upstream Region. Soon he passes the house of Dinipaan of the Upstream Region. He arrives at the house of Wigan. Wigan looks up.

"*Ah nakayah*, Balitok! He has obtained the *hupol*."

"I got it," he says.

Said Wigan again, "Take a by-path to the house of Mombohal (Hammerer). He is the one who hammers out the knives so that you add these to thy *hupol*."

Balitok agreed to this also. Nothing else than that in a little while he takes a by-path to the house of Mombohal. Mombohal is surprised.

"Why! is it thou, Balitok?"

"Because I have heard about thy knives in the Upstream Region."

Mombohal descends, sits alongside; they exchange betels. Said Balitok,

"*Ah nakayah!* Thou, they say, hast irons and makest knives."

"What dost thou want with a knife?"

"We will use it for a *hupol.*"

Mombohal agreed. He takes, too, a knife, gives it to Balitok.

"That's the thing — take the knife, take it back to Kiangan. But we must be invoked in the *hupol* rites, because we are strong in *hupol*. Ours it is to *hupol* the knives of the drinkfest guests so that they be weak."

Balitok agrees. He tucks on his hipbag. "So much for that and I will return."

He pulls up his spear, continues and goes downstream, arrives at Bayukan, turns to Pukauwol, goes downstream to Bangut, arrives at Ampugpug. Time passes unnoted, he goes downstream, arrives at Mongayan. Time passes unnoted. He arrives at Kiangan, goes into the center of the village, thrusts down his spear, turns to the rice mortar. In a little while he is cooled off. He enters the house. He takes down his eating basket, begins and finishes.

"What to do?," he says. "Go ahead and add water to the wine."

His co-settlers agreed. They water their wine. At night they sleep. In the morning [when the sun] is half-way, they notify [invite] the kindred on both sides.

5. When the sun is halfway, they take, it is said, a chicken, bring it into the house; get betels and leaves. Put them with the meat, display them [all] on the basket cover, invoke and invoke their ancestral spirits. He invokes the *Halupe* deities. He passes on to the *Halupe* of the Skyworld and *Halupe* of Dukligan and of Namommon and Gonhadan, this Old Man[7] at Dauyahan. He points [them] at the drinkfest guests. He takes the chicken, bleeds it, burns off the feathers, opens it and [the omen] is *nungitib*. He places it on the basket-cover. He myths and myths these *Halupe*. He finishes. He points at the drinkfest guests. He finishes. He takes the components of the *hupol*. He puts them on the basket-cover. He takes the coconut "matting," also the *kumulitit* vine. He invokes this *hupol*. He passes on to [invoking] Thunder of the Skyworld and Wigan of the Farther Side of the Skyworld. He points the irons toward the drinkfest guests:

"In order that also, alas! the drinkfest guests arrive, but be sound the wine-jars and remain unharmed the gongs and remain unharmed the bodies of the drinkfest guests and be quiet the stones and be fixed fast the fence-stakes, so that they be gentle, so that they be occupied with improvised songs and with (arranging) intermarriages and partnership agreements. And the drinkfest will be finished."

He finishes. He takes the irons, too. He wraps them up.[8] He takes, too, the bamboo and dulls its point. He takes the "matting," and wraps it around. He takes the *kamulitilit* vine and ties it [the bundle] up. He swings it for the spears of the drinkfest guests and the knives of the drinkfest guests. He finishes. He puts it by the *bagat* stud of the house frame. Dark the darkness — they sleep.

6. On the morrow [when] half-way, the able-bodied — how they keep coming in as drinkfest guests! They drink and drink the wine. They get drunker and drunker. *Kanadih* the womenfolk, they pacify them, too. They sing *liuliwa* improvisations. Intermarriage is what they talk about. In the evening of the day, they take the drunks. Their fists are clenched tight, they know nothing of their knives and of their spears. Their wives carry them (home) face upward. They go home by night on their way. The fathers and sons at Kiangan are left alone like the heartwood. They finish the drinkfest. And there was no talk.

It was the source of their becoming abundant in life at Kiangan, and of the increase of their rice, the fast growth of their children.

Kalidi! Thou art being mythed but it is not at Kiangan because it is at the house of the children. Only serve as a pacifier of the drinkfest guests, so that they assemble and assemble in the morning — our kindred, the Mampolya-ites, the Hingyonites, the Kababuyanites, the Bitu-ites, the Anao-ites, and the Piwongites. But be gentled the drinkfest guests, so that they will nudge each other [with invitaions to have a drink]. And let it be that we are like suggesting deities, so that their knives are quiet, so that their spears are quiet and songs and trading-partner pacts and improvisations occupy them. And the drinkfest guests become drunker and drunker, but be closed tight their fists and be they unconscious of their knives and be they unconscious of their way so that they be carried home face upward on backs or with one or more at either end by their womankind and children. And we fathers and sons and brothers to each other who have accomplished the drinkfest will be left alone like the sound heartwood of a [rotting] tree!

17. TULUD PINADING: ENEMIES AS OFFERINGS*

Subject: Use of enemies as substitutes for pigs as sacrificial victims. Used: In rites of sorcery and war. Informant: Ngidulu. Recorded and translated by Barton and Bugbug.

SYNOPSIS

Dotdotan of Tolgayan, a wealthy place-spirit (*pinading*), while enthusiastically drunk at some sort of rituals, announces that he will marry his child to the child of Ingaan, another place-spirit who, however, is poverty-stricken. He sends a messenger and his proposal is accepted. Time passes and Dotdotan decides on a prestige feast. Ingaan is under obligation to contribute by sending pigs to be sacrificed at the feast, but he has no pigs to send.

2. Ingaan flies on a long journey trying to borrow pigs from other place-spirits, but one place-spirit sends him to another till, finally, one of them informs him that some people in Balitang have just returned from a headhunting expedition. Ingaan comes to Balitang, to the house of Barton, whose son, Harold, has just returned from a mock headhunt.[1] Informant Ngidulu directs him against our enemies, the people of Humalapap. Ingaan goes as directed and catches the enemies. He then carries them to Dotdotan, his co-father-in-law, where they are hogtied and placed among the pigs awaiting sacrifice. Dotdotan and his kindred are highly pleased and say that the victims Ingaan has brought "lighten up (set off) the rest of the pigs." A period of flourishing welfare ensues.

3. The priest pronounces a fearful curse on our enemies.

THE TULUD

1. Dotdotan of Tolgayan: The sun is half-way; *ngalana* Dotdotan, he calls together his sitters (priests); they assemble, bring fermentable rice, strip it from the straw, take it down from the house, pound it, give it the first winnowing, [pound it some more] and winnow it the second time. They cook it; it boils and they dry it, paddle it out from the pot and cool it.

When it is cool they add the ferment and put it in wide flat baskets and let it ferment. Time passes. On the third day it is strong; they wash a jar and transfer the wine for further fermentation. They walk about (wait a while) at Tolgayan. They add water to the wine and give it one day more.

When the sun is half way, he calls his fathers. They assemble, pour out the wine, pray, invoke the ancestral spirits, change to the messenger gods, invoke the deities and are possessed by them. They finish, bleed the chicken, burn off the feathers, and open it. (The bile-sac is) *binumga*.

Dotdotan is half drunk, boasts of his wealthiness. "Go ye and propose to Ingaan that we pair our children." In the evening they arrive at Dimale. "You two will pair your children in marriage," he says. Ingaan of Dimale sends (back) the go-between who arrives at

Tolgayan and notifies Dotdotan. Dotdotan agrees, sends back the messenger, who informs Ingaan. Said Ingaan, "Did you appoint a day?" "Yes," says he (the messenger). Ingaan agrees.

Time passes. The third day came. "Now is the appointed day." In the evening they put chickens in carrying coops, pigs in carrying frames. The Dimale people set out. Time passes, it is said. They arrive at Tolgayan. Dotdotan looks up. "The children have come." It is night and they sleep.

On the morrow at mid-forenoon, they call the fathers. These assemble, repay (sacrifice to) the *matungulan*, sacrifice to the ancestral souls, make offerings to the Inumbans. They bleed the chickens, burn off the feathers and open them. They see that it is *binumga*. They accept: "It is good — points to the life of those who will marry and the life of their chickens and pigs." They observe a ceremonial idleness. They walk around.

At the same time the rice wine is strong. Dotdotan of Tolgayan calls his fathers who assemble, pour out their wine, invoke their ancestral spirits, change to the messenger gods, also the *matungulan*. They bleed the chicken, burn off the feathers, open it and the bile is *ningayu*. "It is well," they say. "It points indeed, to the life of the children who give a prestige feast." They fire a pot, put in the chicken.

They bring a cock, stand it on the floor, converse with it, and invoke the life of the givers of the drinkfest. They see that the chicken is quiet. They take off the [cooking] chicken, display it on cooked rice, invoke, cut it up and eat. When finished they chew betels. They take [another chicken], bleed it, burn off feathers and open it, see that it is *binumga*. They take [natural] coconut leaf petiole mat, also *tikam* buds[2] and *kamulitilit* vine, invoke the *na-ototbe* deities, pray the "tying" prayer, finish and tie it up, observe a day's ceremonial idleness.

On the morrow at mid-forenoon, they go for wood, finish. Came the eighth day, they brought cane presses. On the ninth day, they press out the sugar cane, on the tenth[3] they called it *latang* (waiting for fermentation). They notify the kindred on both sides. It comes night. Time passes. On the morrow at mid-forenoon, they talk about the drinkfest at Tolgayan. They drink wine, the wine is magically increased. At evening their co-villagers disperse.

At night Ingaan said to his *biyô*, Lingayu, "Tomorrow will be the *punhidan*."[4]

"We shall be shamed," says Lingayu. "We have no pigs or chickens — let us go look for animals to give for the feast."

2. Ingaan agrees. They take a rice basket, prepare strings for it, carry it on the back, go down in their village of Dimale. They fly

from Dimale, shine on the way, go without noting time, and stop at Hinalipan. Tayaban at Hinalipan looks up, "Why are ye there? Ye've come to my village at Hinalipan?" The two *biyô* answer, "We are looking for animals for a prestige feast. Tomorrow is the *punhidan*, we are ashamed before Dotdotan. He has many pigs and chickens." "Go ye then to Balibali."

They fly from Hinalipan, go in a bee-line, drop down at Balibali. Tayaban of Balibali looks up. "Why are ye there? Is it here ye are coming?" "We are looking for animals for a prestige feast." Said Tayaban at Balibali, "Who is making a prestige feast?" "They're making it at Tolgayan. We have nothing to contribute." "Go to (Mount) Head of Bugan." ... They go thither [where the same dialogue occurs]; then on to Alingangga, thence to Atugu. ... Bumidang of Atugu is startled. "Why are ye there?" "We're looking for animals for a prestige feast; tomorrow's the *punhidan*. We're ashamed before Dotdotan — he has many pigs and chickens. "What to do?" he answers. "Go on to Igayun."

They set forth from Itugu, drop down at Igayun, Tayaban of Iyagun looks up. "Why are ye there?" Said the two *biyu*, "Yes, we are looking for animals for a prestige feast, for tomorrow's the *punhidan*." *Mala* Tayaban of Igayun, "Wait a bit, then. Some people have come back from headhunting."

Mala ot Tayaban of Igayun, he takes his spear, walks on the rice dikes at Igayun, turns toward Ibuyan, goes over the ridge at Bilingan, turns toward Maimok, continues to Lapoban, walks the rice dikes at Abat, enters our village at Balitang.

Asks Tayaban, "Names of these who have been headhunting?"

"The Bartons," we answer. "They are these who went spearing. They speared Laptok of Humalapap."

He takes the meat and cooked rice, time passes and he returns. He walks the dikes at Abat, continues to Lanogan, goes on to Maimok, continues to Ibuyan, arrives at Igayun, gives the chicken to them [the two Tayabans who are waiting there], as also the meat. They eat, it is said.

"Whither are they pointing us?" say they.

"They say for you to point toward Humalapap," he says.

He finds (betels) and they chew, turn them red, it is said. They set forth at Igayun, ascend to Ibalyu. Set forth from Ibalyu, go in a bee-line, turn off their fire at their level place at Humidhid, set forth from Humidhid, drop down on their breasts at Humalapap. They see the large tree[5] at Humalapap, kick it, see that it is smashed to pieces.

In a little while, *mala mo* Lingayu, he jumps into the yard. *Mala Ingaan*, he alights at the smoke-hole (of the house). Soon he jumps down to the floor. He sees our enemies, the kindred of the slain man, opens the door, takes the household, closes the door, takes off his backbasket, ties them in it, sets forth toward Palao, goes in a bee-line, alights at Balibali, sets forth at Balibali. . . . alights at Hinalipan, takes down his eating basket.

On the morrow at mid-forenoon, "Let us go to Tolgayan." They put on their backbasket, descend to Tolgayan. They are catching pigs at Tolgayan, they tie them and run a stick between their legs. "What about it ?" they [the two biyu] say. "Untie the backbasket." They untie the cords. They take out what the two *biyu* brought. They tie them up and run a pole between their legs. They place them among the pigs.

Said the Tolgayan people, "Very fine, indeed, these which Lingayu and his *biyu* brought — serve to set off[6] the pigs."

They are possessed by the deities, kill the pigs, cook the belly fats. When cooked, they take them off, spread on cooked rice, invoke, eat, change to betel chewing. . . . They divide the meat, there is plenty of meat. They share it with the kindred on both sides.

That was the reason they abound in life at Tolgayan.

3. We point Ingaan and Lingayu now against our enemies at Humalapap. *Ngala mo* our enemies — he includes even their small babies. There is nothing left of them — no remainder.

Let it be so with our enemies the Tablak and Humalapap people, so that his house is bewitched, but enter it and afflict him so that thou crunch him so that his sickness will be sudden, so that he wails during his recovery feast and death comes suddenly, so that they tighten his g-string, so that he settles in his death chair, so that his children wail violently, so that his sisters on both sides shout to his soul, so that they clay him [in his sepulchre] with a strong flat stone, so that his house be covered with raspberry vines, so that we will pity him. For headfeast is what ye have been prayed.

18. UMALADANG: DYSENTERY IMPS

Subject: Balitok is afflicted by the Umaladang deities. Used: In rites to cure bellyache. Informant: Ngidulu. Recorded and translated by Barton and Bugbug.

SYNOPSIS

1. The *umaladangs* come up from the Sub-Underworld and afflict Balitok with a fearful belly-ache. After sacrificing to no avail, the Ifugaos divine the source of the affliction by means of the diagnosis stick (*agba*). They sacrifice to the *umaladangs*, who immediately remove the sickness.

2. The priest invokes the same promptness of relief in the present instance.

The Myth

1. *Ngalana* Umaladang of the Sub-Underworld and Iniguan, Hinigalan, Monagad, Hagaang, Ulog-na, and Homohomok of the Sub-Underworld: the sun is half-way. Said Umaladang,

"Let us go upstream and participate in tributes,[1] because they are freed from taboos at Kiangan."[2]

They set out from their village in the Sub-Underworld. They take their time, arrive at Ulu, form a group on the rock at Ulu. Said Umaladang,

"Wait till night and we'll go up to Kiangan."

After a little while it is night; they stand to go, go upstream, enter Kiangan. They assemble round the posts of Balitok's house. Nothing else than that next morning they peep from the corners of their eyes at the [place below] the back door of Balitok's house. It is polluted and cluttered with the straw of rice-bundle butts.[3] *Anhan!* their sickness.

They [the Kiangan people] sacrifice pigs and chickens but there is no result. They use the *agba* stick and the *umaladangs* of the Sub-Underworld are indicated. They do not delay. They catch a chicken, take it to the house, invoke their ancestors, change to the messenger gods, invoke and invoke those who are in the Underworld. They finish. They take the chicken, bleed it, singe it and open it up. They see the seed (bile-sac) and it is *nayo*. They accept: "It points indeed to the cure of the sickness." They fire the pot, force the fire, it boils and is cooked. They take the pot off, spread the meat on cooked rice and recite the myths. They finish, invite the deities, eat, finish eating, and put things away. The *umaladangs* smell it: they say, "They did not delay — they are paying us. Let us cure them."

They blow a cure to the Balitoks. They became well, became strong. That was the reason at Kiangan that they acquired chickens and pigs, the reason their pigs and chickens increased. They farm and farm and the crops fruit and are productive. The enemy and evil spirits keep away from them.

2. *Kalidi!* It is not at Kiangan because it is here at Balitang, at the house of the children that we are mything you. Ye who have terribly afflicted the bellies of the children with strong sickness, relieve ye and lighten ye, so that it be cured, so that he resume his [natural] body, so that he live and his chickens and pigs live. And be the enemies and evil spirits turned aside, because *nadulum* is what [i.e. the rite] you are being prayed.[4]

19. COCONUT GROWS FROM BURIED HEAD*

Subject: Origin of the Coconut; affliction from eating its fruit.
Used: In rites to cure headache. Informant: Kumiha.

SYNOPSIS

1. Balitok of Kiangan, finding time heavy on his hands, decides to
go headhunting. He calls his co-villagers; they perform the preliminary rites and set forth.

2. They take the head of Montinig and raise their victorious cries,
but are disconcerted to find that the head shouts with them. They
bury the head so as to get rid of it.

3. Many years later they go back to the place where they buried the
head and find that a coconut has grown up from it. They take the
nuts and drink of their milk, but are afflicted with headaches. Balitok
sacrifices promptly, whereupon the headaches disappear.

COMMENT

The origin of the coconut or of the large grape-fruit (*pomelo*,
tabuyog) from a human head or of a human being from them is a
widespread element in Philippine folklore. Cf. Maxfield and Millington, 1906, page 106.

I will not assume to say that both Ifugao mythology and the Bible
have drawn from the same sources in this myth, though it would seem
that there is ground for raising the question. The Ifugaos are punished
for eating of the fruit of a tree. There are other myths which point
even more definitely to a common source. For example, in one myth,
"The Hill-Farmers," not included in this volume, there is a miraculous catch of fishes which is foreign to the general course and character
of the myth and which reminds one of the Miracle of the Fishes in the
New Testament. There are also the instances included in this volume:
smiting a rock to draw forth water (myths 5 and 6); the "fall" of
Man, (6), and the parting of the waters (7). Villaverde (page 426)
gives a parallel to the Miracle of the Loaves.

THE MYTH

1. *Ngalana* Balitok of Kiangan every day there [only] walking
around in their village of Kiangan. On the morrow at mid-forenoon
he says he will go headhunting in the Downstream region. He takes
a chicken and prays to the *Na-ótótbe*; he consults a cock and it is
silent. "So it will be with the life of us who go headhunting to the
Downstream Region." He takes the chicken and cuts its throat,
bleeds it and burns off the feathers. They open it and the omen is

nungitib. "So let it be, so that we live who go headhunting into the Downstream Region." They observe a ritual idleness. On the third day it was quiet: there were no falling branches or catchings of chickens by hawks. "So let it be in order that we live who go head-hunting into the Downstream Region." They put rice into their backbaskets and the sun is half way, "Let us set out today who go headhunting into the Downstream Region." They tuck on their hipbags, grasp their spears, set out from Kiangan, cross their village at Kiangan. He sees the cockbird — it is on the right side. They go a second time and the response is good. They go downstream toward the Downstream Region, they arrive at the Downstream Region. They build a shack. They chop down a *bultik* tree, set up the posts, lay the ridge pole and build a fire rack, put on the rafters, the runo cross-reeds and the lower runo thatch. They fold the thatch across the ridge pole and trim the lower edge and it is like a bee-line. *Ngalana* Balitok, he takes flint and steel and strikes fire. He exhorts Dizziness and the Crosser of the Way[1] and finishes. There are no fallings of branches or catchings of chickens by hawks. "So let it be so that we live who go headhunting in the Downstream Region." They cook and boil their food. They take it off and eat, then go to sleep. They awake and it is mid-forenoon. They cook and boil, take off the pot and eat, change to betel chewing. They put on their scabbards, and set out from their shack in the Downstream Region. They go toward Boko.

2. Montinig of the Downstream Region, the Head Intruder,[2] comes forth and hurls a spear and they are on the alert. Montinig of the Downstream Region comes forth and they throw a volley from all sides. They lift up the head. They raise their victorious cries and the head of him they speared in the Downstream Region shouts also. Said Balitok.

"What about this head we have speared in the Downstream Region — there it participates in the shouting?"

They go upstream, arrive at their shack. "*Ah nakayah*, let us bury the speared one for why should it shout when we shout?" They bury the head, they finish and go upstream to their village at Kiangan. They arrive at Kiangan. The able-bodied ask them. "Where is your victim, Balitok?" "We didn't bring it because we buried it at our shack because, when we shout, it shouts with us."

3. Time passes at Kiangan without their noting it and after a thousand of years (many), said Balitok of Kiangan, "Let us go see him we speared in the Downstream Region and whom we buried at our shack." They put on their hipbags, grasp their spears and go downstream. They arrive at their shack in the Downstream Region.

They see the speared one whom they buried in the Downstream Region and; "Why there is a tree which has sprouted from the speared one we buried in the Downstream Region." It had fruited and borne clusters of fruits. They climb it and gather its fruits, cut them open and drink their water.

They go upstream to their village at Kiangan. They take their leisure in their village at Kiangan and they are afflicted by the Head Intruders of the Downstream Region. *Ngalana* Bugan, wife of Balitok at Kiangan, how she complains of her head! And Balitok at Kiangan wastes no time. He takes their chicken in their village at Kiangan and invokes these Head Intruders of the Downstream Region. He finishes, he cuts its throat, bleeds it, singes it and breaks it open and the bile is *nuninloya*. He sets it on cooked rice and invokes Montinig of the Downstream Region, the Head Intruders of the Downstream Region and the Tinikmals of the Skyworld and the Tinamatams, and likewise those of the Upstream Region, those of the Downstream Region, those of the Underworld and those of the Skyworld. Montinig and the Head Intruders of the Downstream Region said,

"The Balitoks at Kiangan lost no time and are sacrificing their small chickens at Kiangan to us. Let us blow, blow a cure, so that we relieve Bugan."

And that was the reason that her head was quickly cured, as if it were untied, as if it were dipped up out of water,[3] as if it were mashed-down vegetation rising again.

Kalidi, it is not at Kiangan for it is at Balitang. And ye who have afflicted the (long)-haired one,[4] blow ye, blow a cure so that she will be relieved, so that she will recover like mashed-down vegetation rising again; for there ye are being mythed, ye Tinikmals of the Downstream Region.

20. ORIGIN OF BOILS*

Subject: Origin of boils and skin eruptions. Used: In rites to cure such diseases. Informant: Kumiha. Recorded and translated by: Barton and Bugbug.

SYNOPSIS

1. Bumabakal dies. His neighbors in the Skyworld object to his being set in the death-chair in their neighborhood on account of the stench and tell his kindred to carry him elsewhere. The kindred take him to the Upstream Region, but the people there also object. They take him to the Downstream, then to the Skyworld, then to Kiangan

— everywhere meeting the same objection. Finally they set the body in the deathchair on Mount Dutukan. The fluids from the corpse run into the river at Kiangan and there cause red and white skin eruptions, especially the disease called *gulid*.

2. The Kiangan people resort to the diagnosis stick (*agba*) in order to ascertain the source of the affliction. Bumabakal is indicated. They invoke his head, arms, legs, belly and liver. They perform sacrifices. Bumabakal smells the offerings and sends back a cure.

COMMENT

This ritual invention is probably based on the association of skin troubles with the skin condition of a corpse, exposed in the death chair — the swelling, discolorations and blisters.

The Ifugaos are not especially repelled by corpses, their stench or their fluids, particularly if they be from their own kindred. Indeed, they believe they derive new life and strength from contact with the fluids. The corpse is carried away by relatives on their shoulders — not by the paid corpse-tender who has for several days been going through the motions of keeping the flies away from it. Among the Northern Kankanai, different lineages struggle for the privilege of carrying away a corpse, believing that they thereby gain luck and fortune. I saw the body of a little old woman pitched through the air between young men of the same lineage in order to keep it from falling into the hands of another lineage.

THE MYTH

1. *Ngalana* Umbumabakal: he perishes and dies. They are going to put him in the death-chair. Said the people of the Skyworld,

"Will he not swell and stink in our village of the Skyworld? Take him to the Upstream Region."

They carry Bumabakal to the Upstream Region and stop at the house of Humidhid of the Upstream Region. Said the people of the Upstream Region,

"Let us not set up [we will not permit] the dead one, for soon he will stink in our village of the Upstream Region."

They shoulder Bumabakal, go to the Downstream Region, arrive at the house of the Napulungot ["clustered village"] deities and the Binongbongs. Said the deities.

"Why do you bring the perished one who died? For he will swell and stink in our village of the Downstream Region."

They shoulder Bumabakal and descend to the Underworld. They stop at the house of the Shakers (Yumogyog) of the Underworld.

Said the Underworld people, "Why do you bring the dead one here ? For he will swell and stink in our village of the Underworld."

They shoulder Bumabakal again, go uphill, arrive at Kiangan. Said the Kiangan people, "Why do you bring the perished one who died hither ? Will he not swell and stink in our village of Kiangan ?"

Said the Skyworld people, "Let us take him uphill to the mountain at Dutukan."

They climb to the top at Dutukan, set down Bumabakal. They make a death chair, make a seat [for the corpse], make a trough [for carrying away the fluids that flow from the mouth]. They set up the body on the mountain at Dutukan. The dead one swells. *Mala* the corpse fluids, corpse fluids of the dead one, they are carried by the flood and stop at Kiangan.

2. *Ngalana* the child of Balitok, his boil is terrible, likewise his white inflamations. He suffers from red inflamations too. Balitok does not waste time, he has the fathers resort to the *agba* stick. The dead one is indicated. *Ngalana* Balitok, he does not delay, gets a chicken, brings it home, invokes the ancestral spirits, changes to the messenger gods, invokes this dead one of the Skyworld: the head of Bumabakal and the throat of Bumabakal and the hands of Bumabakal and the feet of Bumabakal, the belly of Bumabakal, the liver of Bumabakal.

He finishes, takes the chicken, bleeds it, singes, opens it, sees that it (the bile sac) is not well-filled,[1] spreads the meat on cooked rice, myths the dead one on the mountain at Dutukan. He finishes, invokes, puts things away. The steam of the chicken goes without disseminating.[2] This dead one of the Skyworld smelled it.

"The Balitoks of Kiangan lost no time in offering me the fattest of their chickens at Kiangan. I will blow, I will relieve, I will cure the child, the son Balitok at Kiangan," [he says].

That was the reason that the white inflamation at Kiangan dried up, their sickness ceased, as if unwound, as if crushed vegetation rising again. They acquire chickens and pigs at Kiangan, turn their attention to the crop; it fruits and is productive. They travel the vegetation-rotted paths, the enemy and eviel spirits stay far from them.

It is not at Kiangan, for it is at Balitang. If ye have afflicted the hair-cutted one [man] with the boil, blow ye so as to relieve, so as to cure, so that his sickness stops and tomorrow he will be like the *lauwod* vine at Da-une and it will dry up, drop like caked mud. There, ye have been mythed, Dead One of the Skyworld.

21. RED SCABBARDS AND BLACK*

Subject: Origin of boils and carbuncles, from the lime fruit. Used: In rites to cure these afflictions. Informant: Ngidulu.

SYNOPSIS

1. A drinkfest at Kiangan is attended by the sons of Pumihol[1] of the Downstream Region and by the sons of Pumihol of the Upstream Region. The former are wearing black scabbards and are seized with envy when they see the fine red narra-wood scabbards of their cousins of the Upstream Region.

2. On returning home to the Downstream Region, the sons of Pumihol express their discontent to their father. He suggests they pay a visit to their kindred in the Upstream region and obtain red narra wood from which to make themselves scabbards. They act on the suggestion and while in the Upstream Region obtain not only the wood but some lime fruits which they give, on their return journey home, to the children in Kiangan so as to afflict the latter with the boils and carbuncles.

3. The children of Kiangan eagerly eat the lime fruits, whereupon Balitok of Kiangan is afflicted. He wastes no time in sacrificing to the Pumihol of both regions; the latter send him a cure, and a period of prosperity follows.

COMMENT

The myth is of the "invented" type and concretizes various beliefs about boils and their cure. It also illustrates how important in the culture of the Ifugaos is their drinkfest. Many myths of this "invented" type have a drinkfest element.

The association of lime-fruits as a factor in the etiology of boils and carbuncles is a magical rather than a physiological or mistaken-physiological concept. Shape, consistency and color of the one are associated with the other.

The following is a list of some of the Pumihol group; it illustrates how myth characters have come to be added to the pantheon:

PUMIHOL AD LAGOD, Twistering of the Downstream Region.

PUMIHOL AD DAIYA, Twistering of the Upstream Region.

HI DUA N OONGA N DI NAK PUMIHOL AD LAGOD, The two children, the sons of Twistering of the Downstream Region.

HI DUA N OONGA N DI NAK PUMIHOL AD DAIYA, The two children, the sons of Twistering of the Upstream Region.

HI NANGIDAUWIHAN-DA N HI BALITOK AD KIANGAN, Him whom they first afflicted, Balitok of Kiangan.

GOGOBAN-NA, Its getting-hot, or His getting-hot.

BUMABALA-NA, Its becoming-inflamed, or His becoming-inflamed.
ALIMUWÔ-NA, Its getting-hot, or His getting-hot.
KUMIYAKI-NA, Its Itchering, or His Itchering.
GUKGUK-NA D DAIYA, His Gourd of-the Upstream Region.
BUNGBUNGAAN AD DAIYA, Fruit of the Upstream Region.
GUGULU-NA D DAIYA, His Lime-Fruit of the Upstream Region.
TABUYUG-NA D DAIYA, His Grape-Fruit of the Upstream Region.
UDDYO-NA D DAIYA, His Narra Wood of the Upstream Region.
PUMILANGAT-NA D DAIYA, His *Young-Hot-Boil*-ering of the Upstream Region.
BUMINTOL-NA D DAIYA, His *Getting-Hard-Like-a-Muscle*-ering of the Upstream Region.
UMINGA, Earering? (Causing a Boil in the Ear?)
TABUNGAO, (a kind of squash) Softening?
HUMAPIPING, Mumpering (causing mumps?; this being causes a swelling "which pinches but does not burst;" I think it need not be mumps only, though *hapiping* is a word applied to mumps).

THE MYTH

1. *Ngalana* the people of Kiangan: they were talking about a drinkfest. "There is a drinkfest in their center at Kiangan," they said. *Ngalana* the children, the sons of Pumihol of the Downstream Region, they scour their adornments, scour their bolos. "Let us attend the drinkfest at Kiangan."

Mala the children, the sons of Pumihol of the Upstream Region: they also say, "Let us attend the drinkfest," they say, "at Kiangan." They also polish their adornments, polish their bolos.

They go downstream from the Upstream Region; the ones from the Downstream Region come upstream. They meet at Kiangan, arrive at the center in Kiangan. At midday they drink wine. The children, the sons of Pumihol of the Upstream Region come forth (from the crowd). They dance in the yard. The children, the sons of Pumihol of the Downstream Region come forth (from the crowd) and also dance. They look sidewise at the scabbards of the children, the sons of Pumihol of the Upstream Region, they stare [at the scabbards]. They see that [the scabbards] are very red.

They stand, it is said, around the wine bowl, drink wine. The children dip up wine, offer it to the children, the sons of Pumihol of the Downstream Region. He does not accept it. Said the child, "Why do ye [act] that way — why are ye sour?" Said the child, the son of Pumihol of the Downstream Region,

"Yes," he says, "for why ye — your scabbards are very red, and here are ours, very black!"

"Why, these scabbards of ours are from the buttresses of the narra tree of the Upstream Region. Return ye to your village in the Downstream Region, and we will return to the Upstream Region, and let us afflict [the people] at Kiangan so that they will sacrifice to us and we will cure them."

2. The children agreed and returned to the Downstream Region, arrived at their village in the Downstream Region. The others also returned to the Upstream Region. Said the children, the sons of Pumihol of the Downstream Region, bringing their scabbards and giving them to their father, "Why is our narra in Downstream Region like this — a black kind — and their narra in the Upstream Region is red ?"

Their father, it is said, responded, "If ye children like, go upstream and make scabbards, for their narra wood in the Upstream Region is very good, because it is, indeed, *ipil* wood."

The children agreed. "Stay here, Father, and we will go up to the Upstream Region."

They put on their scabbards, settle their knives in them, tuck on their hipbags. They set out in the Downstream Region. Time passes unnoted. They arrive at Baliti. They arrive at Tapaya, go upstream to Hapid, pass on to Naduldul, continue to Kaba, arrive without noting time at Kalupakip, arrive at Kituman, continue to Mongayan, continue to Ampugpug, arrive at Kilkil, arrive without noting time at Pakauwol, arrive in the Upstream Region, arrive and enter. The children come to the top.[2]

"Why are ye there — who have come to our village in the Upstream Region ?"

"Yes, we are looking for your narra wood in the Upstream Region."

Said the children, "What do ye want to do with the narra ?"

"We want to make scabbards."

They take axes, go to the buttress of a narra tree, cut out a piece, make scabbards. They finish, carry them back to their village in the Upstream Region. They [happen to] see some fruit trees. "Go get (fruits) so that we may eat them."

"Those can't be eaten — those are what cause boils."

Mala mo the children, sons of Pumihol of the Upstream Region, he climbs the lime tree and brings down, it is said (fruits). The child gives them. "There, take it," he says, "and go by a by-path to Kiangan so as to give it to the children, so that when they get boils they will sacrifice to us."

The children agreed. "So much for that — we will return now." They return, journey without noting time's passage, arrive at Kiangan. *Kanadi* the children, they take a by-path to Kiangan, hide by the fence.

The children, sons of Balitok, are walking about; he reaches out the lime fruits, the children accept, peel and eat them at Kiangan.

3. The result of that, it is said, was nothing else than that Balitok, at night, when they were sleeping, *anhan*! what a sickness he had: a boil, an inflamed hard swelling. They got chickens and pigs for his recovery rites but without results. They resort to the *agba* stick and, it is said, the Pumihol of the Downstream Region and the Pumihol of the Upstream Region are indicated. They waste no time, bring a chicken, take it to the house, invoke the ancestral spirits and messenger gods, invoke these *pumihol* who are in the Downstream Region and in the Upstream Region. They finish, bleed the chicken, singe and open it. They see its "seed" [bile-sac] and it is, it is said, *nayo*. They accept: "It points to the cure of the affliction." They fire a pot, put in the chicken, force the fire, it boils and is cooked and they take it off, spread it on cooked rice and recite myths for the Pumihol of the Downstream Region and those of the Upstream Region and they invite them. The steam goes without disseminating. Those of the Downstream and of the Upstream Regions smelled it.

"They did not delay — they have offered us a chicken at Kiangan. Let us return them a cure."

That is the reason why the Balitoks, their boils are dried up, turn to ash-color, they recover their natural body. They acquire chickens and pigs. They farm and farm, [their crops] fruit and are productive and the enemies and evil spirits are kept far away, and they themselves become like the central *pango* bead in a string; become like a clump of giant bamboo.

Kalidi, you are being mythed so that if ye be the ones who have afflicted the haircutted one [man], why relieve him, cure him, so that he gets well, becomes able-bodied, regains his normal body — and for his life, the life of his pigs and chickens the shunting aside of the enemy and evil spirits. Because ye are invoked the *nadulum*.

22. NUMPOLOD: THE SELF-CUT

Subject: Balitok's sons learn from a python how to cure wounds. Used: In rites for snakebite and wounds. Informant: Ngidulu.

SYNOPSIS

1. Balitok of Kiangan, with his kindred and sons go hunting. The dogs bay at a python and Balitok's party kill it and cut it up. They build a shack at the site of the kill and, leaving Balitok's two young sons to guard the python meat, continue to hunt.

2. The python's mate gathers a healing grass and goes to the shack.

Balitok's sons in great fright climb upon the shack's cross-girder. The snake goes to the pieces of its mate, nudges them together, licks them and applies the grass. The pieces join, the snake comes to life,: and the two snakes crawl away.

3. The children try out the healing properties of the grass they saw used, by cutting a leg off the game shelf; they rub the leg with grass and it become whole again.

4. Balitok and party come home from the hunt. The boys tell what happened but are not believed, and Balitok scolds them about the absence of the python meat and accused them of having eaten some and thrown the rest away.

5. In proof of their story, one of the boys cuts off his arm, then causes it to grow back by means of the grass and by spitting betel juice on it.

6. Balitok becomes famous as a healer of snakebite, receives many fees and becomes wealthy. The priest invokes a similar cure for the present case of snakebite.

COMMENT

The myth takes its name, "Self-Cut," from the act of the boy in cutting off his own arm. The essential theme of this myth has an exceedingly wide distribution in the conception of jointed snakes that fly to pieces and reassemble, or of snakes that reunite after having been cut to pieces, as, from Illinois: "If you cut up a certain kind of snake, the pieces will unite again and the snake will crawl away." (Hyatt, 1935, No. 1597). A very similar myth is found among the Nabaloi (Moss, C. R. 1920b, page 326). The Khasi have a myth that is remotely similar.

THE MYTH

1. Balitok of Kiangan: his dogs were catching [pigs and chickens] with their mouths. The neighbors exclaim, "Why dost thou not take them hunting, Balitok?" He calls the leader [and ties him up], throws out chicken feed, chooses the biggest and fattest, takes it to his house, invokes his ancestral spirits, changes to the messenger deities, invokes the gods of reproduction, changes to the *Naóthe* gods. He bleeds the chicken, singes it, breaks it open, sees that [the bile is] *nungitib*. "We will live, we who go hunting." They fire a kettle-skillet, put in the chicken and fire and it is cooked ... They observe a ceremonial idleness for one day. On the morrow, when [the sun is] halfway, the Kiangan men eat, put on their scabbards, slip on their backbaskets, take down their *gayang* spears, their *balabog* spears, untie the leader of the dogs. They go to their hills, they look up to

the cock bird [omen bird]. He gives a rapid cry, he sounded his cry. Balitok "clinched" it: "It is our life who go hunting": they went a second time. It was just the same. They go to their observation place, stick down their spears, take off their g-strings, give each other betels and betel leaves; they chew, it is said, betels, they spit and it is red, they tuck on their g-strings, pull up their spears, enter their forest. After a little while the dogs bay, bay at a python. Balitok and party push the grass aside, they spear the python, it drops over and is dead. They cut it in two, carry it to the open place at a bend in the ridge, they build an *apal* shak. They finish it, trim the eaves' edges to a bee-line. They cut up their quarry, put it on the game-shelf. At night they sleep. In the morning when [the sun is] half-way they go to their forest. There were the two children: "Stay ye here," said Balitok, "stay here in the *apal* shack." They enter their forest. They take their time on the mountain. [The dogs] bayed at a wild pig. They run all over their forest at Kiangan.

2. *Mala*, it is said the mate of the python — it pulls a (kind of) grass. It goes to the *apal* shack, it arrives and enters. The children, sons of Balitok, cried "Inay!" They climbed to the pole across the hut, perched there motionless with fear, they looked down [on what happened]. The python it is said climbed up on the game-shelf, nosed (nudged) off the quarry, and [the pieces] fell to the floor. He (the python) took the grass, licked and licked the pieces of meat. The children saw the meat join, crawl together [and become] a snake, the veins and skin reunited. The snakes crawl away and the children come down; they look upon the grass the snake brought.

3. They take a bolo, they step on to the game-shelf; they cut off a leg of it. They grasp a handful of grass, they take the grass and rub (the cut-off leg). They see that its veins and skin reunite. The children laugh.

4. After a little while Balitok and his party bring down their quarry, they carry it, a man at each end of it, they put a pole between its legs, carry it on their shoulders, coming toward the *apal* shack, they arrive and enter. Said the children.

"Our python that we killed is no longer here. Its mate came and applied grass to it and the python woke up; [its pieces] crawled together and the two of them crawled away!"

They were scolded and scolded, the children: "These children know a lot! I suppose you ate a little and, thinking you'd be scolded for it, threw the rest away."

5. *Kanadih* Balitok, caught the children by the hair and shook them. [One of the] children, it is said, cried. He [the child] seized his knife, put it on his other arm, cut off his arm, he looks on it and it is

fallen on the ground. He grasps his arm and brings it to apposition [with the stump] picks up the grass and wraps it around the severed arm, chews betel nuts, betel leaves. He sees that it joins, that the veins and skin reunite. Balitok examines carefully and "Indeed it is true that the python came and grassed its mate, made it alive and they went away." They prepare food, cook, they take it off, "dry" it and dish it out. They eat, finish, put things away, change to betels, take the meat, put it in backbaskets, carry it to Kiangan. They eat the quarry in a general feast.

6. *Ngalana* a Kiangan man, he is bitten by a snake. Balitok did not wait. He takes the grass, goes to the person bitten by the snake, a co-settler at Kiangan. He chews betels, invokes these *tugtugmu* (powers?) which are the python and the Self-Cut. He spits the first betel juice on the snake-bite, turns to the grass, presses it on the snake-bite.

The pain, it is said, immediately ceases, the veins and skin reunite, his body is restored. *Kanadi moh* Balitok, [he treats] both sides of his kindred who heard from each other about Balitok whose grass was strong. It is the reason for his getting pigs and chickens and irons so that it [spelled] the increase of his pigs and chickens, the increase, also, of the rice and the life of his children.

Kalidi! Thou art mythed this myth of ours which is at Kiangan, but [cure ye by] *tugtugmu* the snake-bitten, but pushing out the pain so that the pain ceases and the ache of it, so that it be like the betel vine on the mountain, which dries up and shrivels because *hoplad* ceremony which is *tugtugmu* is what ye are being prayed.

23. KAHLANGAN: DIFFICULT BIRTH*

Subject: Difficult birth caused by a log of wood cut by Kahlangan. Used: In birth rituals. Informant: Ngidulu. Recorded and translated by Barton and Bugbug.

Synopsis

1. Kahlangan of Tinok takes his axe and goes to the forest, where he cuts down and trims a log of the *buhlong* tree, which resembles the "slippery elm" of the temperate zones. He tosses it down the hillside. It slides into the river, is carried by the current and stops under the house of Balitok of Kiangan, whose wife is in labor. Delivery is thereupon delayed. The priests employ the *agba*, or divination stick, to ascertain the cause of delayed delivery and it indicates Kahlangan of Tinok.

2. They lose no time in making the proper sacrifices. Kahlangan perceives that his log has reached a woman in labor and that the

proper sacrifices are being made to him. He goes down to Kiangan and removes the log, whereupon, to the surprise of the woman's companion, birth is immediately accomplished. Also the "blanket and house" of the child, (the placenta) emerges immediately. The priest invokes a similar happy result in the case for which he is reciting the myth.[1]

THE MYTH

1. Kahlangan of Tinok, when the sun is halfway, sees his axe in the Upstream Region, puts on his scabbard, takes his spear from its pegs, descends from his house in the Upstream region. He goes without noting time through his village of Tinok. He sees their forest at Gonhadan. He crosses the outskirts of the village and, not noting time, fords the river. He enters their forest at Gonhadan, scrutinizes a tree on the mountain. He chops it on the uphill side and fells it. He trims the trunk and strips off its bark. He finishes. After a little he tosses the trunk, notes that it reaches the river and is carried by the current. The log takes its time and finally arrives at Kiangan, where it slides up under the house of Balitok.

2. At this time Bugan, the wife of Balitok, is confined, in labor, giving birth. She sees that birth is delayed. The fathers used the *agba* stick and Kahlangan of Tinok is indicated by it. °

They waste no time, bring a chicken, take it to the house, invoke the ancestral spirits, change to the messenger gods, invoke Kahlangan at Tinok. They finish invoking, bleed the chicken, singe it, break it open, see that the bile omen is of the *numboga* kind.

They put fire under a pot, put in the chicken, bring it to boil furiously, it boils and is cooked. They take it off, put it on top of cooked rice, and recite the myth of Kahlangan of Tinok who chopped down a tree. They invoke.

Kahlangan of Tinok heard. Said Kahlangan of Tinok, "My log has encountered somebody." He goes down in his village at Tinok, takes his spear, goes leisurely down-streamward. After a little while he arrives at Kiangan. He comes up to the center, to the house of Balitok. Balitok notices him. "Here is a man."

He goes down and sits alongside, they give each other betels. Kahlangan stands to go. He walks round about at Kiangan. He draws away his tree trunk.

Ah nakayah, the longhaired one who was in labor! That was the reason why she gave birth quickly to her friend;[2] the reason why it came out quickly, why its blanket, its house accompanied it. Her companions utter exclamations, those around are astonished and ask each other questions.[3]

That was the reason why, in their village at Kiangan, they flourished, and their pigs and chickens flourished, and their enemies and the evil spirits were turned aside.

Kalidi, for ye at Tinok are being mythed. Ye who afflicted and blocked the long-haired one who is giving birth, relieve her ye, so that it will quickly emerge and its blanket and house will accompany, so that her companions will exclaim and the bystanders will wonder, so that these people will live and their pigs and chickens will live, so that the enemy and the evil spirits will be turned aside; because ye at Tinok are being mythed with these myths of ours.

24. HIBOLUT: BELLY-SICKNESS

Subject: Affliction of Balitok at a prestige feast. Used: In rites to cure belly-sickness. Informant: Ngidulu.

SYNOPSIS

1. Balitok of Pindungan sees that his pigs are growing tusks. His father advises him to utilize them as sacrifices for a prestige feast.

2. Detailed account of the rites preliminary to the prestige feast.

3. Binlang of Tukyudan hears about the prestige feast and attends its drinkfest. So also does Balitok of Kiangan. Binlang enters the dancing ring and dances. Balitok addresses an insulting speech to him. Binlang threatens Balitok and returns home. That night Bugan, the wife of Balitok, is seized with a terrible bowel sickness. Balitok loses no time in sacrificing to Binlang, whereupon his wife recovers.

COMMENT

This myth is analogous to that of Pumihol (No. 20). Likewise the incidents of this myth, just as in that one, are regarded as entities which must be worshipped by prayer and sacrifice. Binlang may possibly be derived from the root *bolang* meaning "to let down." Besides myth incidents and characters, there are a great number of other *hibolut*: hibolut of the grass, of the chickens, of the pigs, of the dogs, "of our human companions" and so on. The Ifugao pessimistically sees a belly-ache in everything.

THE MYTH

1. *Ngalana* Balitok, son of Ambahingauwon, in his center at Pindungan: he sees that his pigs are growing tusks. Said his father Ambahingauwon, "What about it Balitok? The pigs are growing tusks. Better give a prestige feast so that our wealth in our village of Kiangan be heard about."[1]

13*

2. Balitok agrees. He sees that he has rice wine fermenting and puts it in a jar. At mid-forenoon he calls his fathers. They assemble in the center at Pindungan, pour out wine, keep dipping it up while they are being possessed by the deities, while they are acting the role of deities. They finish, bleed the chickens, singe and break them open, and the bile is *nungitib* and good. Ambahingauwon accepts, "So let it be," he says, "It points and indicates the accomplishment of our prestige feast."

They invoke the *Matungulan* deities and the *Na-ototbe*, sacrificing for the prestige feast. They bring up a cock and consult it, as an oracle. Good — it kept quiet. They take the chicken below and change it for a little chicken, which they bleed, singe and open. Good — it is *nungitib*. Balitok accepted. "It is good," he says, "We will now make the prestige feast." They observe a ceremonial idleness. At nightfall there has been no falling of limbs nor catching of chickens by hawks — it is quiet and night comes.

They sleep at night. At mid-forenoon of the morrow, they strike the gongs, gong their way to get *bultik* wood. They cut it down and chop it into sections. They distribute it and carry it home to Pindungan and divide it among the people. They catch a pig, take it to the house, sacrifice to the *na-ototbe* of the Skyworld, the Underworld and the Upstream Region. Lubog, Manahaut, Sun and Moon come down.[2] They finish, stick the pig, burn off its hair, open it up, cut the meat into large pieces: They fire a kettle skillet, put the meat in it, add fuel, force the fire. It boils and is cooked. They take out the meat, put it on cooked rice. The men eat.[3] When finished they chew betels. The men of Pindungan disperse. All of them pound fermentable rice, winnow it, take it to the house, roast it,[4] cook it. When boiled they roast it by the fire, dip it out into winnowing trays and cool it.

In the evening, they call for Balitok, he sprinkles the yeast back and forth on the fermentable rice and they set it to brew. At night Balitok, son of Ambahingauwon, and companions perform the rites for observing the prohibitions for the prestige feast.[5] They play the gongs and dance.

Came the eighth day, Balitok said, "We will set up the post of the cane press, today." His fathers agreed. They sound the march-gongs, gonging their way to the *bultik*. They chop the trees down, trim off the branches, carry them home to Pindungan. They dig a hole for the main post, carve out tongues, set the posts, erect the press. Balitok approves. He calls the fathers, they catch a large pig, tie it, take it to the house. They "branch" their prestige feast[6]. .... (They sacrifice and kill the pig in the usual way.) ...

The men go home. All day they work on the sugar cane presses.

They work into the night. On the morrow at mid-forenoon, "We will get sugar cane today." They go forth with gongs. They gong the sugar cane. They cut the cane, strip it and bundle it, carry it to Pindungan and help each other with it. They cut it into sections, peel off the cortex, bring up chickens, and "branch" the prestige feast. It was well, no bad event, and they work at the cane presses all day.

Comes nightfall. They stay up all night, counting the kindred on both sides to be invited.[7] On the morn of the next day, *mala mo* their "servants,"[8] who must be dirty and dirty, go forth to the kindred on both sides and notify (invite).

3. By evening, everybody has heard [about the feast]. Binlang of Tukyudan heard about it.

"Tomorrow," says he, "will be the drinkfest of the prestige feast of the Balitoks at Pindungan." They get ready betels and betel leaves, burn lime for them. They repair their scabbard belts, put new rattan ferrules on their spear handles.

It was the same with Balitok of Kiangan, who had heard of the prestige feast of Balitok (of Pindungan): "Let us go to their drinkfest at their center in Pindungan tomorrow." His fathers agreed. They gather betels and at night the young folk gather in the center at Pindungan. They bring down wine [from the house] and pour it into a receptacle. They invoke the *na-ototbe*; they call the deities to possess them, they keep singing the *alim*, do not sleep the whole night. On the morrow at mid-forenoon, they sound their gongs [and set forth].

Said Binlang, in their village at Tukyudan, "Let us go to the drinkfest today."

They pack their betels, go down to the river, clean their jewels, scour their spears of all kinds, go through Pindungan, arrive at the center in Pindungan. They sound their gongs, come to the dancing place, stand around the places under the houses. They pour out wine and drink.

The sun is half way in Kiangan. Said Balitok, "Today is the drinkfest in Pindungan." He calls his co-villagers. They go down to the river, cross to the other side, scour their spears of all kinds, cross the Amdangal tributary, ascend to Pindungan, arrive in the center at Pindungan, play the gongs. They stand around the edge of the dancing place. They go under the houses and drink. About noon they are half drunk. Binlang appears in the dancing place, circles around and dances, and Balitok addresses a speech:[9]

"*Kana katog* Binlang of Tukyudan, who wears a scabbard of palm leaves and coiled vines[10] in place of brass coils, his belly-ache is strong in their village of Tukyudan."

And Binlang roared with anger, "Indeed it is well-known that my belly-ache is strong in our village of Tukyudan, and why dost thou mention it, Balitok ? Thou wilt return to thy village of Kiangan, but if anyone has a terrible condition of his stomach, if it rumbles, if it rattles with wind, we are the ones to whom he must sacrifice meat and rice and it will be well [with him]."

Balitok answered affirmatively and at evening Binlang said, "We will return to Tukyudan," and Balitok also said, "Where are ye, my co-villagers ? Let us return to Kiangan."

His co-villagers agreed and Balitok's party go downstreamward. They arrive at Kiangan and it is the evening of the day and the Balitoks eat and sleep. In the middle of the night, fathers and sons awaken, and *nakayah*! Bugan, wife of Balitok has a frightful belly-ache; she turns over and over.

And Balitok said, "That is what the man said yesterday," and he takes meat and cooked rice and they display the things[11] and he invokes Binlang at Tukyudan and finishes and he recites myths.

They finish and Binlang smelled [the offerings] and her stomach is relieved; it is as if untied; the enemy and evil spirits are turned aside from their village at Kiangan. They become like a clump of the giant bamboo, become like a spreading *baliti* tree, in their center at Kiangan.

Kalidi it is not at Kiangan where I am mything you, because it is at our house in Balitang.

25. TULUD OPA: RITE FOR RETURNING SOUL*

Subject: Wigan brings back the soul of a woman who is giving birth. Used: In birth-rites. Informant: Ngidulu.

SYNOPSIS

1. Wigan, of the Skyworld, hears the priest's invocation and reasons therefrom that some Ifugao's soul must have been stolen. He procures betels, puts wine in a jar and goes across the heavens to the house of Manahaut [Deceiver]. Manahaut is not at home, so he goes on to the village of the *pahang* deities, who stand all clustered around something. Wigan offers them betels, but they come to get these one at a time. He offers them wine, but even for wine they come only one at a time. He thinks of a ruse: he breaks his string of beads. This trick works, for the *pahang* deities all rush to pick up the beads, whereupon, a woman's stolen soul about which they had been clustered, becomes "as plain to be seen as the turban on a man's head." Wigan rushes the soul to the edge of the village, then returns

to get its beads. He destroys the soul's garden so that it will not think of returning on account of its possessions.

2. Wigan asks the soul where it lives and is told that its home is Balitang, where the myth was being recorded. The soul refuses to descend on a rope, lest it be blown to some other village, or on a field drag, lest it slide to some other village. Finally it consents to descend on a spear. The spear turns into a stairway leading down to the mountains to the east of Balitang. On reaching the earth, the soul balks at going further, but Wigan hustles it along to its home and tells it to stay in its "sooty" house. He carries back to the Skyworld a lot of gifts for the *Pahang* deities so that they will have no hard feelings over the matter and will send down a cure for the difficult birth.

3. The result is that the "friend" (foetus) travels quickly, accompanied by his "blanket," (the placenta); the mother recovers her natural body and in general, everything becomes well with them.[1]

THE TULUD

1. Wigan of the Skyworld: the sun is half way and spake Wigan; "*Kana*, an Ifugao is calling to our village in the Skyworld—probably they have tricked the soul of an Ifugao."

He goes down to his houseground in the Skyworld. He sees his climbing pole for betel leaves,[2] sets it up and props it [against the tree on which the betel vine grows]. He climbs up it, arrives at the top, pinches off the choicest leaves and flower spikes, fills up his hipbag, slides down to the houseground. He sees his betels in the Skyworld, climbs up, arrives at the first cluster, jerks it off, slides down to the houseground, goes to his house, plucks off the fruit, fills his hipbag.

He goes into the house, takes down his wine, pours it out into a *guling* jar, finishes, puts on the cover, tucks on his hipbag, puts on his knife, takes his spear, descends. *Mala* it is said, Wigan of the Skyworld, he directs his steps to the house of Manahaut (Deceiver). He sees that the ladder is removed from the door.[3]

He climbs up the steep at Nagangal, changes toward Binggayon, climbs at Tikidon, arrives at the top of Holdangan.[4] He sees the house of Aginaya at Holdangon and Indungdung at Holdanan. *Kaya*! the males of the Pahang deities have gathered and also their womenfolk. They are playing gongs. Wigan enters the village, thrusts down his spear, sits on the rice mortar, untucks his hipbag, takes out betels and betel leaves.

They come one by one to ask betels from him and each returns to his sitting place. He goes up into the house, takes a wine bowl, pours out wine and raises the cup. They come one by one to drink, and each returns to his sitting place.

"How shall I deceive them ?"

Wigan stands up, goes into the yard, breaks his [string of] jewels. They are scattered all over the houseyard. Said the menfolk and womenfolk of the Pahang,

"Alas for Wigan's jewels!"

They rush in a body to the houseyard, search the ground carefully [for the beads]. The soul of the (long)-haired one is [then] as plain to be seen as a turban. Wigan goes under the house, takes it by the hand and draws it rapidly to the edge of the village. Wigan returns, sees the jewels, gathers and strings them, he sees that they are all there, he finds what it (the soul) has planted — taro, sugar cane, yams and bananas. He pulls them up and spreads them in the sun.

"I do it thus so that it [the soul] will not look backward."

2. He takes the haired one who was giving birth homeward. He gives her all her personal effects. They come out upon the top-place.[5]

"Where is thy house ?"

Said the haired one, "Our house is in Balitang."

"Where is thy top-place ?"

"Our top-place is at Madinayup" [top of mountain east of Balitang].

"How wilt thou go — by my rope of the Skyworld ?"

Said the haired one, "I won't go down the rope lest it be blown aside and lead to a strange village and I be lost."

"How wilt thou travel [downward] ? On my rice field drag, so as to slide down ?"

"I will not go on the drag, because it will swerve and go to a strange village and I shall be lost."

Said Wigan, "Well, then, my spear of the Skyworld ?"

The haired one answered, "All right, then, the spear: my grandfather carried a spear in former times."

He pulls up his spear [from where it has been standing stuck in the ground], turns it around and shoves it down on Madinayup. It (the soul) looks downward, it is said, and it (the spear) has turned into footholes like kettles.[6] The haired one descends, stops on Madinayu, is lazy (hesitant, unwilling) about going further, sits on the top-place at Madinayup. Said Wigan,

"Why, then, will it go back ?"

Wigan descends and asks the haired-one, "Where is thy house ?"

"Our house is at Balitang."

"Let's go; lead thou the way."

The haired one stands to go. They follow the ridge at Ibalyu, come to Montubinok, come out [of the forest] at Anuling, descend at

Dayakut, continue to Nahalantukan, cross to Nunbalabag, enter here at our village of Balitang. Said Wigan.

"Look, thou, indeed. Here thou art, at thy sooty house."[7] Let them prepare gifts, thy fathers."

He takes chicken meat and rice and betels and betel leaves and wine and goes outside. He ascends into the Skyworld. He adds bananas and rattan fruits and Wigan takes his time. He ascends at Nagangal, comes to Binggayan, climbs at Tikidan, arrives at Holdangon. He sees that they have not dispersed home — these menfolk of the Pahang and womenfolk of the Pahang. He divides the chicken meat and cooked rice and puts down a portion for each. They share it and none are left out; they have accepted it from Wigan. They send down a cure, cure the haired one.

3. That was the reason that the friend came out quickly, accompanied by its blanket, its house. It startles [with its squalling] her companions, too; those around her ask each other questions.[8]

That was the reason, too, that the haired one was quickly cured, recovered; it was the reason of her life, of the turning aside of the enemies and evil spirits, of the life of her pigs, her chickens.

Kalidi for you messenger gods are being mythed, but return ye home the soul of the haired one, so that her bad feeling, her indisposedness be removed, so that she recover her natural body, for ye have been mythed these our myths, ye *monkontad*.

26. MINULING: LIKE A HARDSTONE

Subject: Hardstone overcomes Softstone. Used: In war rites and sorcery. Informant: Kumiha.

Synopsis

1. Hardstone of Hunduan brews rice wine, becomes drunk and shouts in the manner peculiar to drunken Ifugaos. Softstone echoes these shouts. This offends Hardstone, who considers that he, being the stronger of the two, should be the only one to shout. Softstone does not admit this argument and Hardstone challenges him to a duel.

2. The two slide down to the river and each paves one side of the river bed. Hardstone orders Sun to cease shining and Rain to pour down. The floodhead comes rushing, straightening curves in the river channel and carrying down great trees whose uprooted ends reach out like hands. Hardstone lifts his spear, challenges the floodhead and frightens it into passing on the other side, over the place paved by Softstone. Softstone is destroyed completely and the priest utters a *fiat* against his enemies, invoking a similar destruction upon them.

Hardstone is not, however, satisfied with the complete destruction of his enemy, and calls on the rain to pour down a second time so as to completely destroy his enemy again!

3. Hardstone returns home, brews wine and performs sorcery against his enemy. The few of the Softstones that come home become like brothers and uncles to him and he distributes among them the soft bones (cartilages) of the animals he has slain in his sorcery rites so that the Softstones will become softer. Breaking the taboo against eating an enemy's food completely destroys the Softstones a third time, so that their kindred who escape this third complete destruction cover their houses with wild raspberry vines [so that the dead will prick their fingers if they come back as ghosts and try to get into their houses] and with *balanti* wood used in their *himong* ceremonies.

4. For this reason the Hardstones began to acquire pigs and chickens, had no crop failures, and their enemies and the evil spirits were shunted aside. The priest calls down on his enemies no less destruction than that depicted above, and seeks the same prosperity as that enjoyed by the Hardstones for those in Balitang for whom he is officiating.

COMMENT

This is a typical example of the myths of the "contest" type.

THE MYTH

1. *Ngalana* Muling of Hunduan: he is walking about his village in Hunduan every day. He sees that his fields in Hunduan have a heavy growth of grass, so he works them. He finishes. "I will brew wine. I will perform sorcery."

He brews wine and gives it time to ferment. On the morrow, when the sun is half-way, "I am going to make sorcery in my village of Hunduan." He pours wine and keeps dipping it from a wooden bowl in his village of Hunduan. He goes down out of his house. The sound of his "*guwai!*"[1] is very loud. Softstone of Takap answers and imitates them. Said Hardstone, "Thou art not, indeed, equal to me, because I am the one they (the Ifugaos) call on in sorcery rites, duels and controversies."

Balugabog answered, "It is the same with me: they also call on me in sorcery rites, duels and controversies."

Hardstone responded; they would, he said, go down to the river, "so that we have a duel."

Softstone agreed. *Ngalana* Hardstone, he goes up into his house. *Ngalana* Softstone, he begins to slide one after another down to Dalilig, on the other side from Hunduan. Hardstone came down from his house. "Look thou! Thou art not equal to me. I am the one in my village at Hunduan, whom they call on in sorcery rites, duels and controversies."

Softstone responds in the same spirit. Said Hardstone, "Go across the sand, so that we have a trial of strength." Softstone agreed. *Ngalana* Softstone, he crosses the sand. *Ngalana* Hardstone, he takes sorcery and a turning-aside talisman.[2] He puts them between g-string and body, tucks on his hipbag, takes spear in hand, crosses the sand.

2. They line up on either side. They exchange challenges. Said Hardstone, "Thou art not equal to me." Softstone answered in the same spirit.

Ngalana Hardstone, "Thou, Sunshine, quit shining. Thou Thunder, give forth sharp cracks and roll, so that thou turn on the Rain of the Upstream Region."

Ngalana Thunder, he gives sharp cracks and rolls, turns on the Rain of the Upstream Region, the Rain at Binahagan. It comes down in torrents, swirls down the creeks.

Ngalana the Flood roars downstreamward, straightens out the curves [in the channel], carries on his head the uprooted tree butts; arrived at Hunduan it reaches out with its myriad hands [i.e. the tree roots].

Said Hardstone, "Where art thou, Softstone? Don't run away. Let us wait the Flood for it has come to Hunduan."

Softstone agreed. *Ngalana* Hardstone, he takes his spear, shouts at the rolling edge of the waters,

"Don't pass over me! Thy path is over my enemy, the Softstone."

Ngalana the rolling edge, turns sidewise to the other side, where Softstone lies. It overwhelms him, he turns head to the Downstream Region, feet to the Upstream Region.

Fiat: There is no remainder of him, nothing left of him. Let it be so with the center of our enemies, the Humalapap people, so that there arrive unto him the Manalidals[3] of the Upstream Region and the Umaladangs of the Sub-underworld[4] so that they crunch him, so that sudden his sickness, so that he lies sick a long time in his house, so that he sleeps through his recovery rites and suddenly dies, so that they tie his body with a new g-string,[5] so that his women-folk wail and wail, so that he settles in his death-chair, so that his kindred on both sides raise death cries! They wall him up in his sepulchre with a strong tombstone and we will keep hearing of it, we will pity under the half-way sun, for there ye are being raised up (invoked? aroused?; literally, as above) these whom we invoke at Hunduan.

Ngalana Hardstone, he sees that his enemies the Softstones are scattered in a pool, scattered in a cataract. Said Hardstone, "Thou, again, Thunder, give forth sharp cracks and roll so that thou turn on the Rain of the Upstream Region, the Rain of Binahagan."

It is said it pours down, emptied as from aqueducts in the Upstream Region, emptied at Binahagan, swirls down the creeks, comes downstreamward, straightens out the curves. Carried on its head are uprooted *gakad* (vines) and *tukamug* trees; arrived at Hunduan it reaches out its myriad hands.

Ngalana the Softstone, he is overwhelmed and lost, one after the other, only the dust of them is left; they disappear in the chinks between other stones, go in between them.

3. *Ngalana* Hardstone, "I will go home to my village at Hunduan. He tucks on his hipbag, belts on his scabbard, takes spear in hand, goes home to Hunduan.

"I have put my enemy to flight, I will brew rice wine, I will make welfare rites in my village at Hunduan."

He brings fermentable rice, strips it, takes it down below, pounds it, winnows it twice, heats up a kettle-skillet, puts in water, puts in the rice, forces the fire and it is boiled. He lets it roast dry, paddles it out, spreads it in winnowing trays, cools it, sprinkles on yeast, puts it aside to brew, puts a jar underneath to catch the drippings. Three days pass. He takes [the malt] from the basket and puts it into a jar. He waits (for completing of fermentation). He adds water. At nightfall, "I will now make welfare rites." He calls his fathers, his companions at Hunduan.

They gather and gather, pour out wine, catch pigs, tie them up, trammel them. They invoke the ancestral spirits, change to the messenger gods, invoke the *matungulan*, those of the Skyworld, the Underworld, the Upstream Region and the Downstream Region, Deceiver, the Sun, the Moon, those at Kiangan[6] — the source of their multiplication. They are possessed by the deities. They pour oblations on the pigs. They finish, kill the pigs, singe them, open them up, take the lower belly fat, fire a kettle-skillet, put in water, put in the meat. They force the fire, it boils and is cooked, they take it off, spread the meat on cooked rice. They recite myths about those of the Skyworld, those at Kiangan, Deceiver, Sun, Moon, the source of bad omens who are of the Skyworld, those who are at Kiangan. They invoke them. They sacrifice to all of them. They finish. They divide the meat.

Ngalana the remainder of the Softstones, the enemies of Hardstone at Hunduan, they come home, some of them become like fathers (to Hardstone), others become like brothers. They (the Hardstones) take the knee joints [of the sacrificed animals] and the cartilages, distribute them to the remainder, to the widowed wearing mourning bands. The Hardstones take food baskets, they spoon up [the food] from the baskets, finish, put things away, change to betels, chew betels, lime their quids, spit and the spittle is red and thick.

They bring meat, divide it into small pieces. They take the knee joints and *puu*[7] and take it to the remainder, the widowed and wearers of the mourning bands.

In the middle of the night, *ngalana* the remainder wearing mourning bands and the widowed, they ran away one by one. Some fell (over cliffs). Others became big-bellied (from enlarged spleen) and others became big-bellied [in some other way]. There is no remainder, nothing left of them, they have filled up the chinks, gone in between [other stones]. In the middle of the night, those shouting to the souls slide off,[8] and also the wailers. On the morn of the morrow, Hardstone comes down from his house. He peeps and peeps at his enemies.

In every direction are death chairs. The wearers of the mourning bands and the widows stand back to back. Said Hardstone, "Are there any more of you enemies of mine there?" There was no answer, no sound [in response]. Their houses are covered over with raspberry vines, covered over with balanti trees.

Said Hardstone, "I have done with mine enemies." He carries his spear from place to place. There is no talk, no sound. He removes the taboos incumbent on him.

4. That was the reason, too, that Hardstone has acquired chickens and pigs, that his chickens and pigs live, that he [was able to] turn his attention to farming his crops. They bear fruit and are well-fruited; there is no crop failure. He travels, too, the decaying-vegetation lined paths[9] and the enemies and evil spirits are turned aside. He flourishes, too, like the giant bamboo, like the *baliti* tree.

It is not at Hunduan but here in our village of Balitang that we are mything you prayables who are at Hunduan so as to face you against our enemies of Humalapap. Face ye them so as to carry them up, so that the *manalidal* of the Upstream Region and the *umaladang* of the Underworld travel through them, so that he crunches them, catches them by the waist, so that sudden sickness seizes him, so that he lies long in his house, sleeps through his recovery rites, suffers quick death and is dead, so that they tie him with a g-string and their women wail and wail over him, so that his brothers raise the death cries, so that they seal him in his sepulchre with a strong tombstone; because *hinuganid* is what we are mything you, you prayable beings of ours at Hunduan.

A *tulud* follows this myth.

27. BALITOK OBTAINS PACIFIERS*

Subject: Balitok of Kiangan secures pacifiers for his drinkfest. Used: In rites preliminary to prestige fests. Informant: Lumidik Bugbug (Hingyon). Recorded by: Francisco Bugbug (1937). Translated by: R. F. Barton.

SYNOPSIS

1. On the eve of a drinkfest that he is about to give, Balitok is worried. His wife advises him to secure pacifiers in the Upstream Region. He goes to Tadona, who provides him with a number; then he goes farther and secures still more of them.

2. On the following day, when his guests become maudlin and begin to fight, Balitok has only to raise his hand to stop their enmity and set them contracting intermarriages with each other or trading partnerships or to singing improvisations.[1]

THE MYTH

1. *Ngalana* Balitok of Kiangan, the sun was half way and he spake and said, "Drinkfest tomorrow — and the guests will gather and [are likely to] cause trouble."

Said Bugan wife of Balitok at Kiangan, "Alas! go upstream to the Upstream Region."

Balitok answered affirmatively and they enter their house, they eat; only a little bit they eat;[2] change to betels and betel leaves, and cause it (the spittle) to become red, they spit all around. He settles his knife in his scabbard, tucks on his hipbag, takes his spear in hand and goes, it is said, upstream. He goes without noting time's passage and comes to Pumbokbokan, comes to Mongayan, goes to the other side to Bokyawan, arrives at Lablabong and goes upstream. He arrives at Bayokan, goes up to Tobo, goes not noting time and arrives at the Upstream Region, goes up to Kahoban. Said Tadona, "Why art thou here, Balitok?"

Said Balitok, "I am searching for a strong *halupe*, because we are making a prestige feast. The drinkfest guests will gather and make us trouble."

Said Tadona, "Here are *halupe*, "Charity, Pity, Persuasion Consolation, Lover's Harp, Lover's Harp,[3] and Jews' Harp," and he gives them to Balitok.

Said Balitok, "Are there no villages farther on?"

"There are," said he (Tadona).

And he (Balitok) goes and he brings the assembled *halupe* powers of those who are at Namoman, who are at Ginohod, at Pamoligan, and those who are at Gonhadan. And he returns and he goes without noting time's passage downstream to Tabo, to Buyudon, and arrives at Lablabong, at Bokyawan, Mongaiyan, Pombokbokan and to Kiangan. He ascends and arrives, enters his house and eats.

Said Bugan, "Didst thou get the *halupe*?"

Balitok answers affirmatively.

2. On the morning of the morrow, the drinkfest guests assemble, they drink and drink and they get drunk, they begin to fight, the drinkfest guests become maudlin. Balitok descends, raises his hand and they cease, the drinkfest guests become quiet. They enter the places under the houses and discuss intermarriages and the conclusion of trading partnerships with persons of foreign regions (*bibiyaowan*) and sing songs of good-natured criticism (*liuliwa*).

At evening, the drinkfest guests return and they who have accomplished the drinkfest are left alone. Their pigs and chickens multiply, their rice is miraculously increased, the enemies and evil spirits are turned aside, they become like the central gold ornament of a string, brave their way to wealth, they become like a *baliti* tree.

Kalidi it is not at Kiangan because it is at this house of the children where I am myth-reciting unto you, our Myths who are at Kiangan and who are in the Upstream Region.

28. WIGAN TEACHES RITES TO BALITOK*

Subject: Wigan teaches Balitok the *kibkiblu* rite. Used: In death rites. Informant: Buligan Bugbug. Recorded by Francisco Bugbug. Translated by Barton.

Synopsis

1. Wigan of the Skyworld goes hunting. His quarry runs into the Upstream Region, and Wigan kills it there. He needs fire and, from a tree, descries smoke, which is rising from the house of Balitok. Wigan goes thither to get fire, but Balitok is too sluggish to do any honors as host and compels him to wait on himself.

2. Wigan returns with fire to the place where his game lies; soon he takes a foreleg to Balitok. Wigan asks Balitok why he is so listless and is told that a relative died recently, since which time, rain, mist and sun have weakened all in the family.

3. Wigan teaches the *kibkiblu* rite, whereupon all recover and flourish in prosperity.[1]

The Myth

1. *Ngalana* Wigan, he lounges about his houseground in the Skyworld. His dogs keep using their teeth in the Skyworld: they catch

chickens and also pigs on the housegrounds of the Skyworld. Said Wigan, "Alas! they are always calling to me."[2] He calls his dogs and ties them with a bamboo stick and hitches them to a housepost. He sacrifices a chicken for the *ikbo* rite; he invites his neighbors of the skyworld to help in the rites. He finishes and singes and opens it. He sees that it (the bile) is *nungitib*. He takes a clay pot, pours in water and puts it on the fire. It boils and is cooked. He paddles out the rice and prays. He finishes and prays the "breast bone" prayer,[3] and divides the meat into small pieces and they eat. He finishes eating and they put things away. They change to betels, betel leaves, and lime them. They blow out the first betel juice and it has become red and thick-spittled.

The sun is half way, it is said, and he unties his dogs and goes to look at the cockbird.[4] The bird spake from in front of him. Wigan responded: "Be it so with the life of the hunters." He goes a second time and it is the same. He goes a third time and the bird gives "harsh talk."[5] He enters their forest in the skyworld and the quarry is started. He runs around all over the mountains and turns the game to the Upstream Region and kills it on the level place of the Upstream Region.

There is no fire. He climbs a large tree in the Upstream Region. He looks all around. Smoke is seen rising at Duyugan. He descends and climbs up to Duyugan and sees that it is fenced around,[6] and has a tied gate. Said Wigan,

"Thou man, open it."

"Thou, man, just thou open it," answered the man.

Wigan takes down the tied gate and goes to the other side.

"Thou, Balitok, bring me fire, please."

"Thou, come thou up and get it."

"Where is the pot ?"

"Dost not see, thyself, the pots hung all around ?"

2. He (Wigan) takes down one of them and carries it to the level place of the Upstream Region. He takes the belly fat and puts it inside the pot, pours in water and kindles fire underneath. He forces the fire, it boils and is cooked. He takes it off and invokes his neighbors of the Skyworld. He finishes and eats. He puts things away and changes to betels. It turns red and thick-spittled. He takes a foreleg and puts it in the pot as the share of Balitok at Duyugan. "Where art thou, Balitok, so as to receive the pot ?"

"Thou, bring it up!"

And he takes it up.

Said Wigan: "Why art thou so listless ?"

"Yes, because we are bereft (some of us are dead) here in our village of Duyugan. And the sunshine, rain and drizzling mist weaken us."

Said Wigan, "Did ye bury the dead and did ye not perform the *kibkiblu* rites ?"

"We don't know how. If thou knowest, go ahead."

"Have ye no dried meat ?"

"Why not ? It is hanging under the shelf."

3. He takes the cover off and spreads out the meat and invites these neighbors of his, the Skyworld dwellers, and those at Duyugan, and Trash and Dirt-Crowded-Together and Spitter-by-Blowing-it-Out and Winnower and Spitter-by-Sputing-it-Out.[7] He finishes and descends.

"I am going to ascend to the Skyworld because I am of the Skyworld. If ye be bereft, I am the one to whom thou shalt perform the *kibkiblu* rite, and I am strong in *kibkiblu*, so that even though ye pass into sunshine, dripping mist and rain, ye will sweat well, be like ripening grain, be healthy, grow fast.

He crosses the level place of the Upstream Region, he takes his wild pig and spear, puts on his backbasket, shakes it into place and ascends. He climbs up the steep place, thrusts down his spear. It (shatters a paving stone) like a leaf, like a plume.

It was the beginning and reason that the Balitoks at Duyugan should go under the sunshine and rain and that they should sweat well and be like ripening grain. They go acquiring chickens and pigs and their loans in the outskirts increase as also their sacrifices for other rites than those of sickness,[8] and their rites performed against enemies and their sacrificing of chickens and pigs. They travel and travel the vegetation-rotted paths and the enemy and evil spirits are retarded. They flourish like the *baliti*, like the giant bamboo.

Come hither, for it is not at Duyugan, but at our house here in Balitang: I do the *kibkiblu* for the children who have interred the deceased one, and let them go under the sunshine and rain, but be they healthy like ripening grain.

29. TULUD: BUGAN'S DECEPTION*

Subject: Bugan, wife of Manahaut, carries off enemies. Used: In all sorcery and war rituals. Informant: Kumiha.

SYNOPSIS

1. Manahaut of the Skyworld, declares that he will go down on earth and trick the Ifugaos. His wife Bugan confidently remarks that she had better go, as she is "the one to deceive the Ifugaos." Manahaut confidently asserts his ability along this line and his wife tactfully makes no answer, confident that he will find out for himself that it

is she who is the better equipped for duping males. Manahaut presents himself before informant Kumihan, on earth, and is told to procede against the latter's enemies in Tablak. Manahaut proceeds thither, but the Tablak men are too wary for him.

2. Manahaut returns home empty-handed and his wife reminds him that she told him so in the first place. She then dresses in all her finery, rejuvenates herself and goes to Tablak. She gets the enemy half drunk, sets them to playing gongs, dances for them, calls for a sleeping board, does a strip-tease act, lies down on the board. Thereupon the enemies and their kindred on both father's and mother's sides rush to her, she wraps them in her arms and carries them up to the Skyworld.

3. Manahaut gives the enemy more wine, but they become so disturbing that he sends Bugan with them to Tiningba, who soon tires of them and sends Bugan to take them to another deity further away, and so they go from one to another, deeper into the Skyworld till they reach Lumingay. Bugan, on acceptance of them by the latter deity, returns home immediately — before Lumingay has time to become disgusted with himself for receiving them. Lumingay has no other recourse than to take them across a chasm, remove the bridge-pole and leave them there, where they stay forever, not knowing where they are or how to get back.

THE TULUD

Ngalana Manahaut and Bugan his wife. The sun is half way; says Manahaut, "*Ah nakayah*! The Ifugaos are calling us. Probably they want us in order to point us against somebody.[1] *Ngalana* Manahaut — said Manahaut, "I will go down and deceive their enemies [for them]." Said Bugan,

"I am the skillful one — better let me deceive the Ifugaos."

Said Manahaut, "I also know to deceive the Ifugaos."

Bugan made no answer. *Ngalana* Manahaut, he puts on his hipbag and then his scabbard, grasps his spear, goes to their steep place, he thrusts down his spear, untucks his hipbag and chews betels. He limes them and turns them red. He tucks on his hipbag, takes spear in hand and continues downward. He stops at our village of Balitang.

"It is I, indeed, for whom they have prepared sacrifices."

He takes betels and betel leaves, chicken and rice, and carries them on his head. He goes around the mountainside and upstream to Matong, goes over the ridge to Nunhapang, comes to Ibiyu, goes over the ridge to Imayapit, and upstream to Ubuul, descends to Luhadan, goes down to Ula, continues and climbs the steep, goes round the hill to Tabla, to the house of the Puoks, our enemies.

Ngalana Manahaut, he arrives, thrusts down his spear, sits down on the rice mortar of our enemies, Puok and Batad, takes out betels and betel leaves. Our enemies assemble, but take betels from him, each, one at a time, then each returns to his sitting place.

"How shall I deceive the Ifugaos?"

He pours out wine. Our enemies of Tablak assemble. Only one at a time comes to dip up wine in a cup and then he returns to his sitting place. Said Manahaut.

"I can't deceive the Ifugaos. I'll go back up."

He tucks on his hipbag, seizes his spear, goes up the steep, and climbs up to his village in the Skyworld. He arrives in his village in the Skyworld. Bugan, wife of Manahaut, laughs,

"Thou seest!" she says, "Thou canst not deceive the Ifugaos. Wait, I'll go down; I'll surely deceive their enemies, those Tablak people."

Manahaut agrees. He winds on Bugan's bracelet. Bugan has made herself young, puts a plume in her hair, arranges her loincloth. She starts downward. "When I get there, I'll surely deceive the Ifugaos." She arrives at Balitan.

"Where are these against whom ye are pointing us?"

And we say, we fathers and sons, "Thou art pointed toward Tablak, against the houses of Batad and Puok." Bugan agrees. She goes on around the mountain side, goes upstream to Matong, over the ridge to Nunhapang, descends to Ibiyu, crosses to Imayapit, goes upstream at Ubuul, descends at Luhadan, goes on down to Ula, climbs the steep and arrives at Tablak. She goes to the house of Batad and Puok and their kindred on both sides. They assemble. *Ngalana* Bugan wife of Manahaut, she takes out betels and betel leaves, they receive them, they crowd around Bugan, wife of Manahaut of the Skyworld, *Ngalana* Bugan wife of Manahaut, she brings down a wooden wine bowl. They pour out the wine, she keeps dipping it up for our enemies the Batads and the Puoks and their kindred on both sides. They are half drunk. Spake Bugan, "Don't ye have a gong?" Said Batad, "Bring down the gong." They dance and dance. Spake Bugan, "Have ye no sleeping board?" Batad responds and brings it down, places it on the house ground. They play the gong with both hands, Bugan emerges and dances. *Ngalana* our enemies, they dance and dance with her. *Ngalana* Bugan, she approaches the board lies on her back on the board, thighs open and hands extended. She takes off her loincloth. *Ngalana* Batad and Puok and their kindred on both sides, they rush headlong to Bugan. *Ngalana* Bugan, she closes her arms and legs, wraps round them her loincloth and gets up and, embracing them, carries them away to the Skyworld,

14*

comes to their village in the Skyworld. Manahaut chuckles. "Hast tricked the Ifugaos!" Bugan responded, "I'm skillful in deceiving the Ifugaos."

[2]*Ngalana* Manahaut, he brings down rice wine, pours it out, hands a cup of wine to our enemies the Humalapal people,[3] the Tablak people. He keeps dipping up wine for them. They become drunk, they make a big racket, they bite the coconut cup.[4] *Ngalana* Manahaut, "*Ah nakayah!* Those thou hast tricked, Bugan, are becoming noisy, biting the cup. Take them to the house of Tiningban." Bugan agrees and embraces the Batads and Puoks, takes them up to Tiningban's house. Tiningban agreed, "Ifugaos, tricked by Bugan" [he says]. He brings down wine, he dips it out to them, they become noisy, they bite the cup. Said Tiningban,

"*Ah nakayah!* Bugan, those thou'st tricked are biting the cup! Take them to the house of Dinukligan."

Bugan agreed, she embraces our enemies, takes them to the house of Dinukligan. Said Dinukligan, "Ifugaos tricked by Bugan!" He accepts them, brings down wine, pours it out. They drink. *Ngalana* those deceived by Bugan bite the cup. "Take them to Namakdalan, to the house of Lumingay." Said Lumingay, "Ifugaos tricked by Bugan." He accepts them, brings down wine, pours it out. Bugan laughs, "I'll go back to our village in the Skyworld." *Ngalana* Lumingay, and companions, they keep trying to make the Puoks and Batads keep quiet. They take them across a chasm, remove the bridge.

They do not know how to return; they will stay there forever, they do not know where they are. So let it be with our enemies the Tablak people there, so that thou trick them so that they do not know where to return.

30. TULUD DI NATE: DEAD MAN'S TULUD

Subject: Soul of the dead is dispatched to the Region of Souls. Used: In funeral rites, as the corpse is being carried to the sepulchre. Informant: Ngidulu.

SYNOPSIS

1. Despite all that his kindred, the Bitu people, can do by means of rites and sacrifices to secure his recovery, Barton dies. Taking note of his surroundings, Barton (i.e. his soul) perceives a file of his neighbors in festive garb on their way to a drinkfest in Anao, a region adjoining his home region, Bitu.

2. He puts on his adornments and accompanies them. He becomes quite drunk, enjoys himself and does not return at night with his

neighbors, but instead sleeps in Anao. Next morning the Anao people invite him to go with them to a drinkfest at Pugu, a region adjacent to their own, across a small stream. He accepts and again becomes too drunk to go home. On the following morning, the Pugu folk take him along to a drinkfest in Madekit, in Kudug Valley, across a hill. Again he is greeted cordially.

3. Three sons of Bespeaker, (Imbagayan), who are conductors of souls, on looking down from the Skyworld, see a strange-looking guest at the feast, and recognize him as recently dead. They descend and participate quietly in the drinkfest. The soul again tarries with his hosts of Madekit. On the morrow, these as well as the Conductors of souls take him to a drinkfest at Binokyug, farther down the valley. And on the following day, they all go to a drinkfest in Mongaiyan across the river, and again, next day, to a drinkfest at Bulá, down the river. At this last place, which is the eastern limit of his people's territory, the Conductors of Souls pay him the greatest deference and see that he has an especially enjoyable occasion. At the same time they begin to dominate him, so that, on the following morning, they have no trouble to persuade him to go with them down the river to a drinkfest in strange, little known territory.

4. They go down the river to a drinkfest in Kaba, and on the next day still further down it to one in Kawayan. Barton has now lost all thought of his home. On the morrow, the Conductors of Souls turn him over to the Imbangad deities, who call on certain other deities to cut the thick grass and make the road further down the river easy. Barton now thinks so little about his home that he even leads the way and keeps getting ahead of the others. In the Region of Souls he is received by his ancestors, with whom he henceforth abides. And he does not return to cause trouble to the living kindred in his former home.

COMMENT

Long before I recorded it, I knew that some such *tulud* as this existed, but had never been able to get a priest to teach it or even to admit he knew of it. One day Ngidulu besought the privilege of becoming my debtor in the amount of a small sum of money. I answered him that I didn't understand how he conceived that I should be the one to lend him money when he wouldn't do me so small a favor as to teach me how effectively to lay an ordinary ghost — and didn't he think there ought to be a mutuality in our relations?

"But there's nobody's name that I can use in it," he protested.

I perceived then where the difficulty had been all along and said, "Use mine, and let's do it right away."

A look of astonishment came over his stolid face and quickly gave way to one of cunning. His voice, too, had a nervous, husky quality as he explained that he must have the money first, that his need was urgent, that he had to give it to a man right away, but that he would return immediately and teach me the *tulud*: *an magagala, Apo* [truly right away, Apo], and a very fine *tulud* it would be.

He was evidently greatly in earnest, so I yielded to his entreaty for the money now; but, accustomed as I was to his procrastinations, I was surprised when he kept his word literally. He did come quite soon, and we began the recording. Two or three of the loafers always present during my recordings whispered together. One went away and soon came back with enough others to fill the room.

I gave no particular thought to the curious look of cunning in Ngidulu's face or to the expectant way in which he regarded me for several days afterward, until, a few weeks later, I learned that the Ifugaos have a series of rites called "funeral-while-living," in which, quite logically, this very *tulud* plays an important role.

Sometimes old men, broken in health and helpless, want to die and can't. In such case, they insist that their kindred perform for them the "funeral-while-living," and after that they soon die. I was told of a case in near-by Hingyon in which an old man died eight days after such a ritual. I was also told of the case, some years ago, of Balogan, the father of Timiging of Nahalantukan, about a quarter of a mile away. He called together his "sitters" and told them what he wanted done. They were reluctant to go through rites of such a nature. The old man, however, gave them a bawling out and made them say their parts.

But the longed-for death did not come. He wondered why and it occurred to him that for rich men like himself, there is another region of souls — in the Skyworld, instead of in the Downstream Region to which all souls, rich or poor, usually go. Then it appeared to him that the reason he had not died was that his soul was fated to go to the other region. So he again called his "sitters" and ordered them to repeat the rites but to dispatch his soul this time to the Skyworld instead of to the Downstream Region, as in the first instance. The rites were finished about first cock-crow and he died at dawn.

The sympathetic reader will, I trust, understand my reasons for leaving my name in this *tulud*, just as Ngidulu used it. For it is my triumph over Ngidulu. The young Ifugaos who have gone to school will read the native text — they will read it to Ngidulu.

Then Ngidulu will remember his creditor who lived to collect. He will remember the days when he was working out his debt — the long, hot hours under the iron roof when he was my "sitter," sitting with his heels on the chair seat directly under his own sitter; will remember how torrents of rain falling on galvanized iron would drown out his voice; will remember those interludes when my eleven-fingered cook, who was not nearly so much of a cook as a nooser of snakes, would bring in one of the deadly tree-snakes so feared by the Ifugaos, how the people would assemble to delight in its death throes from a wad of cyanide-soaked cotton down its throat and would shake their heads as they exclaimed, "*Ah poa!* What a strong poison the Melikanos have."

These, to him, grateful interruptions, and much else, Ngidulu will remember, and probably time will have so velveted over the whole period that the exertion that need not have been, had the *tulud* only worked on Barton, will now appear tolerable to him — to him who had no taste for any kind of exertion.

Nor was it any fault of the *tulud* itself that it didn't work, for it is an ingenious, artful and even subtle device. Knowing that Ngidulu has a reflective and naturally logical mind, I will suggest to him a premise by which he may explain its failure in this instance: the subject *had* no soul.

I nowise blame Ngidulu for harboring the hope that he did. For the trap was of my own making. Since I was no kin of his, he was, according to his lights, under no obligation whatever to warn me against it. Besides, I judge no man, for I know what thoughts not infrequently get past the censor from my own Unconscious.

Furthermore, I owe a debt to Ngidulu which the few *pesos* I paid him for his services as informant leave far from liquidated — a debt which cannot be paid in money, although no doubt he would prefer further monetary compensation to any amount of any other kind of acknowledgement.

He was an excellent informant; his knowledge of Ifugao ritual and other lore was well-nigh encyclopaedic. Besides, he liked to get things down right and he soon gained, to some degree, a conception of what was important, what was significant. In bringing to a close a volume that to so great an extent is his as well as mine, the least — and unfortunately, the most — that I can do is to add these informal acknowledgements to the conventional ones already rendered in the preface.

THE TULUD

1. *Kanadih* Barton: the sun is half-way. His sickness is terrific! *Kanadih* his elders (kindred), the Bitu folk, they assemble. They get together [sacrifices for] his welfare rites. They catch a pig, tie its legs, trammel it, carry it to the house. They pour out wine, invite

the ancestors, change to the Suggesting deities and to the *Na-ótotbe* who are in the Skyworld, the Underworld, the Upstream Region and the Downstram Region. They pay back the Matungulan. They finish, *kanadih* and are possessed by the deities. They finish and stick the pig. They burn off its hair, open it up, boil its lower belly fat. It boils and they take it off. *Kanadi dyie*, they spread it on cooked rice. They myth and myth those of the Skyworld and those of Kiangan; they finish and invoke them. They cut the meat into small pieces [and] eat. *Kanadi* the able-bodied take their [shares of the] meat and distribute it [to their kindred]. The able-bodied go home.

Ngalana Barton — he cannot be welfare-feasted (cured by welfare feast). When the sun is half-way, Barton perishes and dies. He takes note of his surroundings at Balitang and there are people. There — *ah nakayang*! the able-bodied, they are in a file, uniformly adorned with white plumes in their hair.

2. Barton begins and finds all his things, puts them on and leaves his house.[1]

He crosses the outskirt at Balitan. He asks the able-bodied:

"Whither are ye going?"

They answer and say: "Attend thou the drinkfest at Anao."

Barton goes to the drinkfest with them. They walk around the mountain at Abat. They go not noting time's passage. They turn to Abatan, turn to Paghok. They go around the mountain at Maimok, walk on the dikes at Lingayan. They enter Ginauúdan.

Kanadi mo Barton, he enters (the village). Nothing else than that the able-bodied meet him and make friends. They go straight to the dancing place. *Kanadi* in a little while the sweat stands out and he goes under cover. He faces the drinking place and they drink and drink. They do not note time's passage. That evening — *kanadih* the able-bodied, they go home. Barton is left behind. It is night and he stays for the night. They sleep. After a while it is morning. They prepare and cook, take off [the pot] and roast it, paddle out [the rice] and cool it. They eat, finish eating and clean up. They change to betel-chewing.

When the sun is half-way, they talk about a drinkfest at Pugu. Say the able-bodied, the Anao people "Let us go to the drinkfest, Barton." He goes along with the crowd of the Anao folk and they go downhill. They come down to Itumok, go, not noting time's passage, to Patukan. They walk along the rice dikes. They turn to Talalang, ford the river to Madekit. The drinkfest guests at Madekit flock to him. "Who is this man who has come to our drinkfest?"

Say the Anao people, "Barton who was adopted by the Bitu folk."[2]

"Why is he here?"

And they say, "Because he has died."[3]

They go down to the dancing place. He plunges into [the dance] and they dance and swing in the dance.

3. *Ngalanda* Giniling and Bagayan and Dumya of Lingahen: they are at the edge of the steep at Lingahen. They look and look and they gaze down on Barton.

"What about that man who is dancing in the dancing place at Madekit whose paleness is different?"

They go back to their village in the Skyworld and enter their houses at Lingahen. They pack up betels, tuck on their hipbags, follow this by girding on their bolos, take spears in hand. They come into sight at the Steep Place, turn their spears around [shod end forward], use them as staffs at Nabultikan. They jump downward and come to Nabultikan, descend to Pugu. They enter Madekit. They take note of Barton who is half drunk.

"Why is Barton there?"

"Because he has perished."[3]

They approach and drink wine. Time passes unnoted.

That evening, *ngalanda* the able-bodied from Anao, they return and Barton is left behind. It is night and they sleep. On the morrow they talk about a drinkfest at Kudug. *Ngalanda* Giniling and his companions persuade Barton [to go]. They go with the rest up the steep at Pugu. They walk on the level around Nabultikan. They descend to Hobob, turn to Kaiyang, continue to Tikdap and go downhill. They enter the village of Binukyug.

Ngalanday the able-bodied of Binukyug, they meet them with wine. *Ngalana* Barton, when he has become drunk, he boasts about his wealth. They keep getting drunker and drunker. In the evening the drinkfest guests go home and Barton is left behind. It is night and they sleep.

On the morrow they awake. *Kanadih* Barton, he does not think about going back home. At midforenoon they talk about a drinkfest at Mongaiyan. The Kudug people set forth and Barton sets forth with them, joins their crowd. They descend and come down, wade [a stream] to the other side, turn to Boka, descend to Higib, go down to the river and ford it. They come up out of it and enter Modaliyong. *Kanadih* the able-bodied of Mondaliyong, they pour out wine, approach Barton and the Ginilings, Lingahen. They drink. *Kanadih* Barton gets very drunk. No thought comes to him of returning home.

That evening, the drinkfest guests return home. At night they sleep. On the morrow, they talk about a drinkfest at Bulâ. *Kanadih* Barton goes with the crowd of Mongaiyan folk. They turn to the river, go downstream, arrive at Impakid, turn to Inyakob, go down to Impatye, walk around the hill to Dotal, arrive in Bulâ.

Kanadih Bagayan and Giniling keep saying, "Make way, ye drinkfest guests, for Barton's passage, for he has perished." Barton arrives and they pour out wine and take it to him. They keep drinking. They keep getting drunk. Time passes unnoted. In the afternoon, the guests go home.

4. It is night and Barton stays over. They sleep. On the morrow, *kanadih* the able-bodied of Bulâ,

"Where are ye, Giniling and Bagayan and Dumya ? Bring Barton along so that we all go to a drinkfest at Kaba."

They agree and persuade Barton.[4] They set forth, follow [the river] to Halop and go downstream, arrive at Kadel, turn to Ligauwe Gap and continue downstream. They arrive at Pantal, turn to Lana, arrive at Baiyukon. They go downstream. They arrive at Banauwọl. They turn to Yungyungan, enter Kaba. *Ngalana* the able-bodied of Kaba, they pour out wine. They have become half-drunk.

"Why is there here a man, come to the drinkfest, whose handsomeness is profound, whose nose is high, and whose eyes are like a spider-web ?"

Said Dumya and companions, "It is Barton, who was adopted by the Bitu people."

They pour out wine and come to him, they drink and drink. Barton has become very drunk. He talks and talks — like a stretched cord (?), like a bamboo harp. Soon there is nothing else in his speech but talk about his wealth.

In the evening the guests return home; Barton is left behind. It is night and they sleep. On the morrow, when the sun is half-way, they talk about a drinkfest at Kawayan. The Kaba folk set forth. Time passes unnoted. They go downstream, arrive at Pangahalon. They go not noting time's passage, arrive at Utupan, go downstream; arrive at Madungul and go on downstream. They arrive at Kawayan, go down to it, enter.

Ngalanda the able-bodied of Kawayan, they pour out wine and proffer it to Barton. They become half-drunk. *Kanadi* Barton, he has no thought of returning and tarries. *Ngalana mo* the Imbangad's of the Downstream Region,[5] they call on the (?) and the Grass-cutters. These cut a path for him. He goes along docilely and keeps getting ahead, keeps leading the way. They bring him to his mothers and fathers and he stays permanently there and forgets about his home, there. No thought comes to him of going back.

Kalidi: Ye are mythed here this myth of us who have suffered a death, but do not ever return. So that the pigs and the chickens may live and the enemies and evil spirits be shunted from N—[6]; so that the sunshine will leave her alone (not harm her).[7] And their children will be ruddy of complexion and be healthy. And they go acquiring pigs and chickens and their purchases of property in the outskirts increase. They will travel and travel the vegetation-rotted [accustomed] paths and the enemies and evil spirits will be hindered from reaching them. They will flourish like the giant (*palutan*) bamboo, like the *baliti* banyan. For ye are being mythed this *tulud* of ours.

Appendix

CLASSIFICATION OF MYTHS AND
BRIEF OF THEIR MOTIFS

1. VIRGIN BIRTH (GENERAL)

See tabulation in Section 5 of Part I.

2. SELF-BEHEADED (INVENTED)[1]

1, Creature without a head. 2, Tendentious *tulud*.

3. KINSHIP ASSEMBLAGE (GENERAL)

1, A god sends a flood which washes two of his children, a brother and a sister, from Skyworld to earth. 2, Slides down also cultural equipment. 3, Brother dams river, flooding the world. 4, Releases flood, creating mountains: for better hunting. 5, Has intercourse with sister as she sleeps. 6, Sister limes belly and detects lover. 7, With sanction of divine parents they marry. 8, Children intermarry, but descendants are sickly. 9, Tendentious.

4. THE NEGRITOS (INVENTED—BASED ON TRADITION)

1, Negrito's arrow misses game, sticks in housepost of Balitok, causing him a stitch in the side. 2, Tendentious.

5. TURNED TO STONE (GENERAL)

1, Brothers, hunting, become thirsty. 2, Elder brother strikes water from stone. 3, Younger brother hastens to drink. 4, Elder brother turns him into stone. 5, Water passes through him. 6, Their sister comes and takes her place alongside younger brother. 7, Tendentious.

6. ORIGIN OF IRRIGATED RICE (GENERAL)

See tabulation in Section 5 of Part I.

7. THE SELF-CAUGHT (RECENT TRADITIONAL)

1, Intermarriage between Upstream Woman and a god downstream. 2, Betels carry message downstream. 3, Difficult birth from pregnancy cravings. 4, Gold ornament changed into granary charm. 5, Tendentious. [See synopsis].

8. HALUPE DEITIES COLLECT DEBT (INVENTED)

1, Deities assist creditor.

9. FEUD BETWEEN BROTHERS (MIXED)

1, Feud between brothers. 2, Parents divorce, each taking a child.
3, Brothers hunt heads from each other's kindreds. 4, Various deities
are invited to reconcile them. 5, Tendentious.

10. THE DIVIDED CHILD (GENERAL)

1, Man dwells alone on mountain, naked. 2, Goddess tosses him her
girdle to wear. 3, They marry, have a son. 4, Goddess cannot endure
man's relatives. 5, They start for the Skyworld, but man cannot make
ascent. 6, Child divided. 7, Tendentious.

11. MAN IMPRISONS GODS (INVENTED)

1, Wind gods destroy fruit trees. 2, Man imprisons gods in their cave.
3, Gods bargain for freedom. 4, They give a talisman for their liberty.
5, Tendentious.

12. WEAVERS' MYTH (RECENT TRADITION)

1, Earth folk obtain loom from Sky-dwellers. 2, Weavers are afflicted
with eye troubles; tendentious.

13. THE TOOTH OF THUNDER (GENERAL)

1, Brothers flee from enemies and creditors. 2, Enraged Thunder god
thunders at thunder-piper. 3, His teeth are caught in wild abaca.
4, Brothers rescue him. 5, He implants his teeth in their jaws.
6, Tendentious.

14. THE IRON-EATER (GENERAL)

See tabulation in Section 5 of Part I.

15. SUN AND MOON QUARREL (GENERAL)

1, Feud between Sun and Moon. 2, Sun blinds moon with lime. 3, Moon
recovers, sets trap for Sun. 4, Sun is impaled, recovers. 5. Tendentious.

16. TIED UP (INVENTED)

1, Wigan secures Pacifying magic for his prestige feast.

17. ENEMIES AS OFFERINGS (INVENTED)

1, Poverty-stricken place-spirit uses human being for sacrifice.
2, Tendentious.

18. Dysentery Imps (Invented)

1, Dysentery imps afflict Balitok. 2, Tendentious.

19. Coconut Grows from Buried Head (General)

1, Headhunting party takes head of a god. 2, Head mimics them. 3, They bury the head. 4, Tree grows from the head. 5, Tendentious.

20. Origin of Boils (Invented)

1, Drippings from corpse cause skin eruptions. 2, Tendentious.

21. Red Scabbards and Black (Invented)

1, Deities afflict with boils. 2, Tendentious.

22. The Self-Cut (Mixed)

1, Ifugaos cut up a python. 2, Mate comes and reunites pieces, whereupon the two pythons crawl away. 3, Tendentious.

23. Difficult Birth (Invented)

1, Deity sends log to cause difficult birth. 2, Tendentious.

24. Belly Sickness (Invented)

1, Man insults deity in ritual speech. 2, Deity afflicts with bellysickness. 3, Tendentious.

25. Rite for Returning Soul (Invented)

1, Theft by deities of soul causes difficult birth. 2, Tendentious.

26. Like a Hardstone (Contest)

1, Trial of strength between two stones. Tendentious.

27. Balitok Obtains Pacifiers (Invented)

1, Prestige-feast giver obtains a Pacifier. 2, Tendentious.

28. Wigan Teaches Rites to Balitok (Invented)

1, Wigan teaches a rite.

29. Bugan's Deception (Invented)

1, Goddess carries off enemies.

30. Dead Man's Tulud (Invented)

1, Soul of dead is lured from one prestige feast to another and finally dispatched to the afterworld.

Notes

PART I. QUALITIES OF THE MYTHOLOGY

1. INTRODUCTION

1. Boas, 1914, p. 374.
2. Beyer, H. Otley, 1913. [See bibliography.]
3. Hoe myths in 1919; 3 myths in 1930; 3 myths in 1935; 2 myths in 1946.

2. THE MAGICAL AND FUNCTIONAL ROLES OF IFUGAO MYTHS

1. For such an invocation, see Barton, 1946, pp. 123, 128.
2. *Ibid.*, 52, 109; 106, 119.
3. Barton, 1938, p. 111.
4. In Kankanai, the word means "guiding," and this is probably the older and, hence, the ritual meaning.
5. Unfortunately, I can give no examples of myths followed by this kind of *tulud*, in this work, as I lost nearly all my Kiangan materials during the Japanese invasion.
6. Barton, 1946, p. 67.
7. *Ibid.*, p. 96.
8. *Ibid.*, p. 203.
9. Marr, N.J., 1936, Vol. 2, pp. 93, 130.
10. Malinowski, B., pp. 62–65.

4. LITERARY ATTRIBUTES OF THE MYTHS

1. Barton, 1946, p. 155, fn. 98.
2. Designs—such as of houses, carved utensils and images, spear head designs, textile patterns, scratchwork on bamboo lime tubes, etc.

5. CLASSIFICATION, NUMBER AND LENGTH OF MYTHS

1. This behavior is probably specific for ducks of this variety. The corresponding behavior of drakes in America gives only a mild hint of it.
2. In passing it ought to be added that myths of the type of the "Self-Beheaded," the "Iron-Eater" and "Pinading" (nos. 2, 14, 17) belong to a class called *Madingla*, or "Raw-Eaters." Recitation of such myths precedes that of the ordinary, more normal kind, with raw meat piled in baskets in front of the priests, and takes place while the meat to be used for recitations of the other kind of myths is being cooked. I think there are seven or eight such "raw-eater" myths.
3. Barton, 1946, pp. 16–18.
4. Moss, C. R., 1920a, p. 284.

6. AFFILIATIONS OF IFUGAO MYTHS

1. Boas, 1898, p. 100.
2. Barbeau, 1915, p. 53.
3. These *lettered motifs* do not always correspond to the *Roman-numbered sections* of the myth as they appear in the text in Part II. Thus, motifs A, B,

C, D do appear in sections I, II, III, IV; but E corresponds to V, VI, VII; the five motifs G–K all occur in section IX; and so on. [Ed.]

4. Loeb, 1929, pp. 149–162.

5. Loeb's published version says "barrel," but in a footnote he says that barrel is modern and that other versions have "bamboo." The children number 7 and later another is found. This brings the motif in line with "h" of the Ifugao myth, in which 8 mythical monsters are created from bamboo joints.

6. Barbeau, 1915, p. 58.

7. *Ibid.*, p. 56.

8. *Ibid.*, p. 53.

9. Cf. Ifugao Myth 1: Myaingit enjoins the mother "It's up to thee now, To look out for Balitok."

10. Boas, 1898, p. 100.

11. All this information is derived from unpublished field materials of Professor Fred Eggan and his oral information.

12. Lambrecht, 414.

13. Among the Ifugao the *pahang* are soulstealing deities. They appear in our 25, a rite whose purpose is similar to this one.

PART II. THE MYTHS*

1. In some instances myths are abridged by leaving out insignificant details of journeys, cooking, betel chewing and the like, or matter that is exactly repetitive of what has preceded. Such abridgement is indicated by periods, thus: ... Where not otherwise indicated, myths were recorded in the Balitang region in 1937.

1. THE VIRGIN BIRTH

1. Maíngit is the son of Amkídul, God of Thunder. The word means "red light" such as that in the sun shower, rainbow and lightning, all of which phenomena have individual names. The god seems to be identified with these phenomena and also with the glow of the rising and setting sun.

2. *Nalhom di binla-da*, literally, "whose whiteness is deep, or profound." The Ifugao's ideal of beauty is a lightish, limpid skin-color, what we might call a "clear" complexion.

3. Two homonyms have the form *dayu* (more correctly, *daiyu*): one means "descend," the other means "rejoice."

4. *Ablatan*: a precipice, invisible to mortal eyes, down which the gods descend to earth, especially to the top of Mount Pangagauwan (Sto. Domingo). The gods also can see, from its edge, what is going on in the earth.

5. He puts his weight on the spear in order to press its shod end into the earth and leaves it standing.

6. I have translated "amber," because such is the color of the beads, but the *pango* is not amber; it is made in the following way: "a core of non-translucent yellowish paste is plated with gold leaf, which is covered with clear yellow glass." Such beads have been found on the beach of Kuala Selinsing, Perak. Winstedt, 1932, p. 5.

7. *Inultikan*: a piece of betel nut, sprinkled with lime and rolled up in a leaf; the ordinary word is *natiktikan* or *nahultikan*.

8. In every Ifugao house the fireplace is at the farther right-hand corner from the door. Above it is the fireframe, which consists of three stories or

*. The title theme may, however, as we have said, be a general motif.

racks. On the two lower, fuel is piled to dry. Straddled on poles across the upper rack is a supply of rice bundles, which will be threshed out as needed for consumption. Amtalao, seeing a chance for magic, in the packed-full fire-frame pronounces the *fiat* which follows in Episode VI.

9. The dual is used. The Ifugao often uses it, as here, to soften reproaches by including himself in them or, even more delicately, to soften the preachiness of advice.

10. The Ifugao haircut is precisely the same as that used by the Ao Nagas. (Smith, 1925, p. 19). "It looks as if a bowl were turned over the head and then a smooth cut were made all round its edge with a pair scissors." Beneath this smooth cut, the hair is trimmed (with a stick of wood and a knife) so closely that it gives an impression as if it had been shaved only the day before yesterday. Above, the hair is not trimmed at all, so that the "rim" spoken of by Bugan stands out definitely and the upper growth of untrimmed hair, as Dr. Smith remarks, "gives the appearance of a sort of helmet." Mr. J.H.Hutton, in a footnote in Dr. Smith's work, adds that the Mishmi and Miyong Abors have the same coiffure, and that the Siamese formerly had it. Bugan's words, of course, amount to a denial of ever having known a man.

11. The posture of the Ifugao woman in labor is the following: The woman stands behind a person—her husband if he have not become "afraid" and run away, or if, being present, he be not exhausted—bent forward on his back as he crouches or kneels, with her arms over his shoulders. Hence it is that in the series of births that follows, Bugan *looks down*, each time, to see the result.

12. That is, the omen bird [*Rhapidura cyaniceps*].

13. The omen insect, *taktak*, makes a sound like its name and, like most of the creatures born of Bugan, is taboo to eat.

14. The birth of various beings from Bugan in this myth and the creation of various creatures from the Divided Child (Myth X) have parallels in very many Polynesian creation myths. Tangaroa, connected with, or personifying the Sky or the Sun, (uniting, sometimes, with a goddess who personifies the earth) produces similarly incongruous "hodgepodges" which are also "forerunners of the human." Williamson, Vol. 1, Chapter 2. In a version from Tonga, it is notable that even the landslide is found. Caillot, pp. 247–259.

15. I was told that if the child be a male, the Ifugaos lay it on the right side of the mother while they cut the cord; if a girl, on the left side.

16. Myths about the birth of heroes so frequently signalize their birth by celestial phenomena that this motif is almost characteristic: Buddha, Krishna, Abraham, Moses, Laou Tse, the Caesars, Quetzalcoatle ... Bouton, pp. 141 to 146.

17. The dual is used. See footnote 9 on this use of the dual.

18. *Munpinhodan*, "right oneself" signifying to give birth. Russian women frequently use the same figure.

19. *Saliagiwan*, a kind of very hard, tough, dark brown wood.

20. The sons of Ambalitayon are, although themselves Kianganites, continually mentioned in the myths as being in feud with Balitok the hero ancestor, and his kin. This hints of clan society, of such a situation as exists in the Naga or Batak village.

21. The top game, as played by Ifugao boys, has a warlike character. One side spins tops for the other side to "spear"—that is, knock down with their own tops. In a sense, the top game is like a game of marbles. The "spearer' is a "taw."

22. This is the time-honored boy's game of building toy terraces, one party

building on one side, the other on the other, near a stream of water. They then turn the water on the "fields" and the side whose fields go down, loses the contest.

23. I am not sure of the meaning of *ayam*: ordinarily it means "chum." Possibly the word ought to be *gayam*, talisman. In any case, the sons of Ambalitáyon charge Balitok with winning by unfair and supernatural means.

24. I do not know whether this manner of falling has any special significance. The phrase recurs continually in the myths. Probably it is the way a vanquished enemy is supposed to fall.

25. The dual is used (fn. 9). Amtalao means to convey to Balitok that since he has no kindred on the father's side to back him up, he ought to keep out of trouble.

26. Note how an Ifugao opens the door when he doesn't know who's there!

27. Embracing of adults is foreign to Ifugao culture.

28. That is, "your hills for consulting the omens."

29. The *pinokla* is a "cock's tail" made to human proportions of palm leaves tied to a wooden and bamboo frame, worn during the mimic cockfight dance at headfeasts.

30. The reciter of the myth here inserts the name and village of his own enemies—not Balitok's.

31. That is, the enemy's rites for recovery from his frenzy.

32. "When the sun is half way we will pity!" is, of course, sardonic.

33. He names omen hills in a different place from before so as to have a virgin field for testing of his increased mana.

34. These are kinds of trees.

35. The Ifugao usually inters his dead, wrapped in shrouds, in a sitting position. As decomposition proceeds, the corpse slowly settles into a heap. The "grave cave" is a sepulchre excavated in a bank or steep hillside.

36. "In Denmark, the slayer and the slain man's kin stand face to face (at the payment of *weregild*) with their paternal and maternal kinsmen as a compact host on right and left." (Gronbech, *The Culture of the Teutons*, p. 355). It may be inferred that such was the battle array, also.

37. That is, those who are in mourning for their recently slain kindred.

38. The statement above that "There is left of them no remainder," is in contradiction with these lines. The Ifugao never lets consistency interfere with his magic. He knows that magic always falls short. It was good magical art to declare them all destroyed, above, but the priest knows they will not be, so now he provides for making peace with those that are left. The Ifugao, killing somebody, shivers in fear of retaliation from the kin of the slain and longs to make friends with them.

39. Only the heads, with possibly an arm or leg or two, of the slain, are carried home as trophies.

40. Strictly speaking, the *tayaban* is a winged supernatural being, but the word is also used in ritual language, as here, to mean a chicken offered in sacrifice.

41. *Ditak* is here used (improperly) to mean the third day's ritual of the celebration after taking a head. What is meant is really called the *binangyn*.

42. "Who feel the way for the omen birds:" that is, those who endow the omen birds (and all beings that give omens) with their powers and who guide them in their omen-giving.

43. The Ifugao kills a pig by running a stick into its chest until it bleeds to death of internal hemorrhage.

44. *Balanti*—the frame from which the palm leaves are suspended when making the "cock's tail" used in the mimic dance previously spoken of (fn.29).

45. The headtakers' paraphernalia consists of a headgear, representing the comb of a cock, armlets with suspended palm leaves representing the cock's wings, and the "tail." On the morning after the mimic dance, these are borne around the house several times, with a recitation of a mostly meaningless formula in which there is a reference to the "house of the wasps"—that is, (I think) the head-hunters' own.

46. Mr. Manghe did not record the *tulud* or "god-pushing" that follows the recitation of the myth.

2. THE SELF-BEHEADED

1. This myth belongs to the group called the "raw-eaters."

2. For the meaning and pronunciation of "y," "n," and "d" standing alone see above.

3. A danger to one of the group draws in the kindred as a matter of course, for, since there is collective responsibility, a threat to one is a threat to the whole group.

4. *Pinigpigan*: The root is *pinigpig*, which is modern speech, means the ring in the nose of an ox or buffalo. *Lunge*: wilted condition of plants or the drooped-over condition of a sick, wounded or drunken man.

5. *Duhidu*: sacrifices rendered useless by counter-sorcery.

6. That is, after tying the pig's legs, he runs a pole between them, above the ties, so as to prevent the pig's kicking itself away from the site of his invocations.

7. *Dinakwat*: a gift from supernatural beings to men of something having mana. I translate the word "Obtainment."

8. During these invocations he has been "pointing" his Obtainment against his enemies. He sees that his invocations are effective because the Obtainment is eating the raw meat of his offering.

9. The sorcery Balitok's enemies have been practicing against him is conceived as having pressed down his house-eaves by its weight. This weight is now removed and the eaves spring upward. In the following line, perhaps I ought to translate, "There's no more raving" for I suspect that this line may refer to the sorcery, conceived as noisy, as well as ponderous.

10. *Tulud*—see Part I. This is the Central Ifugao *tulud*, which consists in passing along the Obtainment from the original acquirer to somebody else living nearer to the village where the rites are being performed, and from him to somebody nearer still, and so on till it is brought to the village.

11. Tobacco is making its way into the ideology: there was no mention of it in any of the myths I recorded 25 years ago.

12. *Didiyan*—from "Di! di!" (from Hidi) sound used in encouraging dogs. I translate "sicked."

13. He throws cracked rice down so as to lure the chickens so that he may catch one.

14. The Ifugao kills a chicken by cutting its throat (formerly with a bamboo sliver but now with a knife); he holds it upside down over a vessel and catches the blood.

15. He plucks out the wing and tail feathers and burns off the rest, after which he inserts his thumbnail under the wishbone and tears the breast back over the abdomen, leaving it attached by the skin of the latter, thus exposing the viscera, undisturbed. He scrutinizes the bile-sac for its omen, then removes

the viscera. He cleans the gizzard and crop, strips out the contents of the intestines. He either replaces the viscera into the abdominal cavity or, more probably, impales them on a spit. He then bends the chicken's neck across the abdominal cavity and folds the breast back into its place over the neck; this compact bunch he then throws into the pot to boil a little—which is all his cooking of it will amount to.

16. That is, he sits resting, chewing betels and catching his wind.

17. He goes to the rice mortar in order to use it as a seat.

18. "Fan" him—swing a chicken in front of him—an attention very acceptable to the deities, generally.

19. *Tayaban*; a winged, predatory being that is much feared.

20. That is, they come like a landslide.

21. The "crunching" here attributed to Self-Beheaded is inconsistent with the concept of a headless body.

22. That is, he goes distributing betels among them and making peace with them.

23. *Kinadangyangan* comprehends both wealthiness and nobility: the two go together in the Ifugao's conception.

3. KINSHIP ASSEMBLAGE

1. A widespread fiction (or is it always a fiction?) in Indonesia. For a discussion, see Barton, 1938, p. 81.

2. I have elsewhere ("How Marriage Prohibitions Arose," *Philippine Magazine*, August, 1938) described a mock combat that always ensued in one section of Ifugao, whenever persons within the forbidden degrees married, between the kindred of the bride and those of the groom. The combat was quite obviously magic whose purpose was to make the two parties unrelated. The reasoning was: Kindred do not fight; these parties are fighting; therefore they are not kindred. In this case the syllogism might be: Kindred live together; these two groups live apart; therefore they are not kindred.

A feature of the decay of marriage prohibitions between members of the same clan is that they first break down between members of the clan that live in different villages.

3. In "7" we see the tendentious ending that adapts the myth to its magical purpose, the relief from childlessness. I see in it a common rationalization for exogamy.

4. [An evidence of Bugbug's acculturation by the Law and Movies. R.F.B.]

5. *Makakaga*: I can't translate. Mr. Bugbug says it means "For Christ's sake!"

6. Falling limbs or the catching of chickens by hawks would be bad omens for the hunt.

7. That is, the omen bird, which is frequently called in ritual language "the cock-bird."

8. If "sisters" are present, this phrase is omitted, at the myth recitation, since reference to sexual matters is tabooed in their presence.

9. A frequent injunction of parents to children of marriageable age.

10. "Settle permanently: *humaligagod*, literally, "turn the soil all around," "spade all around."

11. Mr. Bugbug did not record the final *fiat*.

4. THE NEGRITOS

1. As always when place and date of recording are not cited, the myth was recorded in Bitu, in 1937.

2. The Kiangan referred to in myths is always the *old* Kiangan, about 5 kilometers below the modern town so named. It is on the south side of the Bula river, not far from the gap which marks the limit of the eastward migration of this branch of the tribe. When I first came to the country the site had been abandoned, but I noted on my last trip that two houses had been set up there and some of the many ancient rice terraces reclaimed.

3. This is a simple stick, possibly of runo reed, short enough that the priest can outreach it with his span (middle finger–thumb). After the appropriate preliminary rites, the priest addresses the stick: "Did such-and-such group of gods (or ancestors or other beings) cause the sickness?" If his span overreaches, he names another group, and so on till the stick "grows longer" and his span cannot reach the end of it, whereupon the causative agents of the affliction are believed to be indicated. The stick is also used in the detection of thieves and in other forms of divination.

4. The root is *Alta* (Aeta) a name used generally in Indonesia for Negritos, and in several languages also meaning "slave." The prefix and reduplication here used ought to give the meaning "negritoid" but I doubt that such a sense is intended. The form is probably used for the sake of the meter.

5. TURNED TO STONE

1. "Ngilins"—the gods of reproduction, who have a special control over the lives of men. Quite naturally they are one of the classes that receive especial attention in the rite preliminary to a headhunting expedition.

2. "Accepts"—that is, accepts the omen and clinches it with a *fiat*.

3. Headhunters always sleep under the house the night before they go forth.

4. Such is the phrasing when kindred of the opposite sex are within hearing. But if such be not the case they say, "and pours out from his anus." As is usually the case, the circumlocution is more graphic than plain simple speech.

5. See "Agba—Divination Rites," Barton, 1946, p. 102.

6. The figure comes from the dropping off of mud from the Ifugao's bare legs after he has been wading in the rice-fields or from the curling up of mud on an overflown flat under the rays of the sun.

6. ORIGIN OF IRRIGATED RICE

1. The *padun* is a bamboo through which a cord runs. The cord passed around a dog's neck is thus protected by the bamboo from the dog's teeth. Also a dog on being led from its home by a stranger can be held at a safe distance by means of the bamboo.

2. The Alabat gods are believed to be owners of the game.

3. *Litbong*, "disappearing position of the sun." Hunters consult the omen three times. The omen of the third time refers to the game and to dangers which may befall the hunters and should be a bad one for these—hence good for the hunters. The second omen, "the harsh talk," also refers to the game in this myth, but that is not correct ritual.

4. Fire for this ceremony is always made by friction, with the bamboo fire-saw.

5. That is, he breaks away the charred bamboo envelope from the rice and meat.

6. Harvesters of cowpeas are given the green pods as pay for their work.

The more uniformly the peas ripen, the less need be paid for harvesting them. Perhaps this explains the stress put on uniform ripening. Wigan means to say that they already have a good variety of cowpeas.

7. *Imbalahang an nabuukan*: the first word, literally "like a dragon-fly of the *balahang* species," is the name of a variety of stiff-bearded rice which is planted mostly at the edges of the fields because it is eaten with difficulty by monkeys and wild pigs. The *donaal* species which the myth tells about is the favorite sort; it is without beards.

8. Or, perhaps, "when the plants flower again."

9. "Fanning" rites consist of swinging a chicken and chanting an invocation.

10. That is (after the pattern of modern times), gives them g-strings, rice, chickens, and so on, for their work to be rendered.

11. The Ifugao harvest knife of *kutiwong* type has a blade whose cutting edge is set at a greater angle of about 235⁰ with the handle.

12. The rice bundles are carried in on the shoulder, straddled on carrying poles, or on the head, piled on flat boards.

13. *Pudung*: runo stalks whose blades have been tied in a loop. These are stuck up on a number of occasions: as "ethics locks" when an owner is away from home, as a prohibition to enter; about a village when certain ceremonies are in progress as a taboo sign to keep strangers away; and also as pleasing to certain deities to make fields fruitful.

14. Those for whom a priest is praying are always "children" in the rites he is performing.

7. THE SELF-CAUGHT

1. This dispatching of betels with a message is the only plot element that Ifugao myths have in common with Cole's "Tales of the Mythical Period," and this is the only Ifugao myth in which that plot element occurs. But there is this difference that in the Tinguian "Tales" the betels converse with men, whereas in this myth the betels do not talk but imply a message by their presence. Consequently, we may have here a case of independent origin, and an origin in Ifugaoland. For if the plot element had been brought from a former habitat it would probably appear in other myths, while if it had been borrowed the betels probably would talk.

2. See Beyer, 1935, p. 542. Professor Beyer states that tektites are called "star-dung," or "thunder-dung" by the natives of the Philippines, and in one province, "sun-stones." In Indo-China they are called "thunderdung" or "devil-balls," in Borneo and Malaysia, "thunder-stones," "lightningstones," or "moon-balls," and in the Republic of Colombia, "lightning-stones." They have been widely used as a material for flaked tools and arrow heads and have been found in Philippine graves dating from the prehistoric Iron-Age with a "carry-polish" indicating that they had been carried as amulets. It is also stated that early stone images have been found in Indo-China having polished tektites as eyes.

See also, Busick, 1938, p. 21.

3. A line of four periods in the text, in this and in subsequent cases, indicates the omission of tiresome and unessential details of eating, betelchewing or sacrifice.

4. Classificatory "ancestors" are meant, of course. Bugan was evidently of the senior, property-inheriting line of the family. Descendants of junior lines would be her "ancestors" in many cases, although they would be approximately of her own age.

5. *Tangbalin an ginulitan* "glazed *ginulitan*," rice wine jar of a highly prized kind. Limetubes are bamboo nodes, usually adorned with scratch work patterns, and with use take on a high polish.

6. *Mabla*, literally, "whitish."

7. Falling limbs, swooping of hawks or other untoward events would be bad omens and would prohibit the marriage. The ceremonial work consists in the wife's getting camotes, the husband's getting firewood.

8. "Banutan"—the house ladder, which is made of *banutan* wood.

9. *Dakdak* is a stone that has been brought up to house or field. The sense here is that his head would be taken and carried home by the enemy—like a *dakdak* stone.

10. *Yumyum* is the stroking of a rooster to quiet it before invoking it as an oracle. He means that the enemy would "quiet" him.

11. The *tayaban* is a winged being, of human form, usually nocturnal. It feeds on soulstuff, especially the soulstuff of the foetus and is usually held responsible for miscarriages. It can "turn on fire" so that its body glows like swarms of the tropical firefly. It usually "turns on the fire" when it perches. It frequents large boulders in the ricefields. In the season of water scarcity when the fields have to be watched all night against theft of water, the *tayaban* is greatly feared and frequently seen. Educated Ifugaos thoroughly believe in it and have assured me that they have seen it with their own eyes. Perhaps they saw swarms of fireflies. At any rate the idea of the *tayaban* may have originated from, or been suggested by the firefly.

12. *Atul*: in every old Ifugao village and some new ones, there is a lounging place, of stone, wood or large natural boulders, where the folk congregate, chat and look out over the valley. Cf. Bontok, *ato*, to which the meaning "ward of a village" has been attributed by writers on that tribe. If the Bontok word really has that meaning, the meaning is, I believe, secondary, applied by extension to the section of the village that uses or is entitled to use the *ato*, which, in Bontok is always of stone.

13. The Ifugao word, *mabnang*, means to settle down or sink, but the Ifugaos insist that when used with respect to the *tayaban*, it means "turns on the fire" since that is what the *tayaban* does when he settles to his perch or hovers near the earth.

14. He means that the ropes of the net are worn out from raising and lowering when bats are taken out of it and that the shelf of the shack cannot hold the catch.

15. It is believed that dogs can see *tayabans* in the daytime when they are invisible to human eyes. Their barking with no apparent reason is sometimes thus explained.

16. Compare the crossing of the Red Sea by the fleeing Hebrews. There are many elements in Ifugao mythology that are common with that of the Bible.

17. *Lotang* (1) a ditch or trench around a field, especially a hill-farm, to protect it from wild animals, particularly the wild pig; (2) a mortise.

Although the first *palipal* was, according to the myth, made from upstream bamboo, the Ifugaos, as has been said, always go downstream to Namtogan or neighboring places for bamboo for this purpose.

18. *Honga*, general welfare rites or the consecration of an Obtainment.

19. The *Napulungot* are the gods of the Downstream Region (where the Bula River flows into the Magat); I think the word means "clustered villages." At Namtogan are the gods with whom this myth makes us acquainted. At Nagadangan, Binuyuk and Kapunglahan live numbers of similar deities and

at the latter place a number of gods of reproduction. At Kalinugan, said to be the region of the mouth of the Kagayan River, is a vine whose lower parts have a human form and whose sap is blood. It is a charm against locusts, but must be cut off first in its upper portion, because if the lower part be cut first, the vine will swing and swing forever.

20. *Bokla*—see *Philippine Pagans*, p. 237.

21. The length of time required to sun the rice depends, naturally, on the amount of sun during the period. Usually about three days are required, but perhaps one day of constant sun would suffice. Such days are exceedingly rare in Ifugaoland.

22. A period of 3–5 days during which the gods and powers that increase the juststacked rice are supposed to be doing their work and must not be disturbed. Nobody may work or leave the village during this time.

23. The *pudung* are now being planted for the secondary crops raised on hill-farm, on terrace slopes, and insterstices between terraces.

24. Wages, hire, etc., must not be understood as money payments but as exchanges for labor in the form of rice, g-strings, loin cloths, etc.

8. HALUPE DEITIES COLLECT DEBT

1. The word *bolang*, the name of this deity, has two meanings: "uncover" and "let down" (as something carried in a sling on the back, as a baby or bundles of rice). Both senses are used in this paragraph.

2. Ulnui is the name of the place where the tributary that drains Central Ifugao, including Bitu, where the myth was being recorded, empties into the Bulâ River. The deities ought to follow this tributary. Instéad they continue up the river but see their mistake, turn back and pursue the right road.

3. Those for whom a priest performs rites are always, in the ceremonies and invocations, "children."

4. The priest apparently has no hope of collecting the debt the first time he goes dunning.

9. FEUD BETWEEN BROTHERS

1. *Balbalaiyon-na*, from *bale*, which in modern speech means house. Either it means that he arranged the fuel in house-form or else, possibly, the word house comes from a root originally meaning the place where the fire was built.

2. *Kolili n dinangan. Kolili* is the lower bamboo in friction fire-making, and I am.told the Ifugaos always make fire by friction in this hunting rite. The modern meaning of *dinangan* is flint and steel fire apparatus, but here it means the ensemble of the bamboo fire apparatus.

3. *Hóód*, rice wine put by to use on return from a hunting trip, journey or exhausting work. He drank it from a large wooden spoon.

4. The Ifugao divides a carcass in the gross, giving, say, each pair of his grandparents a portion to divide among their descendants. Or, if he has enough, he goes back further and gives each pair of great-grandparents a portion, or if there are many animals he divides the meat into eight portions so that the descendants of his great-great-grandparents may have a share. The Ifugao reports the magnitude of a feast by telling how the meat was divided. "They divided it into eight," (or four, or twice). The kindred of each line apportion their share to suit themselves. It is this latter division which is spoken of here.

5. This operation may refer either to cooling a heated spear quickly by fanning with a betel leaf (or banana leaf) so as to temper it or else to fanning

up the fire by this means to heat the tang for burning it into the handle. The priest has left out one of these operations. It is evident that the tempering of cast iron, such as was used here, requires a more gradual and gentle change of temperature than does steel.

6. I have not been able to identify the *humang* and *witawit*. Both are used in the attracting-charms of love and hunting. The *humang* is possibly the fire tree. The *witawit* is said to grow on a slippery precipice in the Upstream region.

7. Bad omens which would cause the expedition to be foregone if they happened on the day of ceremonial idleness. The continuous cry encourages the headhunter; the perch on a dead branch dooms the victim. As a matter of fact, though, headhunters consult omens on three days.

8. Lime for their betel chewing made by piling, alternately, layers of snail shells on layers of reeds and then firing the reeds.

9. Bumabakal, Bugan's father, has gone to Gauwaan to officiate in the preliminary ceremonies.

10. *Balangag*, the kind of gong that is played with a stick; there is another kind that is played in the sitting position with the ball of the two hands, called *tabab*. The *balangag* is necessarily the kind that is used when beating time for processions, such as this, funeral marches, etc.

11. Every house in the village will brew rice wine for the feast. The wood is for roasting the fermentable rice for the wine. Note the ritual cooperation.

12. The *alim* is an epic which only rich men (*kadangyan*) have the right to sing. It is sung at rich men's harvest ceremonies, at drinkfeasts and their preliminaries, and at funerals of the wealthy.

13. This press is illustrated in Barton, 1921, plate 42.

14. Two different words, said to mean exactly the same, are used. These "servants" go, playing gongs on the way, two by two, to the kindred dispersed in other regions and other villages to invite them to the feast.

15. The word *mabungot* is one of the hardest words to translate found in the language. Filippinos translate it or the corresponding words in their different dialects as "brave," and I believe it does correspond to their concepts of bravery. They also say that a man is "brave" when we should pronounce him simply "cross," "ill-tempered."

I believe the word expresses a complex of inexorability, agressiveness, persistence in vengefulness, and that these comprise the Ifugao (and usually, the Malay) conception of bravery. Perhaps, in the case above, "inexorable" would be a better translation, and yet it falls short.

16. This phrase is puzzling. It may refer to the spear, it may refer to Lidum himself (for in some invocations the Ifugaos wish themselves to be like runo plumes—that is to have the quick and elastic step that indicates physical well-being), or it may refer to the fragibility of whatever the spear was thrust into. The Bitu priests couldn't explain the phrase. My former informant, Himingale (of Habian) definitely put the last interpretation on it. He always had his heroes thrust their spears into a flat stone, which the men had brought up from the river bed at great toil, shattering it "like a leaf-blade, like a runo plume." Whereupon, a mild protest would follow: "Alas—the flat stone!" The hero would then give the flat stone's fragments a kick, and they would join together and the stone would be made whole again.

17. *Humang*, a kind of plant; *buliklik*, the spotted eagle, which appears during the dry season; *bidut* and *ididalo*, small birds. I cannot explain what significance this "assemblage" has. The informant is becoming maudlin from too much liquor.

18. Informant is a very bright young Ifugao who knows a little English, having attended primary school. Toward the last of this myth recital (which could not be divided into two sessions because the informant lived far away) I felt so exhausted that it seemed I could not type another word. I went to my kitchen for a drink. On returning almost immediately, I noted a big change in the bottle of *nipa* gin from which I had been very cautiously pouring out an occasional drink for the informant and some of the bystanders.

Having noted while in the kitchen that my cook had just cooked a lot of rice, I hastened to get food into the stomach of the informant, for I realized that the amount he had swigged from the bottle during my absence would, on an empty stomach, soon render him incapable of finishing the myth, so that a very hard half day's work might go to pot. This measure, promptly taken, saved the day and brought informant through to only a slightly incoherent finish. It was marvelous luck, though, that the myth was not a longer one.

It was absolutely necessary to provide liquor of some sort for the informants; it is an inevitable accompaniment of invocations and myth recitals in their own rites. Rice wine was the best, because they are accustomed to drink it slowly. But not enough could be brewed, so that gin had to be used a good many times. However, they drank gin as if it were water—would drink a whole tumbler at one draught if allowed to. I learned to practice an unconscionable dilution with water and to keep the bottle outside the room.

Note that in his final, "clinching" phrase, informant enjoins for me a status "along with the Government." He thus showed good will, for that is the most enviable status Ifugao can conceive.

10. THE DIVIDED CHILD

1. This is the beginning of a strained integration which will become apparent in the lines that follow. There is an attempt to rationalize denial to a kinsman of his share in the meat divided at a ceremonial feast. This is a hard thing for an Ifugao to do. Note that the mother says, at first, that they are distant kindred. Later she says that she thought they were kindred, but was mistaken. Furthermore there is not enough meat to go around, and the kindred rub the grease on Kinggaowan in order give him his share. These are indications that an ancient motif is being used which is incompatible with present social relations.

2. *Atob* is a fishtrap made of four stones arranged so as to form three sides and a "roof." It is figuratively used to indicate the deities of the four regions.

3. Pangagauwan: the tall mountain that towers above Kiangan.

4. This version neglects to state that Kinggaowan is naked.

5. That is, the Kiangan people did not observe the taboos about not eating these foods with the game. The *gulid* (skin eruptions—sometimes dhobe itch) that afflicted the hunter and his family was the result.

6. *Lubug* is the general name for the following: *tukukan*, owl; *banug*, a bird of prey, *poktiu*, a kind of bird; *halkhak*, another kind of bird; *halmokon*, another kind of bird; *ido*, the omen bird usually consulted (the *Rhapidura cyaniceps*); *taktak*, a kind of cicada; *waklad*, another kind of cicada; *katibugalon*, the Rainbow; *wegit*, a kind of rat; *kimkimit*, fireflies; *gode*, the landslide. None of these may be eaten, except that a few of the birds are sometimes eaten by aged priests. Compare these with those given by Lambrecht, p. 553. I will add that this author never sent me either a copy of his footnote on p. 714, same series, nor the review referred to in it. Nor can I find a file containing the review—a curious procedure, to state it mildly.

7. It is to be noted that many of these omen beings are attributed to birth from Bugan, daughter of Amtalao, Myth I. No doubt all the other characters of that myth are invoked as well, since they belong to the class of the omen deities, but the priest mentions only Amtalao in this myth.

8. Cf. Villaverde, 1912, p. 299 *et seq.* First published in English translation in Beyer's "Origin Myths among the Mountain Peoples of the Philippines," together with an analogous myth (in abstract form) from the Nabaloi Igorot, collected in 1910 by Dr. Dean S. Fansler.

The Villaverde version was originally recorded in 1894, from the informant Duminong of Kiangan, in Spanish. It gives some details not included in our own version: for example, Bugan made a god, Balitok of Luktag, out of her half of the child.

11. Man Imprisons Gods

1. Informant shortly before teaching this myth had slain Buyagaowan, one of his Bangbang enemies, for which he served six years in the penitentiary for the pagan tribes of Northern Luzon, and afterward returned home. His throat was cut as he lay drunk across the trail on his way home from a drinkfest and he was robbed of ten pesos, a few years ago—about 1935. The murderer had not been found in 1937.

2. That is, the war priest, who is supposed to wear a little plume of white feathers in his hair. For the "torching", see Barton, 1946, p. 143.

3. The priest invites Bugan not to Lamot where the headfeast is occuring in the myth but to Pindungan, the village where the myth was being recorded, and he names the kindred of the man he has recently slain there.

4. Indicating death in the house.

5. This should not be taken as indicating that any importance is attributed to the bile-sac of a pig. Ifugaos are guided by the omen given by the bile-sac of the chicken. Only in two instances is an omen read from the pig's bile—one of them a marriage rite. Still, the priests always look at a pig's bile and perhaps they feel a little better if it be a good one but regard it as being of no consequence if bad. In a myth it is always good, of course, if mentioned at all.

6. Prayables; deities, myth incidents, spirits, charms—anything that may be invoked.

12. Weavers' Myth

1. Looms are set up under a house or granary; two women work at the process. One sits on a block of wood or a board on the ground, with the lower end-stick in front of her. She passes the warp around this, gives the ball of yarn to her helper (standing) who carries it to the upper end-stick, passes it around that, then returns the ball to the sitter, and so on.

2. "Kon dakami ot tungulan"—*tungul* is something given in an exchange. Lidum is, of course, asking for sacrifices.

3. Monkulabe—a deity of weaving.

4. *Binudbudan* are loom fabrics the warp of which is tied and waxed at certain places for making a sort of primitive and crude batik work which Ifugao women of some villages know how to produce. I translate *tinaguan* as "figured pieces." Literally the word refers to representations of the human figure.

5. Informant's grammar is muddled because he has become drunk. He had insisted on the sacrifice of a chicken, else he would not teach this ceremony. The reason probably was that his wife was weaving at the time, for in the end-

ing he turns the benefit of the ceremony to his own household. Ngidulu was, in
comparison with most priests quite temperate, but in the present instance we
had no rice wine and had to use gin, mixed with brown sugar in order to get a
color that would fool the deities. An Ifugao drinks gin as if it were water. It
makes little difference to an aged priest, though, whether he be drunk or
sober—the myth recitation comes automatically. Of course it makes a difference in his pronunciation.

The names of the weavers' deities are given in Barton, 1946, pp. 29–30.

13. THE TOOTH OF THUNDER

1. The Ifugao knows that his enemy is making sorcery also and he believes
that if his own sorcery meets that of the enemy head on, the two will neutralize
each other, so to speak. Hence, he wants his own sorcery to "dive under" that
of his enemy so as to continue on to its target. As to his enemy's sorcery, if it
continues on, he trusts his *kiwil* or turning-aside talisman to shunt it away.

14. THE IRON-EATER

1. Washing children away by rain is also found in Myth 3.
2. The meaning is that some time passes before the next incident.
3. Meaning that the minnows have gone under the cliff.
4. The trip by water is a motif in most of the great hero stories. Cf. Rank:
p. 12 [Sargon]; p. 13 [Moses]; p. 15 [Karna]; p. 17 [Apollo]; p. 22 [Perseus];
p. 41 [Romulus]; p. 45 [Hercules]; p. 53 [Siegfried]; p. 55 [Lohengrin].
5. We have encountered the last three in the myth of the Self-Beheaded, no. 2.
6. It would appear that Lumawig has himself become transformed into a
duck-like being such as his descendants are.
7. ... "ta magomgom di apangal-na," "so that clenched be his fists."

15. SUN AND MOON QUARREL

1. The Ifugao does this when raving-drunk.
2. In my early recordings, in Kiangan, I frequently did not write out the
whole of the clinching phrases.
3. These are all names of villages in the Kiangan region.
4. The *huga* are sharpened bamboo sticks set in the ground slantingly so as
to inflict a leg wound in him who walks into them. They are used to protect
soft rice dikes against trespassers who might injure them by walking over
them, used against enemies and also mischievously set sometimes by children.

16. TIED UP

1. When the alcoholic content has risen almost to the point when it would
kill its own bacteria, the Ifugao adds a little water so that fermentation may
continue. Thus he obtains more rice-wine than he otherwise would and, it is
said, rice-wine of even better quality.
2. That is, gives its assent. The text of such a consultation of the cock is
given in Barton, 1938, p. 157; 1946, pp. 123, 128.
3. This "matting" is a natural growth at the base of coconut leaves, which
resembles a fabric. It is used to enclose the other objects, being tied with the
kamulitilit vine.
4. That is, so that the guests will not pick up the stones and throw them,
or pull up the stakes and use them as spears.
5. Gong-players seem to be in especial danger; other guests may want to
play the gongs themselves. See Barton, 1938, pp. 153, 195.

6. *Hupol* means pacifying magic. The word used for spears is the generic *pinalat*, meaning "made into a shaft." The derivation probably shows that the original spear had no inserted head.

7. I know nothing of this Old Man. There is probably a myth about him.

8. In cases that I observed no iron objects were wrapped up, but only little wooden and bamboo models of knives and spears that had been whittled out.

17. ENEMIES AS OFFERINGS

1. This mock headhunt was enacted by some people living near Anao. The leader carried it out for the sake of a second burial of his father's and mother's bones. Four or five men went along with their wives, hoping that the child-lessness of the latter would be relieved thereby. My son, who was visiting me at the time, accompanied the party and secured some pictures and wrote descriptions of the rites. This myth was recited at the "headfest" rites he gave along with the others on returning.

This myth belongs to the "raw eaters" series (see Part I, section 5, note 2).

2. *Tikam* tree buds have the precise form of a spear head. Usually little wooden knives are whittled out and also tied up, as is a little cooked rice and some rice wine malt. These, wrapped in a bit of the natural mat that grows at the base of coconut leaf stems and tied, tie up the appetites and passions of the guests.

3. The priest is a day ahead in his reckoning: the *latang*, or waiting for sugar cane juice that is added to the rice wine to ferment, is on the ninth day; the drinkfest occurs on the tenth day.

4. *Punhidan*—the day after the public drinkfest, when many animals are killed and meat is shared with all lines of the families. Ingaan, being co-father-in-law to Dotdotan, is under obligation to make a substantial contribution to help out.

5. The Ifugaos believe that large trees protected households from evil spirits such as these. The evil spirits have to kick the tree to pieces in order to get at the household. Cf. Cole, 916, p. 182. Every Kankanai village has one or more sacred trees.

6. I have so translated *pinútalan*, from *pútal*, "light."

18. DYSENTERY IMPS

1. "Participate in tributes"—*makibaiyad*. The root is *baiyad*, meaning indemnity, tribute, or price (probably a modern sense). It is also the name of rites for curing belly troubles, in which there is sacrifice to a certain group of deities, also called "the *baiyad*." [Barton, 1946, p. 70.]

2. An annual epidemic of dysentery rages after the romoval of the harvest taboos and this is largely due to the fact that the people gather and eat raw the soft end of the shoots of rice that spring up from the stubble in the fields. The bundle of shoots is thrown or dipped in the rice field water which always contains dysenteric amoeba and sometimes the bacillus of dysentery as well. The Bureau of Health traced, a few years ago, a very serious epidemic of bacillary dysentery in Mayaoyao to the fact that a Mayaoyao man living at the upper part of the valley had returned from the lowlands ill with the disease and had infected an upper field. Water from this running into the lower ones carried the infection down the valley.

3. The Ifugaos use the threshed out straw as toilet "paper."

4. The *umaladang*, *Pumihdol* and *liblibaiyu* groups of deities are especially interesting in that they show how the Ifugao, in his god-creating, has deified

symptoms, just as in the case of the *halupe* deities he has deified states of mind. See Barton, 1946, pp. 47, 62, .64.

19. Coconut Grows from Buried Head

1. From the time the party leaves this shack (which is built in the edge of enemy territory) the headhunters may not drink water, for it is enemy water and taboo, hence likely to make them dizzy. "Crosser of the Way" refers to the omen bird.

2. *Makiulu*, literally, participator-in-the-head or, perhaps "frequenter of the head": I translate: "head-intruder."

3. The word used, *hinadaan*, usually means meat or vegetables dipped up out of soup; perhaps it here has the sense of "rescued."

4. In this myth recitation the priest assumed a woman to be ill, hence in the myth Bugan, the wife of Balitok, was the sick person. If the patient had been a male, then in the myth, Balitok himself would have been the one who suffered headache.

20. Origin of Boils

1. A flaccid or empty gall bladder indicates that the vesicles of the skin eruption will dry up.

2. That is, does not disperse and diffuse, but goes straight and in full concentration to the desired objective.

21. Red Scabbards and Black

1. The root is *pihol*, meaning to wring or twist, and no doubt refers to the sensation of a growing carbuncle. With infix *-um-* the word might be translated, "it twists" by analogy with *umudan*, "it rains." More accurate, if it be understandable, would be "twistering." Dr. Cecilio Lopez characterizes the affix *um* as the "*nomina agentis* (internal)" and says, "The general meaning of this verbal prefix is 'inner motion,' expressed most approximately by the English 'to become.' This meaning, which is probably the most primitive one, is, however, not to be found in all the different employments which the language has, in the course of time, come to give this affix." (*Preliminary Study of the Affixes in Tagalog*, p. 29). Dr. Lopez's characterization applies equally to the same affix in Ifugao, and in the name of this deity the affix has its primitive meaning. Pumihol is conceived as a being whose essential nature is to "twist"; not only does he himself "twist" but he produces the same "twisting" in others. Probably most of the sickness-producing deities or spirits are conceived after this pattern.

2. According to the priest, and as this phrase intimates, these beings have travelled through the earth. They are similar to the *umaladang* deities of no. 18 in this respect.

23. Difficult Birth

1. A different version is given in Barton, 1930.

2. "Friend" is a circumlocution used to designate the foetus, and "blanket" or "house" are circumlocutions to designate the after-birth. The circumlocutions are necessary for the purpose of avoiding words suggesting sexual relations, tabooed in the presence of kin of the opposite sex. On such an occasion as a birth rite, both male and female kindred are, of course, assembled together.

3. That is, they ask each other, "What is it—a boy or a girl?"

24. BELLY SICKNESS

1. For a consideration of the prestige feast rites, see Barton, 1946, pp. 127 *et seq.*

2. These are war gods. They come down and possess the priests.

3. There must have been a phrase left out here: they never put meat on cooked rice unless they afterward recite myths.

4. The wood that we saw obtained is for the roasting and boiling of rice to be used for wine. The rice is first roasted, then slightly boiled.

5. These prohibitions, continence, half-fast, etc., are incumbent on the giver of the prestige feast, his wife, and the *manikam* or priest who takes the lead in it and its preliminaries.

6. I do not know definitely what is meant by "branching" the feast; I only know that it refers to singing a part of the rich man's ballad, the *alim*.

7. The drinkfest is a public occasion—anyone is free to come, but a ceremonious invitation must be sent to *all* the kindred, else the latter will be offended.

8. These "servants" are only ceremonial servants and feel honored by being invited to perform the function. They must not bathe during the course of the feast. They go with a gong throughout the home region and surrounding regions to invite the kindred.

9. At Ifugao prestige feasts, when a leading man dances, he is frequently addressed by another standing near the dancing ring with a speech containing remarks complimentary to himself and laudatory of his family and kindred, interspersed with friendly banter, perhaps, if friendly relations afford basis for it. In the present case the speech (*gopa*) was insulting. Another version (recorded in Kiangan) gives Balitok's speech as follows:

"*Gopa, gopa*, Binlang of Tukyudan! Thy scabbard is of light soft wood. Thy war knife is crooked. Thy hipbag is a bladder. Thy tree-bark g-string is always soaked" [referring to his chronic bowel looseness].

10. It is interesting that some of the Melanesian peoples do use coiled vines as bracelets and leglets.

11. He puts the meat (probably pig jowls which are taboo for the Ifugaos to eat and which, cut off with the skin attached, are dried and kept for purposes of sacrifice to the lesser deities) on cooked rice. In another basket he displays the "things"—that is, a g-string, bush knife and scabbard, strings of beads, a blanket, etc., as offerings to the Binlangs.

25. RITE FOR RETURNING SOUL

1. In birth-rites there are sacrifices to the ancestors, Matungulan, Napalungot, Nihngodan (gods of reproduction of the Downstream and Upstream regions), Nahigayan (gods of reproduction of the Skyworld and Underworld), and the Pahang group. The first sacrifice is of chickens. If it brings no results, a pig must be sacrificed. If there are still no results, sacrifice of a carabao is indicated.

The *duyun* or prayer to the deities is:

"Ye are being given a chicken [or pig, carabao] in exchange. If ye have afflicted the (long)-haired one who is giving birth, be it enough and relieve her so that the "friend" quickly emerge, accompanied by his "blanket," so that he startle (with his yelling) her companions, so that they will ask each other "Which is it?" so that his body will grow rapidly and be healthy, so that he lives, so that the enemy and evil spirits be turned aside, so that the pigs and chickens live, for ye are being invoked, ye matungulan [or other class as the case may be].

2. Every third or fourth house in an Ifugao village has a pole which serves as a ladder for climbing the trunk of the tree on which the betel vine grows. These trees are usually large ones, and the vine itself may grow up to a height of 40 feet.

3. That is, the house-ladder has been either hung up or its upper end pushed away from the door and held from falling by a cord. This is a sign that nobody is at home. The ladder is so disposed of in order that chickens and rats cannot climb up it into the house.

4. Note how the priest knows the details of the geography of the Skyworld, which is conceived as a mountainous region like the Ifugao's known earth. The males of the *pahang* live in a separate village from the females. See list of these deities, ten each, in Barton, 1938, p. 154.

5. That is, Ablatan, a sky tableland from which a precipice reaches down to earth.

6. The footholes in the Ifugao's paths up steep places are similar in shape to the Ifugao's flattish Chinese kettles.

7. Besides being no mean antiquarian in the matter of beads, jars, gongs, and so on, the Ifugao loves old houses. "Sooty" is no term of depreciation, quite the contrary. The inside of an old house is jet black, but the soot accumulates so slowly that it does not rub off. The Ifugao likes it. Immediately after a death, a cry is raised to the soul of the deceased: "(Name)! Return thou. Thy sooty house is here."

8. About the sex of the child.

26. Like a Hardstone

1. "Guwai!" is the characteristic drunken cry of the Ifugaos. In this myth, I have translated the names of the characters which are: *Muling*, "Hardstone" and *Balugabog*, "Softstone."

2. The Ifugao has no more conception of fair play than have some nations in war. In ordeals and duels, however, the two champions are searched to ascertain that they do not carry turning-aside talismans. It is said that the umpire even looks into their mouths sometimes to see that no talisman is concealed there.

3. Name of a group of deities—from *dalidal*, the pounding of green bark so that it can be stripped off a stick. These deities treat Ifugaos to the action implied in their class name.

4. The Umaladang are an especially abhorrent group of deities that live in *Dagahna*, a region beneath the Underworlds, and who afflict men with belly-aches and bloody fluxes. See above.

5. The preparation of a corpse for burial begins thus.

6. That is, those at Kiangan from whom they increased, namely, Tadona, Balitok, Bugan, etc.: hero-ancestors.

7. Unless the word was recorded wrongly and should be *puhu*, heart, I am unable to translate.

8. As soon as a man dies, the Ifugaos raise a shout to his soul to return and "bring back the souls of the pigs, the chickens and the rice." The meaning here is that what these shouters to the souls of the dead stand on is tipped and they fall off—presumably into nowhere.

9. That is to say, the ancient, deep paths, over whose sides the vegetation hangs and rots.

27. BALITOK OBTAINS PACIFIERS

1. Obviously a myth of the "invented" type.

2. The phrase is magic to cause the drinkfest guests to eat only a little.

3. Three different names for the bamboo Lover's Harp give names to three *halupe* gods: Bikbikong, Alalbe, Iyuding. The latter is a metallic Jew's Harp, whose tongue is jerked by means of a string.

28. WIGAN TEACHES RITES TO BALITOK

1. The myth is a typical example of the "invented" type.

2. Meaning that the neighbors are always yelling to him that his dogs are chasing their pigs or chickens.

3. This is only one of many rites entering into the *Kibkiblu* ritual. See Barton, 1946, pp. 180–182.

4. "Cockbird"—omen bird.

5. The third omen prognosticates the death of the game.

6. That is, the house whence the smoke arises is fenced.

7. The deities here named were omitted from the list of the "Spitters" in my 1946 publication, p. 73, *q.v.*

8. *Pinihpia*.

29. BUGAN'S DECEPTION

1. That is, Manahaut has heard the invocation of Kumiha, the Ifugao priest, on earth.

2. From this point on the tulud is the reverse of the ordinary one in that it sends the deities farther away from the site of the rites instead of bringing them nearer to it. This, of course, is in order to get thoroughly rid of the enemy.

3. Tablak is a village in the Humalapap region.

4. Biting the coconut drinking cup is the Ifugao's classic symptom of intoxication.

30. DEAD MAN'S TULUD

1. It is worthy of special notice that the Ifugao corpse, sitting in its death chair, is togged out in new skirt or g-string and is adorned as if for attending a drinkfest.

2. *Inapo*; lit. "made a grandson (granddaughter)." Original meaning probably, "taken into the group," "adopted." In modern speech it indicates the realtionship between parents whose children have married, or between parent and son-(daughter)-in-law.

3. The bystanders titter nervously and cast doubtful looks in my direction.

4. Bulâ is the limit of the territory of the Central Ifugaos. Hence even the now demoralized soul needs some persuasion to induce it to go further. Hence also the special deference shown to the soul at the Bulâ drinkfest—"Make way for ....."

5. *Imbangad*: lit. "who were returned," a class of deities who meet and conduct the soul into the Region of Souls.

6. N—, name of the dead man's wife.

7. The widow or widower wears a blanket over the head for several days after bereavement to keep off, it is said, the strong light which would be harmful.

Bibliography

WORKS CITED

Alexander, H. B.
  1916. "North American [Mythology]," *The Mythology of All Races,* Vol. 10.
  1916. "Latin-American [Mythology]," same series, Vol. 11.

Barbeau, C. M.
  1915. "Huron and Wyandot Mythology," Vol. 11, publications of the *Geological Survey of Canada,* Ottawa; Anthropological Series.

Barton, R. F.
  1919. "Ifugao Law," *University of California Publications in American Archaeology and Ethnology,* Vol. 15, No. 1, pp. 1–186.
  1921. "Ifugao Economics," same series, Vol. 15, No. 5, pp. 385–446.
  1930. *The Half Way Sun.* New York, Brewer and Warren.
  1935. "Izpolzovanie mifov kak magii u gornik plemen Filippin," *Sovetskaya Etnografii,* No. 3.
  1938. *Philippine Pagans—Autobiographies of Three Ifugaos.* London, Routledge.
  1938. "How Marriage Prohibitions Arose," *Philippine Magazine,* August.
  1941. "Notes on the Northern Kankanai," in Barton Research Records ("BRR"), Vol. 3, unpublished.
  1946. "The Religion of the Ifugaos," American Anthropological Association, *Memoir* 65. (*American Anthropologist,* Vol. 48, No. 4, Part 2, pp. 1–219.)

Benedict, Laura
  1916. "A Study of Bagobo Ceremonial, Magic and Myth," in *Annals of the New York Academy of Sciences,* Vol. 25, pp. 1–308.

Beyer, H. Otley
  1913. "Origin Myths among the Philippine Mountain Peoples," *Philippine Journal of Science,* Vol. 8, D, No. 2, pp. 85–118.
  1921. "The Non-Christian People of the Philippines," *Census of the Philippine Islands: 1918,* Vol. 2, pp. 905–957. Also issued as a special reprint, in English and in Spanish, Manila, Bureau of Printing, 1921.
  1935. "The Philippine People of Pre-Spanish Times," *Philippine Magazine,* October, Vol. 32. Also, in greater detail, under the title "Prehistoric Philippines," in the *Encyclopedia of the Philippines,* Vol. 8, pp. 21–62, Vol. 8, pp. 21–62, Manila, 1936.
  1935. "Philippine Tektites," *Philippine Magazine,* November, Vol. 32.

Boas, Franz
  1898. "The Mythology of the Bella Coola Indians," *Jessup North Pacific Expedition,* Vol. 2, Part 2. (*Memoir* of the American Museum of Natural History).
  1914. "Mythology and Folktales of the North American Indians," *JAFL,* Vol. 27.

Bouton, J. W.
1883. *Bible Myths and Their Parallels in Other Religions.* New York.
Busick, Ralph
1938. "Rizalites—Philippine Tektites—with a Description of the Pugad Babuy Site," *Papers of the Michigan Academy of Science, Arts and Letters,* Vol. 23, pp. 21–27.
Case, Levi E.
1909. "The Ifugao Flood Myth," *Philippine Journal of Science,* Vol. 4, A, pp. 256–260.
Cole, Fay-Cooper
1913. "The Wild Tribes of Davao District, Mindanao," Publications of the Field Museum of Natural History, Chicago, *Anthropological Series,* Vol. 12, pp. 48–203.
1915. "Traditions of the Tinguian. A Study in Philippine Folk-lore," same series, Vol. 14, pp. 1–226.
1916. "The Tinguian," same series, Vol. 14, Part 2, pp. 227 *et seq.*
Dixon, Roland B.
1916. "[Mythology of] Oceania," *The Mythology of All Races,* Vol. 9.
Evans, Ivor H. N.
1923. *Studies in Religion, Folklore and Custom in British North Borneo and the Malay Peninsula.* Cambridge.
Gifford, E. W.
1924. *Tongan Myths and Tales,* Bernice P. Bishop Museum of Polynesian Ethnology, Bulletin 8.
Gronbech, V.
1931. *The Culture of the Teutons.* London.
Harris, Omori
1937. *Japanese Tales of All Ages.* Hokuseido Press.
Hutton, J. H.
1921. *The Angami Nagas.* London.
Hyatt, H. M.
1935. *Folklore from Adams County, Illinois.* New York.
Lambrecht, Francis
1932-5-7-9. "The Mayawyaw Ritual," Vol. 4, Nos. 1–4, *Publications of the Catholic Anthropological Conference,* Washington, D.C.
Loeb, E.
1929. "Mentawei Myths," *Bijdragen tot de taal-, land-, en Volkenkunde van Nederlandsche Indie,* deel 85.
Lopez, Cecilio
1937. *Preliminary Study of the Affixes in Tagalog.* Manila, Philippine Language Institute.
Maine, Sir Henry
1875. *Early History of Institutions.* London.
Malinowski, B.
1936. *Myth in Primitive Psychology.* London.
Marr, N.
1936. *Izbranny Raboty.* Moscow–Leningrad.

Maxfield, B. L., and Millington, W. H.
1906. "Visayan Folktales," *JAFL*, Vol. 19.

Moss, C. R.
1920a. "Nabaloi Law and Ritual," *University of California Publications in American Archaeology and Ethnology*, Vol. 15, No. 3, pp. 207–342.
1920b. "Kankanay Ceremonies," same series, Vol. 15, No. 4, pp. 343–384.
1924. "Nabaloi Tales," same series, Vol. 17, No. 5, pp. 227–353.

Moss, Eleanor T. C.
1932. "Stories of the Bontok Igorot People in Alab." Thesis presented for the degree of Master of Science in Social Administration, Western Reserve University; unpublished.

Nimuendaju, Curt
1945. "The Eastern Timbira," *University of California Publications in American Archaeology and Ethnology*, Vol. 41, No. 1.

Rank, Otto
1914. *The Myth of the Birth of the Hero*. New York.

Russell, Paul F.
1935. *Malaria and Culicidae in the Philippine Islands: History and Critical Bibliography 1898 to 1933*. Manila.

Smith, W. C.
1925. *The Ao Naga Tribe of Assam*. London.

Teit, James
1912. *JAFL*, Vol. 25, p. 294.

Thompson, Stith
1929. *Tales of the North American Indians, Selected and Annotated by Stith Thompson*. Cambridge.

Vanoverbergh, Morice
1919–28. "Songs in Lepanto Igorot as It Is Spoken at Bauco," *Anthropos*, Vols. 14–23.
1938. Same title, Vol. 33.

Villaverde, Juan
1912. "Supersticiones de los Igorrotes Ifugaos," edited in Spanish and annotated, by Julian Malumbres, *El Correo Sino-Annamita*, Vol. 38. Manila, Sto. Tomás Press. See also annotated English translation by H. Otley Beyer, assisted by J. M. Garvan and E. B. Christie; Manila, 1912–14.

Williamson, R. W.
1933. *Religious and Cosmic Beliefs of Central Polynesia*. Cambridge.

Wilkin, G. A.
19 . "Malayan Sociology," *Papers on Malay Subjects*, Second Series, No. 5. Singapore.

Winstedt, R. O.
1932. "The Prehistory of Malaya," *Journal of the Malayan Branch, Royal Asiatic Society*, Vol. 10, Part 1.

Zelenin, D. K.
1914. *Velikorusskie Skazki Permskio Gubyernii*. Petrograd.

CPSIA information can be obtained
at www.ICGtesting.com
Printed in the USA
LVHW111455121219
639936LV00050B/397/P